I NEVER MET
A STORY
I DIDN'T LIKE

I NEVER MET
A STORY
I DIDN'T LIKE

 MOSTLY TRUE
TALL TALES

TODD SNIDER

DA CAPO PRESS
A MEMBER OF THE PERSEUS BOOKS GROUP

Designed by Pauline Brown
Set in 12 point Dante by the Perseus Books Group

Library of Congress Cataloging-in-Publication Data

Snider, Todd.
 I never met a story I didn't like : mostly true tall tales / Todd Snider. — First Da Capo Press edition.
 pages cm
 ISBN 978-0-306-82260-5 (pbk.) — ISBN 978-0-306-82261-2 (e-book) 1. Snider, Todd. 2. Singers—United States—Biography. I. Title.
 ML420.S6729A3 2013
 782.42164092—dc23
 [B]
 2013034606

First Da Capo Press edition 2014

Published by Da Capo Press
A Member of the Perseus Books Group
www.dacapopress.com

Da Capo Press books are available at special discounts for bulk purchases in the U.S. by corporations, institutions, and other organizations. For more information, please contact the Special Markets Department at the Perseus Books Group, 2300 Chestnut Street, Suite 200, Philadelphia, PA 19103, or call (800) 810-4145, ext. 5000, or e-mail special.markets@perseusbooks.com.

10 9 8 7 6 5 4 3 2 1

This book is dedicated to my hero/sister Shannon and her children; my wife, Melita, and her paintings; Burt Stein, Jerry Jeff Walker, Margie Mercer, Mike and Marie Osheowitz.

To Peter Cooper, for listening to me babble for years but more importantly for typing it down for a few days so we could have a book. All I had to do was say 90,000 words. It only took me an hour or so.

Thank you to the characters in the book, all of whom I would readily admit are much more reliable witnesses to these events than myself.

And to Bob Mercer—I will believe you are dead when I have gnawed on your skull with my very own teeth. Hilarious.

CONTENTS

BY WAY OF AN EXPLANATION

Almost everything I say is true.

Ask anybody.

Hi, buckaroos. Here's that book I keep saying I'm going to write. I got Tony Bennett, Bill Elliot, and lots of other big names in here. I could have called it "Smoking Grass and Dropping Names," because it's mostly that. No way it's not a book, though. Look at it. I totally wrote this. High five.

CHAPTER 1

JIMMY WOULD LIKE TO SEE YOU

Charleston and Byron came to the door, knocked, and said, "Jimmy wants to see you."

Charleston and Byron were bodyguards.

Jimmy was Jimmy Buffett—still is—and Jimmy Buffett was my boss. And he wanted to see me.

Why?

Because he wanted to throw fruit at me. And not in a playful way.

Why fruit? Because it was Jimmy Buffett's dressing room, at the dome in Miami. Fruit was handy.

Fruit hurts, it turns out. It hurts your feelings and fucks up your western shirt. I had on a western shirt, and Jimmy said it looked like shit.

"Nobody wants to see some jackass in a cowboy outfit!"

Anyway, Jimmy was explaining to me about the Internet. I'd never heard of it. This was the summer of 1995. I didn't have a computer. I thought computers were for scientists. I wasn't a scientist, and I'm still not. I'm a folk singer. And if you've heard of me, Jimmy Buffett has something to do with that. He took an interest in me when a bunch of other people didn't. He signed me to his record label, which meant a lot to me.

I'd been a fan of Jimmy's since I was very young, had all the records, and had seen him play at least six or seven times.

And he took me out on tour with him, which involved putting me in front of fifty thousand people that night in Miami.

Fifty thousand people was 49,912 people more than I was playing for on the night Jimmy took an interest in me.

And now Jimmy was angrily explaining the Internet. "There are people on the Internet who are mad because you're not playing 'Talkin' Seattle Grunge Rock Blues' at our shows," he said. So now there's an Internet. And it's kind of aggressive. "Talkin' Seattle Grunge Rock Blues" was on the radio, but it wasn't supposed to be. Another song, "Alright Guy," was the one we had made a video for. We went to Atlanta, and we had goats, midgets, fireworks, models, walkie-talkies, and a director with a beret.

But all the goats and berets in Atlanta didn't make radio people play "Alright Guy." Instead, some of them started playing "Talkin' Seattle Grunge Rock Blues." I don't know why people liked it, though I liked it and still do. Jimmy wanted me to make a video for it. I said I would do that if the video could be just me smashing a car. Just smashing the fuck out of it. No singing, no close-ups of my face, and no guitars, unless we were using them to help us smash the fuck out of that car.

Jimmy didn't like my car-smashing idea, which meant nobody liked my car-smashing idea. And Jimmy was my boss. We didn't wind up making a video. But they were still playing "Talkin' Seattle Grunge Rock Blues" on the radio sometimes, which is why the Internet was mad at me and why I was dodging fruit twenty minutes before I was supposed to go onstage in front of fifty thousand Parrotheads. (I don't mean "Parrotheads" as a slur, like "midgets.")

Jimmy had written down five of my song titles on an envelope.

"I want you to play these tonight," he said. And by this point, he wasn't throwing the fruit.

"I want you to play these every night on this tour," said Jimmy Buffett, one of the most popular singers ever.

Ever.

Jimmy Buffet.

And after more than two decades of traveling and singing, he was giving me tips. This guy who'd done all this, and he was showing me how to do it. He was telling me the songs of mine that would be best for me to play on a tour like this, in front of his crowd. His hard-earned crowd, I might add.

Too bad for Jimmy that I was going through my sunglasses at night phase. Really. Shades inside, at night, walking into the same places I'd been hanging out at for three years. Here were my reasons, such as they were: "Hey, guys, I just happen to wear shades inside at night now. Oh, it's not 'cause I have a record contract. It's totally unrelated. I don't know why you're trying to take it there. We all used to just be cool and wear whatever we wanted. I'm not changing, you're changing." So

I explained to Jimmy. "You would have never let anybody tell you what to play," I told him, "and I'm not going to ever let anybody tell me what to play."

Right?

Sure.

"You're an ungrateful prick!" Jimmy yelled, hurling grapefruits at the cowboy outfit in question, citrus smacking against pearl snaps.

The grapefruits weren't the worst of it. The pineapples were the worst of it.

"And an idiot!"

Smack. Orange and yellow. Seeds and pulp and pricklies. Where were Charleston and Byron when I needed them?

Finally, he stopped. And we stared at each other. And I said, "Can I go?"

Jimmy Buffett put both hands over his face and sighed, really big. Looking back, I think maybe he was mad at himself for letting me get him mad. Why would he give a shit?

By the way, Jimmy taught me the phrase, "No good deed goes unpunished." It wasn't until years later that I realized he was trying to tell me something about the way I behaved. I thought he was just telling me about the world.

I turned and walked out of the room, and then I walked down a corridor where Bob Mercer was standing in front of my dressing room door.

Bob was like a dad to me until the day he died, in 2010.

At the time he was the president of Jimmy's Margaritaville Records. This did not make him Jimmy's boss, but it did make him one of mine. Beautiful guy. I'll talk more about Bob later.

In his British accent, Bob said, "What was all that shouting I heard, Sunshine?"

Bob called me "Sunshine." He called a lot of people that.

I said, "I'm going home. I'm quitting the tour."

He said, "Hilarious," and I kept walking.

I went out the back into the parking lot, walking through the tailgate parties that were winding down. The show was scheduled to start in ten minutes. When I got to the edge of the parking lot, I started to leave the venue. But I didn't. I walked to our van and smoked a joint and leaned against it, trying to think how I would get home. And then up walked Bob.

"God, I love shit like this," is what he said, only he didn't say it. He didn't have to say it. It was all over him like a plainly lettered sign. He loved shit like that. Chaos and confrontation and reckless behavior made him calm. He was the eye of my life's hurricane.

Bob said, "You two are a lot alike, you and Jimmy." He really did say this. "Is there any way I can talk you back inside to do your set?"

I said, "I don't think there is a way."

He said, "I'll tell you something that you don't know. Jimmy just found out his father is deathly ill. He found this out about four hours ago. His dad—and Todd, he's very close to his dad—has only two months to live. Absolute maximum."

So Jimmy Buffett—my boss—could have used a friend that day. Instead, he got Mr. Sunglasses at Night.

"Is it not cool for Jimmy to make a song request?" Bob said. "I've seen you take 'em."

Of course that's true. I hear that logic now. At the time, I was just mad and shocked.

I said, "I don't think so, Bob. Am I still going to have a job tomorrow if I don't?"

He said, "Sure," so I said, "I think I'm leaving."

He went inside, and then out came Shamus, our sound man.

Shamus was crying. "I'm crying," Shamus said. "That's why they sent me out. They said you wouldn't be able to look at me crying and still go home."

It was actually kind of hard to see him crying, 'cause my shades were smudged.

No, I could see him. And he was right. He was right to cry, because I was about to blow a good time for everybody. I wasn't the only one giving his life to this. There were five of us. But I was apparently the only one willing to chuck it all. Seeing Shamus that way made me realize that I wasn't willing to chuck it all for everyone else, only myself.

"Okay," I said to Shamus. We walked into the venue, back down the hall, out to the stage, where Bob and Jimmy were waiting to see if I was coming back.

I saw Bob first. He was grinning. Then Jimmy stepped toward me, not smiling but not angry, either. Before I could apologize, Jimmy, my boss, said, "I'm sorry, man." That's an apology Jimmy Buffett did not owe me. Anybody dumb enough to not receive a gift from Jimmy Buffett with grace should be pelted with fruit.

"I'm sorry, Jimmy," I said.

And he said, "I had a weird day."

Jimmy walked onstage into the spotlight, and the crowd roared. Into the microphone, he introduced me to all these people as his new buddy and son and as the guy he was bringing into his record company. He gave me a glowing introduction, effectively handing his people—fifty thousand of them, remember—to me. He told fifty thousand people that I was a good singer and song maker.

While he was doing this, I huddled with the band. And said, "When he says my name, let's do the intro to 'Margaritaville.'"

"Margaritaville" is Jimmy's best-known hit. He wrote it himself, and it was his first big, popular song. It's about a hard-luck guy who finally realizes that he's responsible for his own undoing. And people just love it. We love the melody. We love the arrangement. We love the part where the guy cuts his heel on a beer can pop top. We love it enough that we buy Margaritaville kitchen appliances and visit Margaritaville chain restaurants across the country. Many of us even take vacations to Key West, where we look for the guy in that song. In lieu of that, some of us become the guy in that song.

You might think everyone's heard that song. But statisticians estimate that there are a million people in the United States alone who have not. Statisticians also estimate the US deaf population to be right around one million people.

Deaf people. You can't tell 'em anything. Well, you can, but you've either got to talk real loud and slow or use those gang signs. Jesus Christ, a guy could get shot.

That said, opening for Jimmy Buffett and coming out with "Margaritaville" is a fucking terrible idea. In show business, we call that "stealing someone's act." It's a great talent of mine, but this was not the best time to employ it.

Let's recap. Before going onstage, I'd defied my boss's orders and threatened to walk out on the one good chance that anyone ever handed me. By anyone, I mean him. And now I was about to do something unforgivable, to perform his closing song as my opening number. Today, if someone did that to me, they wouldn't get a second number. That's why Celine Dion never opens for me anymore.

It would be like opening for late-seventies Steve Martin by walking out with a plastic arrow through my head and hollering, "I'm a wild and craaaaazy guy!"

So we went with it.

Just after Jimmy Buffett told fifty thousand people to give me a chance, me and my band kicked into "Margaritaville." And I'm pretty sure every last one of those fifty thousand people immediately recognized the well-worn opening riff and thought to themselves, "Uh, this isn't gonna be good." Jimmy wasn't even all the way off the stage yet when he turned around and looked at me, dagger eyed.

But Jimmy didn't know I had a plan.

Just as the opening riff faded, and it was the singer's turn to sing, "Living on sponge cakes, watching the sun bake," my band kicked into a song of mine off our album, a rock song called "This Land Is Our Land," based on the chords to Skynyrd's "Sweet Home Alabama." Because Woody Guthrie already had a song called "This Land Is Your Land," I based my tune on "Sweet Home Alabama" so no one would think I was being derivative. Or something.

As soon as Jimmy heard the lick change from his to mine (or kind of mine), the daggers disappeared, He laughed out loud, grinned out louder, and threw up his hands to signal a touchdown.

We played great that night, and the tour went on, and Shamus stopped crying a few days later. I think I might have slipped that old "Seattle" song back into the set, too.

By the way, I am sad to inform you that Jimmy's father passed away . . . in 2003, at the age of eighty-three, eight years after he only had two months, maximum, to live.

Which brings me to the point of this story: Bob Mercer was hilarious.

CHAPTER 2

JERRY JEFF
WALKER'S BALLS

The story of Jerry Jeff Walker and me starts at Trog's.

This was 1986. I was in my teens, and I'd just moved to San Marcos, Texas, from Oregon. Trog was six foot eight and weighed about three of me. There will be more on him later, mostly reiterating his gigantic size, but for now I will just say that he was generous, in that he let me sleep on the couch at his apartment, and forward thinking, in that one night before I went to sleep he put a cassette tape in the boom box, and we all listened to Jerry Jeff Walker's *Gypsy Songman* album. After that I listened to it over and over again on my own.

I don't know if you've heard *Gypsy Songman*, and since this is a book I may never know. I don't know if you've heard

Jerry Jeff Walker at all, either, but I hope you have. He's known as "The Gypsy Songman" or "Scamp Walker," the drifting, grifting, scamp type, Texas singer-songwriter who wrote "Mr. Bojangles," a song about a how a young Jerry Jeff Walker gets thrown in a New Orleans drunk tank and meets up with another guy who turns out to be a real good dancer.

The song is better than my plot summary.

"Mr. Bojangles" was made famous in a version by the Nitty Gritty Dirt Band, and it has been recorded by Sammy Davis Jr., Harry Belafonte, Bob Dylan, King Curtis, Tom T. Hall, and a bunch of others.

"Mr. Bojangles" is Jerry Jeff's best-known song, but it's not necessarily his main song. He's got one about hitchhiking called "Stoney" that I love, and one called "Charlie Dunn" that is about a guy who makes boots, but that also seems like it might be about finding joy in your life.

I recorded a whole album of Jerry Jeff's songs and started it with one called "Takin' It as It Comes."

"Well you're damned if you do, and you're damned if you don't," he sang, and I sang. I continued, with his words: "Makes a man stop to wonder whether he will or he won't / But I'm in my prime and I'm enjoying my time / I'm too busy chasing life to stop living mine."

See drifter, gypsy, grifter, scamp. Jerry Jeff was all about taking it as it comes. He has a song called "Pissin' in the Wind" that's not a lament so much as a statement of purpose.

I loved it all the moment I heard it.

One day, a few months after first hearing *Gypsy Songman*, I heard that Jerry Jeff was going to be playing at Gruene Hall (pronounced "Green Hall"), and that we should go. I said, "Fuckin' A we're gonna go."

For those of you who don't share my expansive vocabulary, "Fuckin' A" is an emphatic affirmation.

We got there two hours before the show was supposed to start, which as it turned out was more than three hours early for the show. We got right up front, and I could see that there were no amplifiers or drums set up. This was going to be a solo gig, if it was going to be a gig at all. After everyone else got there, there was tension in the room, because nobody had seen Jerry Jeff. The place was packed, and the guest of honor was absent.

Finally we heard a roar from out by the front door; I looked back, and there he was. Cowboy hat, T-shirt, bandanna around his neck, jeans stuffed into calico boots, acoustic guitar over his shoulder. No case. The crowd had to part for him, as he walked up real slowly to the stage.

Then he got up there, plugged the guitar in, and went, "Hey, buckaroos," and it was on. I'd never been called a "buckaroo" before, being from Oregon. He stood on that stage and played song after song, all by himself, shrugging his shoulders sometimes but otherwise not moving much. He played chords on the guitar, without any of the supposedly impressive, wheedly, way-up-on-the-neck guitar hero leads that my older brother liked. Jerry Jeff didn't want to be our hero, he just wanted to sing us some songs, to drift and grift his way through another blurry night.

Jerry Jeff failed miserably that night, at least on that score. By the third song, he was my hero. By the fourth song, he was my destination.

In some ways, I already was what he was. He was singing all this freeloader gypsy shit, and I was a freeloader gypsy. People who knew me called me "The Load," 'cause I was always bumming a place to stay. It seemed to me right then, watching

Jerry Jeff, that there were exactly three chords' worth of difference between a freeloader and a free spirit.

So he had me at "buckaroos." He just looked like he didn't care about anything. And I didn't either. Except now, if I gave a shit about anything, I gave a shit about becoming Jerry Jeff Walker.

The day after I saw that show, I went to my buddy Mark Watkins's house, had him show me the chords to "Sweet Home Alabama," and took (let's say "borrowed") his guitar. I was off and running, and I played every day. And anytime Jerry Jeff was playing anywhere, I'd go. I must have seen him play twenty times a year for a few years there. My life was bus tables, play guitar, go see Jerry Jeff.

Finally I wrote a song about busing tables, with those "Sweet Home Alabama" chords I knew. I played it for the manager, Bubba, at the bar where I worked, Peppers at the Falls.

Bubba thought it was hilarious.

Bubba was a pushover.

It went like this:

> *I work at a restaurant, busin' tables by the Falls*
> *All day I pick up half-eaten food*
> *And for a break I clean bathroom stalls*
> *I know if I get hungry, though*
> *There's something I can do*
> *I just tell Bubba that I need a break*
> *And make a plateful of bus tub stew*
> *Bus tub stew, bus tub stew*
> *They only took about a bite or two*

I know, I know, but at least it's food
Bus tub stew.

It was my first song. And Bubba decided I had to get up at his bar and play that song. This was maybe a month after that first Jerry Jeff show. An acoustic duo was playing at Peppers, and Bubba insisted that I get up and do "Bus Tub Stew" in the middle of their set. I got up, and it actually went over like crazy.

It hooked me like a drug.

It was scary, though. We're talking about stepping into the light and getting onstage. Now this was one light, and "onstage" meant being two inches higher off the ground than everybody else. But for me, getting on that stage was climbing up to the high, high dive. It was terrifying and thrilling. It was a dare. And I took the dare.

After that, every time that acoustic duo played, I hung around to play my song. I wasn't Jerry Jeff Walker, but I was That "Bus Tub Stew" Guy.

It's fun being That "Bus Tub Stew" Guy. It's not as much fun being the acoustic duo that has to cede their stage for "Bus Tub Stew" every night. One of them finally got mad at me and said, "Haven't you ever heard of Cheatham Street Fucking Warehouse, man? They have an open mike every Wednesday, and you can go play 'Bus Tub Stew' there."

An "open mike" is a deal where a bunch of different people can get up and play a few of their songs, regardless of whether they are well known or not. Usually none of them are well-known, or else they wouldn't be playing for free. It's mostly for beginners. And for many, open mikes have been the first step toward a life filled with hotel keys.

By this time I had two more songs. One was called "Stand Up If You're 19." It was a protest song about how they had just changed the drinking age from nineteen to twenty-one, and how I was pretty angry about that and thought everyone else should be, too. The other was called "Money Makes Fools of Us All." That last one was about my parents.

So I went to Cheatham Street Warehouse in San Marcos, Texas. It was owned by a guy named Kent Finlay, a real song-writers' friend. At Cheatham you had to sign your name on a list, and the order of the names on the list was the order in which you'd play your three songs. I was lucky in that I had exactly enough songs.

Once I signed, I looked at the name in front of mine, be-cause when they call that guy's name, that means I go next. Looking back, I don't know what made me think that would be helpful to remember, but I still remember. The guy before me, his name was Aaron Allen.

I will never forget that name. Aaron Allen, Aaron Allen, Aaron Allen. After they said Aaron Allen, I told myself, it's time to get up there in front of people.

Aaron Allen got up there, and he sang this one song, and it seemed like it was really good, and everybody was kind of excited.

"Simple love, simply told, is the language of the soul," he sang. "Better as you're growing old, simple love." My songs didn't say stuff like that in them. Mine said I ate people's left-overs. Write what you know. The next song he sang was a Willie Nelson song called "Truth #1," and I thought, "This is bullshit!" I'd seen the sign outside, as big as day, that said you had to sing your own songs. There was no mistaking its meaning.

I walked over to the bartender and I said, "Listen, lady"— the ladies love it when you say "Listen, lady," trust me—"that sign said we had to sing our own songs, and that's what I came down here for."

She said, "Yeah."

I said, "I heard this song on a Willie Nelson album."

She said, "Yeah."

I said, "Uh . . . well, . . ."

She said, "Oh, I see. . . . Okay, let me explain. Willie Nelson is the person who made this song famous, but Aaron wrote it. It's Aaron's song." I said, "Oh," then paused, thought a second, and said, "Is there any way that I can get further down the list a little bit or a lot, and maybe let some other young people play before I play my stuff?"

She said, "No, you play when you're supposed to play."

So Aaron Allen played a fucking Willie Nelson song that he'd written out of his own head and heart, everybody went nuts, and then they invited me up. I was eighteen years old. I got up and played every one of my three songs, but the whole time I was thinking, "Aaron Allen, Aaron Allen, Aaron Allen. . . . That guy knows Willie Nelson. He's probably smoked pot with Willie Nelson. What difference does it make what I'm playing, when that guy over there smoked pot with Willie Nelson? What's he do all day but probably rhyme his feelings and tell people what Willie Nelson is like? This guy lives his life and sleeps in, and if something bums him out he makes it rhyme, and somehow he probably gets paid for all that. Now THAT'S a job."

As soon as my part was over, which was real soon, I walked right up to this guy and said, "Aaron Allen, my name is Todd Snider. I want to do what you do."

"You just did, didn't you?" he said.

"Yeah, but I want to be good at it."

"Well," he said, "that's different."

I said, "Whaddaya mean?"

He said, "You've got to get better," and I asked him how you do that. And he said, "Nobody knows. That's the magic."

I thought, "That's not the magic. That sucks."

Then I said, "C'mon, man. Certainly you've got to know something about getting better at making up songs."

He said he didn't know anything, but that he met a guy once who had some advice about how to get better at that.

"I was sitting beside the guitar-shaped pool at a place called the Spence Manor on Music Row in Nashville," he said. "I was with some songwriters, and one of them said he knew how you could always be getting better at making up songs.

"That guy said, 'If you want to be a songwriter and you always want to be getting better at making up songs, you've got to keep your life in a situation where you can pack up every single thing you own in the whole world inside of fifteen minutes and be moved out of wherever you are. And, if you keep your life in a situation where that kinda shit happens to you every once in a while and you are forced to execute that maneuver, I can't promise you a good life, but you will always be getting better at making up songs.'"

Now, I don't know if that was true or not, but I bought into it. And I tell you, it has taken a lot of discipline to keep my life as fucked up as it is.

Not bragging, just saying.

I even have a song called "The Devil's Backbone Tavern," which I sing to help me maintain that discipline, and every time I sing it I send it out to Aaron Allen, in whatever town he's fifteen minutes from being out of that night.

———

Onstage, I sometimes say that my first night at Cheatham went poorly, but it didn't. It was incredibly encouraging. I hadn't planned to talk, but I got scared, and in my fear I started talking. To this day, I still do that: both getting scared and talking. The singing part was all right, too.

After I finished hassling Aaron Allen, the owner, Kent Finlay, came over and said nice things. He said, "You could be like John Prine or something."

I said, "Who's that?"

He said, "You don't know Prine?" And then he said, "Or like a Kristofferson."

Later, I would come to understand what high praise that was. At the time, I didn't know.

He asked where I was living. I told him about my situation, by which I meant the couch that passed for my home. He said, "Well, come on, you want to hear some records? Me and my wife are up all night."

I went to his house. He played me "Brian Hennessey," "I Gotta Get Rid of This Band," and "If That Ain't Love, What Is?" by Bobby Bare. He played "Me and Bobbie McGee" and "The Pilgrim, Chapter 33" by Kris Kristofferson. He played Johnny Cash's version of Guy Clark's "Desperados Waiting for a Train." He played Billy Joe Shaver's "Old Chunk of Coal" and John Prine's "Paradise" and "Hello in There."

He pointed out what he called the twists and secrets of all those songs.

I stayed on the Finlays' couch that night, and then that's where I started staying all the time.

Kent Finlay gave me a PA system and found me gigs. Most important, he gave me an education in music and showed me songs I would have crawled across cut glass to write. Without Kent, I would never have been able to approach my goal of becoming Jerry Jeff Walker.

Except Kent didn't dig Jerry Jeff Walker.

He said some of Jerry Jeff's songs were good, but he thought Jerry Jeff couldn't compare to Kristofferson, Prine, Guy Clark, Shel Silverstein (who wrote a bunch of Bobby Bare's greatest songs, plus Cash's "A Boy Named Sue"), and a bunch of others. Kent was right, in a way. Jerry Jeff couldn't compare, because he wasn't comparable. He was Jerry Jeff, righteous and alone.

Kent actually tried to turn me off of Jerry Jeff once and for all, the night he explained to me that it was stupid for me to want to be Jerry Jeff Walker, because Jerry Jeff Walker wasn't even Jerry Jeff Walker.

Kent told me that Jerry Jeff was not a Texas guy at all, that he was born Ronald Clyde Crosby and raised in the great prairie lands of Oneonta, New York. Jerry Jeff, in Kent's eyes, was something of a phony. He wasn't Jerry Jeff Walker, gypsy songman. He wasn't authentic. He was this kid in the Catskills who one day woke up and decided, "I'm Ron Crosby, but I don't have to be." At least that's how I imagined it, and for me it was gas on the fire.

In the moment I found out native Texas gypsy drifter Jerry Jeff Walker was actually Ronald Crosby, I thought, "Now THAT'S balls. I'm in, for life."

In that moment, I knew I didn't have to be Todd Snider, the Oregon kid who'd played football. I knew, I'm not who I've been told I was; I'm who I want to be.

I'm Todd Snider, but I don't have to be.

I did briefly contemplate changing my name. But just being a folk singer—a thing that went against everything my jock-loving, Republican family adored—was enough. Besides, L. L. Cool J. was taken.

How sweet would that have been, though?

I spent about three years writing songs, playing bars, going to see Jerry Jeff on my nights off, and trying to schedule my own stuff around his stuff.

I saw lots of other people, too. One of the "jobs" Kent Finlay had assigned me in his very real role as my songwriting instructor was to go see a guy named Billy Joe Shaver on a Monday night at Cheatham Street Warehouse. Billy Joe had written an entire album for Waylon Jennings, and he was an awe-inspiring songwriter. He'd put so many years into crafting songs and performing them, and I watched him play at a little Texas shithole in front of not more than eight people, not more than three of whom were listening. And I thought to myself, "I want that job."

Billy Joe was drinking from a bottle after the show when I went to get his advice and tell him how great he was. He told me, "Just keep reading the Bible and it'll all work out." Then he said, "And stay off the whiskey. I'm only drinking tonight 'cause I've got a sore throat."

Meanwhile, I kept writing letters to Jerry Jeff that I intended to give him, but I kept them all to myself. My first interaction with him was one time at Gruene Hall when he lost his guitar pick and asked if anyone in the audience had one. I did, so he did.

I wound up moving to Memphis, where I got some regular gigs and made clear my admiration for Jerry Jeff Walker. He came to play a show one time at the Peabody Hotel, and I was in the audience, kind of front and center, and when he walked offstage he pointed at me and gave me a look of recognition. That was the first time he acknowledged that he realized I was attending a lot of his shows and sitting in the same spot. I was young and had a job working at a place where they made hot tubs. I swept up at that place. You had to keep a broom going there all day, 'cause they made the hot tubs out of fiberglass, and the fiberglass shards would turn to dust and fly all over the place. If you didn't sweep, you'd have a foot of fiberglass dust piled up every two hours.

In Memphis I eventually got enough gigs to retire from the hot tub game, and I made friends with people who owned a place where people performed. One time Jerry Jeff performed at that place. They asked if I wanted to open for him, and I said, "Fuck, yes." I played my twenty minutes that night and did pretty good. When I came offstage there was some lady who had snuck backstage, and she was asking Jerry Jeff to sign a poster. He signed it, but didn't seem necessarily happy about it. She saw me and said, "I heard you, you were good. Will you sign this poster, too?"

I'd never signed an autograph before. Well, I'd signed one when someone thought I was Kurt Cobain. This was the first time I'd signed, "Todd Snider."

She said, "Jerry Jeff, can we use your back?"

"Yeah," he said. "Hurry up."

I put the poster on Jerry Jeff's back and said, "This is the highlight of my life, man."

Jerry Jeff said, "Boring life so far, kid."

———

Three years went by, and I made my first album and my second album. At the beginning of the tour for the second album, me and my band got invited to play at Jerry Jeff Walker's Labor Day Weekend festival, with Jack Ingram, Charlie Robison, Natalie Maines, Junior Brown, Joe Ely, and Robert Earl Keen.

Oh, and Jerry Jeff. He opened and closed. When he opened, I watched him from the crowd. He finished, and I went backstage, ran up to him, wrapped my arms around him, and said, "I love you. You're my king."

He looked for security.

Really.

I noticed he was kind of panicking, and I said, "I'm Todd, I'm playing today."

He said, "Oh, man, I saw you in the crowd with that funky hat and I just thought you'd snuck backstage."

After that, he was good. Though he didn't believe me when I said, "I have every album that you've ever made, memorized."

He said, "No, you don't."

My hero was wrong.

But I had a good set that night, we had a few beers backstage, we exchanged phone numbers, and from then on we were friends.

Five months later, in March 1996, I got invited to play his birthday party. I had this story to tell before my song, called "The Devil's Backbone Tavern," and the story was really about

Jerry Jeff; when I played it that night at The Orpheum theater in Austin, people loved it. And Jerry Jeff loved it.

Backstage, everybody was drinking. After the show, we all went out somewhere and partied, and at a certain point certain people in the party started to un-party. The group dwindled. But some of us ended up in a hotel room, and then that some of us started to dwindle again, and it got down to me, Jerry Jeff, and Ramblin' Jack Elliott.

Ramblin' Jack Elliott, by the way, was born Elliott Charles Adnopoz. He traveled and studied under Woody Guthrie. He inspired Bob Dylan. Bob Dylan, by the way, was born Robert Allen Zimmerman in Duluth, Minnesota.

Damn, I wish L. L. Cool J. wasn't taken.

Jerry Jeff, Ramblin' Jack, and I started walking down the halls of the Driskill Hotel in Austin, looking for more parties. And we found them. And when those dried up, we walked up 6th Street. That's what we were doing when the sun came up.

The morning after Jerry Jeff's birthday party, I was okay. That afternoon, I was throwing up blood and freaking out. Don't judge. You'd freak out, too, if you were throwing up blood.

A few months later I went to rehab for morphine addiction. In those months I made an album called *Viva Satellite*, played a big show in LA where I walked offstage and told the crowd to fuck off (an old Jerry Jeff trick), trashed my hotel room (an old Jerry Jeff trick), and got dropped from my record label (an old lots of people trick). Then I went into rehab, because I was doing too much morphine.

And, yes, any morphine is probably too much morphine. When you say to someone, "I think I am taking too much morphine," you are without a doubt taking too much morphine. If you live outside of a hospital room and you have any idea how to obtain morphine at all, you are taking too much morphine.

Damn, though, it's so good.

When I got out of rehab, Jerry Jeff told me to come out on vacation to his house in Belize. I went with a mentor and Jerry Jeff associate named Keith Sykes and with my friend, songwriter Jack Ingram. We drank Biliken beer and smoked dope, all day every day.

Me and Jack had a big awareness when we'd sit around playing songs with Jerry Jeff and Keith around 2:30 in the morning. We realized that their 2:30 A.M. performances were tighter and better than the ones we did at 9 P.M. in front of people who had paid to see them. We saw that Jerry Jeff and Keith were listening hard to each other and responding to what the other was playing and singing. They weren't making drunk, banging-around music; they were making music that should have been recorded. We thought, "We're just not as fucking good as they are. We need to be playing our guitars more and working on our singing, so we can someday be that good at 2:30 in the morning."

I went to New York City and mixed the *Viva* album. ("Mixing" is where you take all the singing and playing that everyone did at different times and blend them together so that it sounds like everyone was singing and playing at the same time, absolutely perfectly. But please don't tell anybody.) Then I went on tour and went back to the morphine. Not good.

Luckily, I'd met the love of my life (really) in rehab, and we were going steady. Still, I was stinging from being fired by my record company, and Jerry Jeff could tell I was raw and hurt. He invited me and my new love, Melita, down to Belize for his annual fan club weekend, just to get away.

When I got down there, Jerry Jeff threw me to the sharks.

I know you hate it when someone uses the word "literally" to make a point. I know I hate it. But here it bears inclusion: he literally threw me to the sharks.

He told me he wanted to take me snorkeling, and that he knew a really pretty spot. We went out in the boat, and he gave me flippers and told me how to do it: flop in backward, blow the water out of the snorkel, and then swim near the top of the water and check out all the coral and shit.

Then he said, "You go first."

I fell backward out of the boat, blew the water out of the snorkel, and opened my eyes, and as God is my witness there were six or seven sharks. There were sharks everywhere around me, and stingrays right below me. I was four feet from the boat, with sharks between me and the boat, immediately. And then a dozen or more stingrays in close proximity.

Okay, it turns out that this was a place where people who aren't folk singers know that they feed the sharks and stingrays until they become nearly domestic, so that the snorkel people can see them up close. Snorkel people hand them food, and it's a real thrill. Lots of people pay someone to take them to this exact spot. Feeding the sharks is kind of like feeding ducks at the pond, except the ducks look like they're going to fucking eat your face.

Jerry Jeff didn't tell me about the domestic shark deal. I saw the sharks, realized I couldn't get back to the boat, stuck my head above the water, and saw him howling. He was just so happy. Just glowing with joy. And he said, "Swim back!"

Yeah, Jerry Jeff, there's sharks in front of me.

"It's okay," he explained to me, from the boat. "Just swim at them! You have to swim at them!"

I swam right at them, and they scattered as I came closer. Scattered just like ducks.

But enough with the ducks.

Look, plenty of people will tell you that drugs make you paranoid.

I'm not sure that's true.

Well, it's kind of true, but it's not true that you're paranoid while you're actually doing drugs. The deal, in my experience, is that when the drugs run off is when you get paranoid. It's not like getting whiskey drunk and starting a fight. The fight's going to be in another couple of days, after you come down from the drugs.

So, trust me, if you're gonna do morphine, make the commitment to always do morphine. Get a ton of it, if you're going to do it. You don't know where to get a ton of it, do you? I'm reachable, via Da Capo Press.

Okay, I'd been fired by my record company, but I should have been fired. Nobody was mean to me, nobody ripped me off, and nobody tried to make me something I wasn't. I'd been treated like a king, and I failed. Nobody did anything but good to me, and I tanked. I have friends who got fired from record deals, and it was because of the record label guys. My record label guys were great. Nobody made us change our clothes. We didn't have a single excuse.

Jerry Jeff probably knew that I would have felt less desperate and hurt and paranoid if I'd had someone to blame for my music business failings, and that may have been part of the reason he and Susan invited Melita and me to come to Belize. But once I got down there, things didn't go well. We were down there with Jerry Jeff and Keith Sykes, and I felt like they were treating me like a step 'n' fetch it.

Keep in mind that a year before this, I'd have cut off my toes to play step 'n' fetch it for Jerry Jeff Walker. It was probably because of my failure that I didn't want to do that anymore.

Melita and I began kind of hiding off from the group by ourselves, and I got it in my head that we had to go home. We got out of there at 6 A.M., when I knew everyone would be asleep. It was the morning of a Mike Tyson fight. I love Mike Tyson. I actually stole weed that morning from Jerry Jeff's wife Susan. I had it in my mind that I wanted weed for the Tyson fight, and I had it in my mind that she'd understand.

We got on a small plane that took us to some bigger place, where we had to stay to get a flight back to the United States the next morning. I had in my possession, for the first time in my life, a credit card. We got a hotel room with the card and used it again to get the Tyson fight on our TV. Then we got some whiskey and laughed at the absurdity of what we'd done. We'd just used a card that to me looked just like the hotel key, and they were giving me cars, rooms, whiskey, and TV fights. The other absurdity was that I'd turned on my hero and didn't leave a note or anything.

I thought I'd never speak to Jerry Jeff again. I was sad and bothered by that once I sobered up. Or rather, once I got enough of my favorite drug back in me to think close to clearly.

I thought I'd blown it.

I knew I'd blown it.

After a couple of months I wrote Jerry Jeff a letter, explaining how embarrassed I was and how sorry I was. I didn't get any response back. And that bothered me.

Then I was booked to play two nights at the Cactus Cafe in Austin. After the second song of the first night, I heard Jerry Jeff yell, "That's my boy." And once I knew he was there, I did a couple of his songs. After that show was over, we went to his house and played guitar all night.

We didn't talk about the letter. He taught me how to play his song "Hill Country Rain," and we acted like nothing ever happened.

We've never talked about any of this, ever.

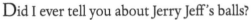

Did I ever tell you about Jerry Jeff's balls?

We were in New Orleans, where Jerry Jeff had just bought a house. My band, the Nervous Wrecks, was on tour. It had been a long tour. I was carrying a tackle box that contained peyote, weed, pain pills, a big bag of cocaine, some assorted fishing lures, and some stickers and buttons and shit.

I should add, I don't do cocaine, and I didn't back then. I just keep all the drugs that have ever been given to me. I don't want to be rude.

At the New Orleans show I found out Jerry Jeff and Susan Walker were in town to see our show. In the dressing room after the show, they came up and I said, "Susan, do you want some drugs? I've got tons." She said, "You've got more than one choice?" I said, "Yes." She said, "What's the menu?" and I told her what I had. They laughed when I said, "Cocaine."

I said, "Let's do some." I knew Jerry Jeff used to be a blow guy. His nickname years ago was "Jiffy Jack Snowdrift." Also, "Mr. Blowjangles." He said, "I don't do that anymore," but he sounded a little tempted. Maybe a little drunk, too.

Being a good friend, I said, "C'mon, let's do this." I lobbied for it. He was like, "Fine, we'll go back to the house, do that, smoke a little weed, and walk around the Quarter for a little bit. We'll have a blast."

Yes, we're going back to the seventies. It was time travel in a tackle box.

So we headed back to Jerry Jeff's. It was me, Elvis Hicks, and Shamus Bacon.

I mention Elvis and Shamus by name because Elvis has children, and Shamus might one day, and I want to be sure their kids know that they used to be cool. And do blow. At Jerry Jeff's house.

By this point, Jerry Jeff and Susan clearly thought that I was doing blow all the time, 'cause I had so much. But I was a JV in a varsity uniform. I had no idea how much I was supposed to take, and I had no tolerance built up.

Somebody cut out a bunch of lines, and they were really, really big. Hey, that's okay. To whom much is given, much is expected, and I'm a shirt-off-my-back kind of guy. So we all passed a mirror around and everybody hits these two huge rails. We decided to do two more real quick, before we went.

Jerry Jeff spoke up. "A line of cocaine will make a new man out of you—and he'll want some, too."

After another round of rails, Elvis produced a hog leg of a joint. We passed it around and laughed and talked about where we were going to go.

Okay, brothers and sisters, we are now exiting the firsthand knowledge portion of this story for a minute. We'll come back, but for now we're moving into the from-what-I've-been-told section.

All of a sudden, they said, I turned real white, leaned back, and started doing the fish-in-the-bottom-of-the-boat thing, then fell onto a glass table and threw up. They were like, "Holy shit, get him into the bathroom." Jerry Jeff, Elvis, and maybe some of the others picked me up, and I responded to their kindness by throwing up again. On them, of course. They tried to get me to a toilet, and I threw up yet again. Then they got me into a shower, and turned the water, freezing cold, on.

I have a brief memory of me in the shower with all my clothes on and a lot of yelling going on. Then it was lights out, completely.

They said they sat around, made sure I was stable and was fine and asleep, and after about an hour of watching, everyone except Susan went out for a drink. Susan stayed to keep an eye on me.

Later, and I remember this part, I was asleep on the couch in the same room I threw up in, and I was awakened by the sound of someone moving around and mumbling. As I woke up a little, I could tell it was Jerry Jeff, pacing and mumbling, "Never fucking again." I didn't have my eyes open.

Then he walked over to where I was on the couch, stood over me, and leaned down to shout in my ear, "Never again! You hear, me, boy?!!"

That's when I opened my eyes. And the first thing I saw, twelve inches from my face, was Jerry Jeff Walker's balls. I could describe this vision in great detail. I will not. You're welcome.

I backed my head up away from his balls and saw that he'd been pacing around, completely naked.

He's a naked sleeper.

"You hear me, then!" he shouted. "Never again. Never a'fucking gain."

I heard him.

I saw him.

Cocaine is a shit drug. I hear people say it's sexy. Sexy my ass.

Every time someone offers it to me, I see Jerry Jeff Walker's balls.

And now you do, too.

I'm older now than Jerry Jeff was on the night when his music first changed my life. He and I sometimes do shows together, when we can find someplace to play where we both want to go.

Jerry Jeff always liked Santa Fe, New Mexico. The only thing he didn't like about that town is they had some rules about how you couldn't walk around everywhere with your dog. Jerry Jeff likes to walk around everywhere with his dog. So he went to great lengths to convince the city that without his dog around, he was prone to nervous breakdowns.

The nervous breakdown thing is completely untrue, but once you start changing names, where do you draw the line? Jerry Jeff don't care.

Now his dog is a "service dog," and he can walk anywhere with Jerry Jeff. That dog has complete Santa Fe immunity now. That dog can smoke a fat joint right in front of a cop, and by law the cop has to pat him on the head and hand him a snack.

So not long ago, Jerry Jeff and I booked a gig together in Santa Fe. The show was a song-swap. We sat onstage at some theater, and I listened hard to everything he was doing, trying in vain to be as good at 9 P.M. as Jerry Jeff and Keith Sykes were at 2:30 in the morning.

So many years have passed since the time I first saw Jerry Jeff, and in those years I have practiced writing, playing, and singing for thousands of hours. I lived by the code of Aaron Allen's songwriter friend's plan long enough and well enough that I was finally able to settle down into a place that'd be much harder to leave. And if you looked at Jerry Jeff and my tax returns, where we have to fill in what we do for a living, we write down exactly the same thing.

I'd like to tell you that all this has made us equals, but it hasn't. Onstage with Jerry Jeff that night in Santa Fe, I felt the same as when I was nineteen, watching him. This time I had a better seat, though not much better: I always found my way to the front row back then. He's not Jerry Jeff Walker, my colleague. He's Jerry Jeff Walker, my hero. And he knows that and uses it against me at every opportunity.

"What's with the hat?" he asked me in Santa Fe.

Turns out that it was summer, and you're supposed to wear straw hats in the summer and felt in the winter. I didn't know that.

"What you got a winter hat on for?" he said. Then he tried to give me his, for the fiftieth fucking time in my life. It doesn't fit, Jerry Jeff. It has never fit. Too big, and so are the boots.

After the gig Jerry Jeff and I walked to the bar at a hotel called La Fonda on the Plaza. We closed the place down, drinking beer and talking about everything.

Not everything. We never talked about that letter I wrote him, apologizing for Belize. But most everything else. We spent a lot of time talking about his albums and how he made them. I like to hear how he found the songs. I could interview him for hours, and every once in a while he'll get tipsy enough to let me.

He and Joe Ely—another legendary Texas music guy—spent a bunch of time together in Santa Fe, so he talked some about Joe. I told him a story that Joe told me. "Joe said he was playing in Lubbock one night and you were playing in Austin, but that when he walked offstage in Lubbock, you were on the side of the stage, 'cause you'd flown up in your plane," I told him.

"You talked him into coming back to your plane and going to Vegas with you, and he said you guys gambled all night and that after the sun came up he went to a hotel room and went to sleep and didn't wake up until a day and a half later. At which time, he took a shower, tried to gather himself and figure out what the fuck was going on, and walked down to the casino. He said when he got to the casino, you were there, sitting at the same table from two nights before, wearing the same clothes. He said when he walked up and sat down at the table, you said, 'Where'd you go?' like he'd just been gone for thirty minutes."

Jerry Jeff pondered this information and said, "Yeah, what of it?"

At some point, I asked him whether he was happy. And he said, "I got a million bucks and a plane. That's all Elvis ever wanted. I gotta piss."

Then he got up, and apparently his million bucks and a plane remark had been overheard by the guy sitting on my other side.

"Who is that?" he asked me.

"He wrote 'Mr. Bojangles.'"

"'Mr. Bojangles'? Shit."

"Yeah, shit is right. He's my idol."

"Yeah, we can tell. We can all tell," he said, nodding toward the bar's last handful of drinkers.

Last call came at 2 A.M., and Jerry Jeff and I were the last two people to straggle out. We walked out of that hotel and out onto the sidewalk, there on the downtown plaza. Our own hotel was just a couple hundred feet away. As we turned a corner, we heard what sounded like a banjo and a harmonica, playing "Mr. Bojangles." Turns out it sounded that way because it was a banjo and a harmonica, playing "Mr. Bojangles." We walked toward the sound.

The guy with the banjo and harmonica was not a performer kid. If he had been, he wouldn't have been working at 2 A.M., when there were no cars and no foot traffic. This was a bedraggled guy, not a kid. A homeless guy, kind of crazy looking, with a harmonica around his neck, his hat on the ground in front of him, and nothing in the hat.

It looked like a winter hat to me.

That guy looked up at us, without recognition. He didn't know Jerry Jeff Walker was standing there. He may never have heard of Jerry Jeff Walker.

"I met him in a cell in New Orleans," he sang. "I was down and out. / He looked to me to be the eyes of age, as he spoke right out. / He talked of life, he talked of life." They were the words from Jerry Jeff's song. Jerry Jeff and I stood there and watched this guy sing them, in front of a closed-down old blues bar, and I could feel us both getting choked up. And I was asking myself, "Should I tell this guy that he's playing Jerry Jeff's song, and that Jerry Jeff is standing right here?" But, no, I figured that if Jerry Jeff wanted to let this guy know who he was, he'd tell him.

He chose not to. When the song was over, he said, "That sounded great," and then he put a fuckload of cash—every bit of cash he had on him—into that guy's hat. And then we walked off to the hotel, and I just couldn't leave the moment alone.

"Maybe the highlight of my life," I said.

"Boring life so far, kid."

CHAPTER 3

THE BEEF

Todd Francis was The Beef.

And in our country's glorious bicentennial year of 1976, The Beef spent his time jacking baseballs out of Alpenrose Main Field in my hometown of Beaverton, Oregon.

I was nine, and I had just started my baseball career as a right fielder for City Rubber Stamp. Perhaps you've read about my skills on the diamond. If not, I can tell you that I batted ninth and played right field, which is pretty much where they always put the best player on the Little League team. That's just known.

Coach Wynn had given me the nickname "Tough Tiger Todd." He'd handed out lots of nicknames to the other kids and had given those nicknames some thought. "Little Dave? You're so quick out there, you'll be 'Scooter.' And Tim, we'll call you 'Stretch,' 'cause you really get that mitt out there at first base." I could tell when he got to mine he was kind of improvising, though. "Aaaaaaand, uh, Todd . . . let's go with, uh, 'Tough Tiger Todd.' Alright, gloves on, everybody!"

One night, I woke my wife up. This was much later. I did not have a wife at nine. I told her that I wanted her to call me "Tough Tiger Todd." But she didn't. And she doesn't, unless she's telling that story.

Okay, so we've established my baseball abilities. My brother was older and better than I was, so he got to play in a higher league, for a team called Shiloh Inn. Todd Francis was in my brother's league, playing for Far West Federal Savings.

Now, the main thing about Little League was that at the end of the season, they'd have the best players join an all-star team that hopefully would win district, go to state, win state, go to regionals and win that, and then go to Williamsport, Pennsylvania, for the Little League World Series. My brother made that all-star team, as did The Beef.

The Beef came from the Francis family. He was one of ten kids, and those ten were by a mile the wildest kids in our school. I'd go to their house after school and watch as people coming down the sidewalk would cross the street to get to the other side of the road so they wouldn't have to walk directly in front of the Francis house. The Francises were terrors, and they dominated anything they wanted to dominate. One of them went on to win a Super Bowl with the San Francisco 49ers. Another has won Emmy Awards for his work at ESPN. All of them are very successful in their businesses, though back in 1976, you would never have seen any of that coming. I remember when I got into high school and started going out at night with some of the Francis brothers, their mother would say, "If you get arrested, don't tell 'em you live here." And there may have been ten Francis kids, but there was only one Beef.

It's hard to describe how good at baseball that kid was when he was twelve. He was better than all the other kids, by a long, long way. More important, he had this reaction to pressure that was unlike anything I've ever seen. It was almost like a nervous tic, except instead of freezing up he would succeed. When Todd Francis got up with the bases loaded or with the game tied or on the line, he would hit the very first pitch out of the park 98 percent of the time. It was the talk of the town. If it happened today, it would be a YouTube sensation, the talk of every town. And Todd was so funny and such a leader and so charismatic, he not only was the most popular guy among the youth social group, he was pretty popular in the parent social group, too. I remember my father giving him the keys to his car on more than one occasion, when Beef was twelve. People just loved The Beef.

So, all-star season started, and everybody thought we had a good team. By "we," I mean "they." I wasn't on the team, but I still cheered for them like they were Dylan and the Stones rolled into one. I was ten, and went to all their practices, just to be around it all.

The first all-star game was under the lights against Sunset Valley at Alpenrose. Sunset Valley had a kid named Timber Meade that everybody was afraid of—everybody but The Beef, of course. He was supposed to be the baddest-ass pitcher there'd ever been in Oregon, and this was a single elimination tournament, where if you lose it's all over. Early on, those guys got up 1–0 on us, and we couldn't touch Timber Meade.

But in the bottom of the sixth inning, still down 1–0, Timber Meade made the mistake of walking the guy in front of

Todd Francis. So there's a runner on first, with the game on the line. In Little League, you only go six innings. The first pitch Meade threw Todd was not even close to being a strike. It was a fastball, high and way outside. Didn't matter to The Beef.

First pitch.

Home run.

Behind the outfield fence, there were power lines, the highest of which was maybe fifty feet in the air. Beef put it over the highest lines. Over the wire, and game over.

For years, people in Beaverton talked about it. "Remember when Francis put it over the wire?" That never happened again at that park.

From there, we went on to win district, and Beef hit three grand slams. When the bases were loaded, his nerves reminded him to do it.

I have established that Beef had a tic that compelled him to hit the first pitch out of the park when the stakes were high. I have the exact opposite of that. Later on, I'll tell you about going on *The Tonight Show* and having my eyes kind of bug out from the pressure. That's what people said, anyway, but they only said it if they were among the millions of people who watched the episode of *The Tonight Show* where my eyes were bugging out. So, it's almost like it didn't happen.

I've already told you about a show in LA where I needed to do well for my record company, but instead told my record company to fuck off. Then there's the time I threw up on my hero. You might even find other examples of me clearly not putting it over the wire against Timber Meade in the bottom of the sixth.

The all-star team then went to another town that was hosting the state tournament, and Todd had a couple of grand slams and a couple of game-winning home runs. He'd had nine home runs in twelve games at this point. Then they went to regionals, in San Bernardino, California. By this time, they were playing in big places, with two thousand seats. It was intense.

The first game was against Northern California, and Todd hit a home run to win it. Then against Hawaii he hit two grand slams. And then they were in the championship, the game that would decide who got to go to the Little League World Series and be on ABC-TV. They were playing against El Cajon, California. The first time Todd got up, the bases were loaded, so of course Todd hit a grand slam. As he rounded the bases, Beef did a little dance, put a hand over his head, and twirled his finger around, like he'd seen the Portland Trail Blazers' Bill Walton do. He did this because Bill Walton was a stoner basketball god, and imitating him was a way to represent the Pacific Northwest when parents from Southern California were booing The Beef.

Next time up, the bases weren't loaded, so Todd hit a little dribbler down the first base line. It was too early in the game for him to hit a first-pitch home run. The first baseman fielded it and stood in the base path to tag Beef out. If you're the runner, the only way you can get out of being tagged out in that situation is if the fielder happens to drop the ball as he tags you, so Todd did everything in his considerable power to see if he could make that happen. Mostly this involved running into the guy at full speed to jar the ball loose.

In hindsight, maybe The Beef's move was a little over the top. But at the time, we were convinced we were being screwed when they kicked Beef out of the game. It was total mayhem. Police escorted the umpire out, because our parents were so livid. They wouldn't even let Beef watch the game from the dugout. They locked him in a room. And we lost that game, and it was over.

We all went back home. Beef kept on playing baseball after that, and he got drafted into the pros, played in the Seattle Mariners minor league system, and got hurt pretty quickly. Now, he coaches. He says his system is that when the parents are there, he gives a speech about how it doesn't matter if the kids win or lose. And then when the parents leave, he says, "Now that your parents are gone, you little fucks, I'm gonna show you something." Then he stands and swings the bat with a swoosh that they can hear, an inch from some of their faces. And he says, "That's what I'm gonna show you little fuckers how to do."

Then he explains that it pretty much matters whether they win or not.

—

When Beef was in the eighth grade, everybody knew he was by a mile the kid you wanted on your side if you were in trouble, and the kid you did not want to be in trouble with. A new family moved into town. We'll call them the Dickwhistles, which is how I think of them. Their father was a real stumpy, pit bull–looking tough guy, and their son looked like their father. He was a pretty tough kid. I don't doubt he was the toughest kid where he came from. But he was not the toughest kid where he'd come to.

Mr. Dickwhistle was one of those guys who thought that the good way to fit in when you're in a tough situation is to pick out the biggest guy and then drop him. Then you've established yourself. But this only actually works if you happen to be tougher than that biggest guy. If you were going to try to drop the toughest guy in our neighborhood, you were going to dilly with The Beef. That's what Petie Dickwhistle set out to do, and one day after school, for no good reason, he picked a fight with Todd Francis.

No one had ever done this before. A couple of poor kids got fought on by The Beef, but that was not their choice. He wasn't a bully, but he had his line, and a couple of people had crossed it before.

Petie Dickwhistle, a new kid with new ideas, picked a fight with Beef, and Beef was obliged, and it went pretty awful for Petie, really quickly. It was over before what would have been half of round one. Todd was quick and strong and big and confident. Those were four important things to have in a fight, and he had more of them than Petie Dickwhistle. The Beef seemed bemused by the situation.

The kid got a bloody nose, and he gave up and went out the front door of the school. We didn't know this at the time, but he went to a car where his dad was. And then his dad must have said something to him, and so he came back in and wanted some more.

That's when it started to get un-funny. Now there's a black eye, a bloody nose, and a bloody lip. Todd hit Dickwhistle directly in the face maybe a dozen times, and Dickwhistle maybe hit Todd in the shoulder once or twice. Everybody's watching, and Dickwhistle falls down again and goes crying back out the front door. Then he comes back in and wants some more. And this time, thirty seconds after he comes in that front door, his father comes in behind him.

To watch.

Round three was pathetic. The Beef didn't want to be doing this but didn't know what else to do. And this kid was getting the shit beaten out of himself and was going to get grounded if he didn't continue to do so.

Todd hit him maybe two more times, and you could see that there was no motivation there. So Todd, at fourteen years old, stopped and turned to Petie Dickwhistle's father and said, "It seems to me that you're the one that wants to know if you could beat me up, and we could solve that right now."

The look of fear in that man's face was much greater than the look of fear that had been in his son's face when this whole thing started.

I remember thinking at that time that Todd, The Beef, was very different.

A ton of people saw this. They saw that man back down with the old, "I can't fight a kid thing," but everybody knew that was not exactly the problem. I believe if that man thought he could beat up Todd Francis that he would have, but that he knew deep down he would have ended up going home looking a lot like his son—which he already did—but in a different, less pleasant, bloodier way.

When The Beef said that to the father, he didn't have that nervous thing like when the game was on the line. The game wasn't on the line, and he knew it. The game was a foregone conclusion.

The Francis kids started a tradition that I hold dearer than Christmas or Thanksgiving. The tradition was that they would write their names in this tunnel that you had to go through if you're going from Beaverton into Portland. The tradition started with the oldest, Phil Francis, in 1971. The deal was that in your senior year, you'd go to the tunnel one night around three in the morning. It was scary, because cars were zipping by and there was very little room between you and the cars.

You can also get arrested for being in there, but that wasn't as scary as the cars zipping by.

Now, in this tunnel you didn't actually paint graffiti. You took your shirt off or took a towel from the car and you just wiped your name onto that tunnel wall by wiping away dirt. It was really cleaning. Technically, it was part of the solution. Year after year, every spring, a bunch of people would do that.

Usually, you'd put "Class of Whatever" on the tunnel wall after your name. Or you'd put something about how you ruled or you kicked ass. Some of us did both. We ruled and we kicked ass, according to the tunnel we'd wiped.

When it was my turn, I just said that I ruled. "Todd Snider rules." I went with that. I briefly considered the Tough Tiger Todd thing, but it had never really caught on.

From all that, I went on to near-minor fame in the folk music game. I started with three chords, minus one, which turned into a tour that started in 1994 and continues to this day.

In 2001, I came to Portland to play McMenamins Pub, a building downtown with a glass bubble in front of it.

Wait, let me sidetrack for a moment.

There was this guy who coached Little League football, and who seemed normal at first but then started to show signs of delusion that scared the other parents. Then one Friday night at a Beaverton High football game, when the kids were all coming out to do their warm-ups, this guy—I'm guessing he was about thirty-eight years old at the time—comes out and starts doing wind sprints. He had on full pads and a helmet. When someone asked him what he was doing, he said he was about to try out for the Rams. After that, the parents wouldn't let him come around anymore, and they told us kids that he didn't take his medicine and it made him act crazy.

One day I was in the grocery store with my mom, and that guy was there. This was post-sprints. She was polite and asked him what he was doing. He said he was currently in negotiations to get The Beatles back together and play McMenamins Pub.

Alas, something fell through.

So, much later, I played McMenamins, without any Beatles at all. The place held about 150 people, maybe a few more. On the way to the show, I was riding through the tunnel with my tour manager, Spike, and I told her the whole story about the graffiti tradition and how it was technically cleaning. And then we went down and did the gig, and at the gig there were three or four of my high school friends, who were pretty drunk by the time the show was over. I happened to be pretty drunk, too. I asked my old friends what they liked to do when they were having fun, and they said they liked to do karaoke.

As musicians, we see karaoke as machines that put us out of work.

I also think karaoke depletes the ozone layer. But these were my old friends, and I agreed to do it. We went to this little bar and got pitchers of beer. I knew I didn't have to worry about it, because Spike was the driver. Most of her job, I would say, was to take care of me after the show. In those years, that was a harder job than it is now. Not a lot harder. A little harder. We drank and sang karaoke. I did Guns N' Roses. My buddy did Tom Petty. I felt like a scab, but I had a good time, and I don't even remember the last half of it. I don't know how it ended. I don't remember leaving the bar or getting back to the hotel. Another big part of Spike's job was to tell me what happened between midnight and 4 A.M. Quite often, it was really interesting stuff I wished I hadn't missed.

I woke up in my hotel room downtown the next morning. I knew for sure when I woke up that I hadn't hit anything with a car and hadn't had some kind of public issue. I woke up and probably had a drink, so I wouldn't get a hangover. That's really the only way to beat a hangover: become a full-blown alcoholic. None of that vitamin shit works. Staying drunk works. I've tested this, at length.

I met Spike at the van to start heading down toward California. We started heading through that tunnel. As we got closer to it, I saw what looked like might be my name. And as we got even closer, I could see that it also said something else.

Really close, it was clear that it said, "Todd Snider rules."

I turned to Spike, not completely pleased. "Is that what happened last night?" I said. "Tell me I didn't do that."

"Who the fuck else do you think would?"

"Goddamnit, Spike," I said. "This is why you're out here. You think I give a fuck if I'm in tune, or on time? Everybody knows I don't care about either of these fucking things. THIS is what I care about: I care about not doing shit like this. I know this is just a business relationship, but I thought we were friends, kind of. You could have at least said to me, 'Don't write RULES after your name,' but you didn't. You probably stood there and giggled your face off."

We headed into the day, and I remember making up a song called "Rose City Blues" on a bag from Wendy's, the hamburger chain that used to have an ad campaign based around the slogan, "Where's the beef?"

Where's the beef?

He's swinging bats at kids.

ROSE CITY BLUES
By Todd Snider

We wrote our names in the tunnel back when
Coos Bay was as far away as we'd ever been
Pine trees climbing up winding hills
Fishing boats and paper mills
Multnomah County's where I come from
Hometown to Bigfoot and the Burnside bums
Rain clouds hangin' down low and grey
God knows I wish it would have rained today

Tonight I've got those old Rose City blues
Tonight I've got those old Rose City blues

Tonight I'm drivin' through some other town
Radio on with the windows down
Old song comes on from a long time ago
How on earth did that DJ know?

Tonight I've got those old Rose City blues
Tonight I've got those old Rose City blues
Rain rain rain
Pouring rain doesn't bother me

We wrote our names in the tunnel back then
And last night we went down and did it again
One sip too many from that old loving cup
Rose City people never do grow up

Tonight I've got those old Rose City blues
Tonight I've got those old Rose City blues

—

When I got home from that tour, I got a call from a friend that I'd been to high school with, saying she was sorry she missed my show but that her family had been on vacation.

I said, it was okay. You didn't miss much."

She said, "Well, it must have been a little better than okay, 'cause one of your fans went down into the tunnel and wrote 'Todd Snider rules!'"

I said, "No shit?"

Anyway, remember a minute ago when I told you about the crazy coach who ran out onto the field before the game in full uniform, because he hadn't taken his medication? The guy who was going to get The Beatles back together? Well, sometimes I get a little skittish, too. One time, I was in Oregon on vacation with my wife. We'd flown out there and were driving to Port Orford to see my mom. Ever since those douche bags flew those planes into those buildings in New York, all of a sudden you can't carry pot on a plane anymore. You can't just stuff it in your underwear. This angers me. What the fuck am I going to blow up with a half-ounce of weed?

The after-party, that's what. High-five!

Nevertheless, on a journey to see my mom, I had to make absolutely certain that I was going to have pants on the ground. For those of you who don't know the phrase "pants on the ground," it means "a place to pick up marijuana." And those of us who are concerned with having pants on the ground are not concerned with the derivation of the term. I have no idea, and don't care.

So, I called The Beef. He met me at a hotel with some hippie lettuce for me to take on my two-day trip to see my mom.

The night we saw him, we got high, and he left me with four really big joints. That was not quite enough to get me through a couple of days, but I thought I could conserve it, and I hoped there'd be something going down at Port Orford, too.

The next day I had some coffee, but I didn't light up in the morning. I thought, "I'll wait until we get to the beach." Which meant that I was probably going to drive too fast to the beach. Sobriety fucks up my focus, you understand? But rest assured, during this whole time of writing you this book, I have been totally and completely focused.

We started heading down toward Port Orford, and we took the scenic route. We headed out to the coast, took a left, and headed south, through Tillamook County. We were planning to go through there, past a pretty place called Florence and on down to Port Orford.

So I was driving, and speeding the whole way. Melita kept trying to get me to slow down. But if I haven't smoked dope, I can't focus. I don't know if I have mentioned that before.

We got outside of Tillamook County, and there was a construction thing going on where they were trying to haul tree stumps from off the side of a hill. I noticed that all the construction workers' cars were pulled over and parked sort of halfway off the road. I saw another guy in the middle of the road holding a stop sign. You had to go to the opposite lane just to get to him, and when I got to him, he had an attitude. He was cranky with me, and I looked around and saw that with this job they were all doing, it was going to be two hours until they finished. I honked at the guy like, "Are you fucking serious?"

He gave me the "Come here" gesture, or the "Go through." I wasn't sure which. I drove past him and got to some other guy with a sign. Just as I was about to go past that guy, too, another worker tried to stop me. He acted like he was going to get out in front of my car. So I flipped him off.

I probably wouldn't have done that if I'd have been stoned. If I'd have been stoned, I'd probably still be sitting behind those parked cars, listening to the radio. Somebody would have had to come and jostle me and tell me to go ahead. But I wasn't stoned. So, I flipped that guy off and went about my business. I drove another thirty miles, with four joints in my pocket. Then I saw the familiar glow of red and blue lights, and I pulled over.

The cop said, "I heard you had a little trouble back there."

"Yeah, I'm sorry," I said. "I lost my cool and flipped that guy off. But I'd been sitting there a long time and finally got to go through. I thought they were being rude to me, and I didn't understand it. I thought I did everything right, and I never got past ten or twenty miles per hour."

"That is not at all what they're saying," he said. "I'm going to have to arrest you for reckless endangerment. Can you get out of the car?"

I could. Sure.

The guy put me in the back of his car, and he walked up and told Melita that she'd probably need to go to a bail bondsman.

They took me to the jail. By the time I got there, I'd told the cop that I'm a singer. He asked what kind, and I said, "Kind of like Jim Croce." We were getting along. I was being nice. He trusted me.

But then when we got to the jail, a woman processed me and told me to come in and change clothes. "Really?" I said. "Can't I just sit in the cell in the outfit I have on now? My wife's going to get the money for the bail.'"

"She'll be here in twenty minutes," the cop said.

They put me in the drunk tank, but they never made me give them my clothes, which had four joints in them.

It's a bad feeling to be locked in a little box. It hits you quick. I've had it about eight times. But I read the paper, and I made up a song called "Tillamook County Jail." I'd been carrying a line about the "Alabama Lie Detector Test," which is when they get the truth out of you by beating you up, so I put that line in the song, but it's fiction. Nobody in Tillamook laid a finger on me. Everybody was nice.

I sat in the cell for about four hours, and I read the paper. And then my wife came to get me out. She had clearly been crying.

I got in the car and said, "I've got a song."

Sometimes she's really excited that I get songs.

Not all the time.

This one didn't jack her up too much. But I was excited about it, and I still had my weed.

So, I thought everything was going to be fine. We got a hotel in Florence, and then when I got home I got a lawyer and they offered me five days in jail. I asked my lawyer if they could turn that five days into a price tag, so he worked on that. And then all of a sudden, it was not jail but rather money and thirty hours of community service. That didn't go so well, because they told me they wanted me to teach kids about drugs, and that was a total miscommunication. I was showing kids how to make bongs out of apples, which really wasn't what they wanted.

Okay, maybe that's not true. But I tell that last bit onstage, and I'm not afraid to stand here and tell you that I support hard drugs being marketed to children. Hard drugs make you feel good. It reminds me of porn. I don't see why we have to take that away from kids, either. They should know about it early, so they'll know how to get it on when their bodies are ripping. But at the time when our bodies are the most banging, we're having the most awkward sex of our lives.

I'm for hugs and for drugs.

A few years after this Tillamook County stuff, I was at a drinking party, recounting this whole story to our friends. I was explaining how I came up, saw these guys doing their work, wasn't sure what to do because of how they parked their cars, and wasn't sure how to get in the lane away from the workers' cars.

Just at that point of the story, my wife stopped me and said, "What do you mean, 'The work people's cars?'" I said, "That big line of cars. The parked cars for the workers." She said, "Those weren't parked cars for the workers, there were people in those cars. That was the line you were supposed to be in."

I said, "Why didn't you say anything?"

She said, "I don't know."

So, now I know what I did. And I actually, honestly, would like to use this platform as a place to say I feel horrible about that. And to those guys who put themselves in danger while their wives and kids count on us not to act like dicks as we drive past them, I want to say, and do say, that I would give anything for that moment back. I'm completely remorseful. And none of it would have happened had I smoked some weed.

Right, Beef?

High-five!

TILLAMOOK COUNTY JAIL
By Todd Snider

I'm sitting here waiting in the Tillamook County Jail
Hoping that she's not so mad now that she doesn't even pay
*   my bail*
If I was her I'm not so sure I wouldn't keep on moving down
*   the trail*
I'm sitting here waiting in the Tillamook County Jail

Got a lump on my head and a boot print on my chest
From what the guys in here call the Tillamook County lie
*   detector test*
Well I did my best but as you mighta guessed
It's a tough test not to fail
I'm sitting here waiting in the Tillamook County Jail

One phone call, two Tylenol
Four cold gray walls closing in
If I ever do get out on that highway again
I ain't ever goin' back to Tillamook County
No I ain't ever goin' back to Tillamook County

It all started when I had a little trouble with a guy on a
*   highway crew*
And that lyin' son of a gun told 'em I done some things I
*   didn't do*
They came running for me down 101, lights flashing on
*   my tail*
And now I'm sitting here waiting in the Tillamook County
*   Jail*

One phone call, two Tylenol
Four cold gray walls closing in
If I ever do get out on this highway again
I ain't ever goin' back to Tillamook County
No I ain't ever goin' back to Tillamook County (nope)

I'm sitting here waiting in the Tillamook County Jail
Now I'm still hoping that she's not so mad now that she
*   doesn't even pay my bail*
Coming down on vacation, gonna leave on probation
Have to send all my money through the mail
I'm gonna send all my money to the Tillamook County Jail

CHAPTER 4

K. K. RIDER

Here is the story of how I became the lead singer of a band called K. K. Rider. It's one of those classic show business stories about a kid being in the right place at the right time.

Back in Memphis in the early '90s, long after Jerry Jeff and lots of other stuff I haven't told yet, I lucked into a recording contract with Jimmy Buffett's Margaritaville Records. Bob Mercer, whom I have spoken about before and will speak about again, was the president of the record company at that time. He was a great guy with one minor wrinkle, which was that he didn't want me to play in Memphis for a good six months before the record came out. He didn't want to dilute the brand, and he explained to me that I was the brand.

The problem was that at the time I was paying my rent by playing around Memphis two or three nights every week, including every Thursday at a place called the Daily Planet. I needed the money. Bob had the idea that I could live off my advance until the record came out, but my advance was all gone, spent on groceries and other essentials that definitely, for sure, did not include gambling and good times.

There was a loophole, though. There's always a loophole. All you have to do is stare at the loop long enough and you'll find the hole. Here, the loophole was that I could play just as long as I wasn't playing as myself. One day, I started flipping through the *Memphis Flyer*, looking at the "Musicians Seeking Musicians" listings. There were lots of bands—metal bands, soul bands, wedding bands—and one of them was a country cover band called K. K. Rider that needed a rhythm guitar player.

Country songs, you know, are pretty easy to play. You just strum around the "Johnny B. Goode" chords until you get to the part where everybody stops and the singer yells the chorus, which is usually a slogan of some kind. You know, "Ain't Goin' Down 'Til the Sun Comes Up," or "There Ain't Nothin' Wrong with the Radio," or "I'm from the Country and I Like It That Way" or "You're Not from the Country, So Fuck You."

I went to try out, and when I got there I discovered that K. K. Rider was, in fact, a guy I knew named Kelly Kellit. He used to heckle me at my gig by requesting Dylan's "Sad-Eyed Lady of the Lowlands" all night. That song has twenty-something verses, and it drags on, to the point where I never honored the request. I always liked Kelly, and I figured he liked me, too. I was right, and I got the gig without even trying out. I was gainfully employed.

At the gigs, K. K. wore a white hat and a white jacket with tassels under the arms. He'd close his eyes up there and sing his heart out. Now that I was rhythm guitarist, I had to stand about five feet back from and off to the left of K. K., where I would strum along with the rest of the band.

Mainly, K. K. Rider played a Memphis pool hall. It was what you'd expect: a little, honky-tonk type joint with low ceiling full of smoke and rowdy people. There was one unexpected twist to the place: a red, velvet rope swing that swung toward and away from the bandstand. At either end of the swing's arc, the owner of the pool hall had attached golden bells to the ceiling. Waitresses would get up in the swing with their short skirts, and when one of them got close enough to the bell, she would ring it, and it was half-price drinks for the next hour.

It was a nice gimmick, as is every gimmick in the world that involves short skirts and/or half-price drinks. Everybody always laughed and cheered when the waitress rang the bell.

One night we were playing an old country song called "Don't It Make You Wanna Dance." K. K. was singing his heart out, and you could tell 'cause his eyes were closed. Tassels were flying. I was back and to the left. Suddenly, I heard the familiar hoots of the crowd and I looked up to see a cute young girl up on the red velvet rope swing. She came toward us and away from us, getting a little higher each time, and when she reached the bell and rang it, everyone smiled and laughed. Even the band, except for K. K. He was singing his heart out, eyes closed, and he missed the whole thing.

After this cute young girl was done, she got down out of the swing and a not-so-young, not-so-cute woman got up into it. She had stringy red hair and skinny arms. Her jeans had been pretorn at the factory (I always wanted that jeans-tearing job), and she was wearing a sleeveless, 38 Special T-shirt. Not the gun, the band. No one thought she had the authority to trigger another half-hour of half-price drinks, or that she had anything to do with the official bar or billiards businesses at all. It was clear to all of us that this was one of those famous-last-words moments, one that was of the "Hey y'all, watch this" variety.

This woman, it turned out, had no intention of treating the swing gently. She pumped her legs back and forth, energetically, in a way that would be fun to do if you were, say, outdoors or in some other space that did not feature a ceiling with metal bells on it. She picked up speed and altitude, going faster and higher. At one point, the owner darted out from behind the bar. I assume he had insurance concerns and wanted to get her down from the swing, but her boyfriend intervened. He was as skinny as she was, with jet-black hair and a mustache. He had on a sleeveless, 38 Special T-shirt (same band, different tour). He appeared to believe, based on what I could gather from my vantage point, that his woman's right to that rope swing had been taken care of when he paid her cover charge.

Surprisingly, the owner disagreed.

The arguing soon escalated to the point where this guy and the owner were touching chests, like guys do sometimes before they get to the pushing.

As a result of the chest bumping, they failed to see that this woman was swinging way faster and higher than she had been even ten seconds before. She reached the first bell and rang it, and then the second bell, and rang it. She continued to move between them, and as a result of her accelerated speed, the dings got closer together and louder, until they weren't dings so much as thuds. Anyone watching—which was everyone, except her boyfriend and the bar owner and K. K. Rider, who was singing with his eyes closed—could clearly see that this woman was hurting herself.

Eventually the boyfriend became aware of the thuds, and he turned to see what was happening to his girl. It was at this point that he did the dumbest thing he would do all night. Well, I shouldn't say that. I don't know where they went after. I just know that at that moment he made a fateful decision to reach out and grab the rope attached to the swing. This stopped the swing short and propelled the woman off it, through the air and toward the bandstand, where K. K. was singing his heart out. I was in my spot, five feet back, five feet to the left, playing great rhythm guitar on "Don't It Make You Wanna Dance."

So, this woman flew through the air, all the way to the stage, where she landed directly between the monitors and the microphone. The microphone went down on its stand and then back up, like it used to do when James Brown was singing. But James Brown sang with his eyes open. K. K. was not aware when the microphone went down, and as a result he was not aware when it came back up and smacked him square in the mouth.

He was also not aware of what happened in the moments following the microphone smacking him square in the mouth, on account of it knocked him out. Went onto his back, right next to the woman, who was also flat on her back. Their bodies formed a "T," right at the base of the microphone stand, which had somehow miraculously righted itself.

I was still strumming the song, which, fortunately, is pretty easy to play. But at that moment it occurred to me that I knew the words, so I stepped over my K. K., closed my eyes, and sang with all my heart:

Don't it make you wanna dance
Don't it make you wanna smile
When you're down, down, down in the country
Pick and sing awhile.

You hear that story in show business a lot. Right place, right time.

⁓

When my album came out, I left K. K. Rider. I ran into him now and again in Memphis, but by the late '90s we had lost touch. I wondered sometimes where he had ended up.

A few years ago, I found myself in a hard little town called Carbondale, Illinois. I quickly realized we were in a tough city, and in one of its toughest clubs. It brought to mind a sweet song I made up with Robert Earl Keen and Bruce Robison, called "We've Played Some Shit Holes But This Takes the Cake." The gig was a zoo, too. The crowd pressed up against the stage, yelling in a threatening manner. One guy was so drunk that he came up onto the stage and tried to push me. I was singing with my eyes closed, of course, and when I opened them I saw my tour manager, Elvis, tackling the guy.

After the show, I found out Elvis had tried to throw the guy out, but the club wouldn't let him. The guy was a local VIP, because he owned a titty bar in Carbondale. Fair enough.

I was booked to play the same club the very next night. In the afternoon, I killed time by taking a long walk around Carbondale. When I got back to the hotel, I had a message to call a bar called Bi's. The girl behind the counter giggled and told me it was a strip joint. I assured her I had no idea why a strip joint would be calling me, but I don't think she believed me. I went up to my room, called the number, and the telephone was answered by none other than . . . K. K. Rider.

"Hey man," he said. "I came down to see you last night, and your fucking tour manager tackled me."

Tough luck. Tough club. Tough town. Tough titties.

CHAPTER 5

MEETING BILL ELLIOTT

Every night when I play, they have speakers just for me. They're right at my feet, and I can ask the sound guys to fill them with any kind of mix I want. No matter what a show sounds like to anyone else, it sounds perfect to me: the right balance of vocals and instruments, the right bass. The crowd and I hear two different shows. From where I stand, they all sound great.

These special speakers at my feet also allow the sound guy to relay private messages to me. They come through these speakers, and nobody but me hears them.

Like, "You okay?" Or, "Your wife made it." Or, "It's almost curfew." Or, "You're drunk, get off." Or, "Shut up and play."

One night I was playing an outdoor show in Chattanooga, Tennessee. My buddy Will Kimbrough was playing guitar with me that night. I was playing some kind of folk song about wolves and trees: deep environmental stuff. And somewhere in the middle of the set, out of the blue, from the monitor speakers, came a voice: "Hey, man, you like NASCAR?"

And I kind of do. Sort of, anyway. I mean, for the most part it's about a guy hauling ass and turning left for about four hours. I could probably do that, but my brother digs it. So I stepped away from whatever wolves-and-trees song I was playing, moved out so the sound guy could see me, and nodded clearly in the affirmative.

I sang another verse, this one about the sky, maybe, or moss, and then there was another solo for Will, during which the voice appeared again. "You want to meet Bill Elliott?"

Bill Elliott? Hell, yes, I wanted to meet him. In fact, I remember once hearing my brother say that Bill Elliott was his hero. And I remembered that Bill Elliott was nicknamed "Awesome Bill from Dawsonville," because he was from Dawsonville, George, and because if you're drunk enough, "awesome" rhymes with "Dawson." I stepped away from the microphone and nodded again, even more enthusiastically this time.

After the show, Will and I were sitting in a room backstage. It's similar to the one we sit in most nights. We get free celery and carrots and ranch dip and booze, even. We get towels. We get all kinds of shit, and nobody can touch it but us. You want celery? Talk to the hand.

That's right, I said, "Talk to the hand." And here's why: when it comes to slogans and fashions and bands, I like to be what I call "post-hip, pre-retro." That sweet spot, right when something isn't cool anymore and before it becomes cool in an ironic way. The cutting edge of uncool.

There we were, in this room with all our free shit, and up the stairs came the sound man, trailed by Bill Elliott. Before we could even shake hands, Awesome Bill from Dawsonville poured himself a tall whiskey and was knee-deep in our own private ranch dip.

After he ate a couple of carrot sticks, he turned around and told us he loved the show. I asked him if he would sign my guitar, and he did. But he signed it so big and so obnoxiously that I knew I'd never use the guitar again. It was more like something you'd win at a race than, say, Willie Nelson's guitar.

I was starting to think that I didn't like Bill Elliott, but I wanted to be nice because he was my brother's hero. So I told him, "Man, you're my brother's hero."

"No shit," he said.

"No shit," I said.

Then he said, "Let's call your brother," and I thought, "Cool, now this is getting fun."

My brother was asleep, but he woke up to answer the phone. "Hello," he said, and Bill Elliott yelled, "Mike Snider, you old limp-dicked cunt face, it's Bill Elliott, and I'm about to go chase pussy with your brother."

Now I was thinking something more than that I didn't like Bill Elliott. Now I was thinking, "It's a good thing this guy can haul ass and turn left pretty good, 'cause he's a dick." But knowing he was my brother's hero, I bit my tongue and poured myself an even taller whiskey than the one Bill Elliott had poured. As a result of my interest in protecting my brother's interest in Bill Elliott, or possibly the whiskey, Bill Elliott started to seem almost cool. Will and I asked him what I guess you'd call race driver questions, which he answered with a drunken flourish. I suggested we walk across the street to the bar to get another drink. Everybody agreed that was a great idea, since all we had left backstage was celery. As we walked, I heard myself sing, to the tune of the Barry Manilow hit, "Mandy," "Moe Bandy / When you came and you sang with Joe Stampley / Well, it blew me away, Moe Bandy."

I laughed and laughed and laughed, and so did everyone else. I still don't know what made me think of it, but to this day I can still make myself laugh by singing that song. It's funny because it's true.

Now we were walking down the street, singing this new Moe Bandy song, arm and arm like frat guys as we staggered into this old bar.

I took a stool and told Bill the first round was on me. I ordered a Jack Daniels on ice, and so did Will. Bill ordered some crazy, expensive-ass thing, and lost a couple of the points he'd made with Will and me, but you make allowances for your brother's hero.

We drank. We talked. Then Bill Elliott turned to me and said, "I'll be right back, man, I've gotta piss." He went into a narrow hallway where the restroom was. And no sooner did he disappear from view than the bar owner rushed over to us with a worried look on his face and said, "That guy didn't tell you he was Bill Elliott, did he?"

No fucking way. I couldn't believe it. This guy wasn't my brother's hero after all. This guy was my hero.

CHAPTER 6

SONGS FROM
THE DAILY PLANET

Back in Oregon, when I was a kid, my father was really into sports. He was a big jock, good at everything he tried, and very interested in being good at everything he tried. My brother and I tried to follow in his footsteps. He could, and I couldn't.

That didn't mean I didn't try. I gave it everything I had. I have detailed some of my adventures in baseball, by which I mostly mean that I spent time watching The Beef become a hero on the diamond. Football was another area in which I attempted excellence. By the time I was a junior at Beaverton High School, I was on the varsity football team.

I'm not saying I played varsity football, I'm saying I was on the varsity football team.

If you've never played high school football, I'm just going to tell you real quickly what it's like.

If you're on the football team in high school, that means you and about fifty other guys are going to get together for four months out of the year, every day, for about ninety minutes a day. You're going to take off your comfortable outfits and put on uncomfortable outfits. And then you're going to go outside, whether it's raining or freezing or really hot or really cold. Doesn't matter. You are going to go outside in those uncomfortable outfits, and you're going to run into and away from each other, all in relationship to the movement of a ball.

Now, while this is all going on, you're going to be screamed at, consistently, by adults whose lives revolve around the ways in which you run into and away from each other. Sometimes they scream something kind; usually they scream something else. Sometimes they're screaming right after school, sometimes at another school, and sometimes they even have people pay money to gather around and keep track of what you do while you're doing it. Sometimes it's under the lights, and that's when they get kids from another school to run into and away from you. But, basically, all you're really doing is what I described before: guys, ball, running. Your parents will tell you that you are representing the community. Or at least that's what my parents told me. And they said that if things went well, we could win district. I didn't even know I was from a district, let alone that it was up for grabs and that somehow I was responsible for attaining it for everybody, by running around in my uncomfortable outfit.

So one afternoon I was at football practice, and they had this thing they made you do where you push this big sled that has pads on it. The coach stands on it and yells at you while you push the sled. This never happens during the game, but they make you practice it anyway. Not only do they make you practice it, you have to wait in line.

There I was, waiting in line to push something. And I noticed that across the field there was another group of kids. And I noticed that these kids were still wearing the clothes they wore to school. Very comfortable clothes, I might add. Loosely flowing garments. And they were smoking cigarettes, which I heard was bad, but while they were doing it they were also talking to some girls who were standing around, which I heard was good. And the girls were also wearing the clothes they wore to school.

So I tapped an older guy in front of me and said, "Who are those guys over there?"

"Those are the burnouts, man," he said.

"What's a burnout?"

"The burnouts hang out in the smoke pit."

"What's a smoke pit?"

"A smoke pit is where the burnouts hang out."

I asked the coach. I said, "Coach, what's a burnout from the smoke pit, man?"

And he said, "Oh, Snider, I would hate to see you turn into some kind of burnout from the smoke pit."

He paused. He looked up. He looked back down.

"Son," he said, "I am not trying to disparage any of the other kids at this school, but those kids over there, they're just a bunch of dirty sheep standing around in a field doing nothing."

"I don't want to be that," I said, and went about my business.

Then, about a week later, I was in the cafeteria, siting there, and this kid came in and sat next to me. I clearly recognized him as one of the burnouts from the smoke pit. I didn't know what to do. He started talking to me, and I found, to my surprise, that he seemed as nice as any of the other kids. And then he said to me, "Hey, man, have you ever tried psychedelic mushrooms before?"

"No," I said. "I've never tried anything like that before."

"Would you like to try something like that?"

"Sure, I think I might like to try something like that."

So, he handed me this big handful of psychedelic mushrooms, and I ate them. About thirty-five minutes later—it may have just been a half hour, but it seemed like thirty-five minutes—I realized that there was no way I was going to go to football practice that afternoon. I just didn't feel that it was a good idea anymore. Instead, I decided to go stand in that other field with those other kids. And when I was standing in that other field with those other kids, I saw the life that had been planned out for me from a distance for the first time.

There they were, the football team. And I don't mean to disparage any of the other kids. I'm just saying that it could be argued that they looked like a bunch of dirty sheep standing around in a field, waiting to push a grown, screaming man on a padded sled.

And just as I was taking in this information, I looked up at the goalpost. And the goalpost turned into candles, and just as I was taking that in, they turned into Roman candles. They went up into the sky. And just as I was taking that in, I looked over at that sled I had been pushing for a couple of months, and I saw my friends lining up to push that sled. Only now it wasn't a padded sled, it was Fred G. Sanford from the hit situation comedy *Sanford & Son*. And he was screaming, "Push, you big dummy!" And then he was holding his chest out like it was the big one, screaming, "Look out, Elizabeth, I'm coming to join you, honey!"

Next, the pad they were pushing morphed from Fred Sanford into Jesus Christ himself.

I never noticed how much Jesus and Fred Sanford look alike.

I'm not trying to be sacrilegious. In fact, I was put out by the fact—the indisputable fact—that my friends were pushing Jesus Christ. But they were pushing him, nonetheless. And then, just as I was about to get really upset, he morphed into this other guy that wasn't Jesus or Fred Sanford, but who kind of looked like some kind of guy that might have hung with Jesus in the day.

I was staring at this guy, this guy who wasn't a sled any longer, and these football players were pushing him. And as I stared at him, he looked over and made eye contact with me. And then he yelled across the field, "On a scale of one to ten, what is your favorite color of the alphabet."

I nodded my head, "Yes."

Then, "Hey, man, do you have two tens for a quarter?"

I did not have two tens for a quarter, but I knew in that moment that I was never going to go back to high school football practice again for as long as I lived.

That doesn't mean I'm down on football.

To this day, I still follow Coach Boyer and the Beaverton Beavers, because I think this could be the year we win district.

Also, because we have the coolest goalposts in the whole state of Oregon, and probably the world.

I've been telling that story about the goalposts and the 'shrooms all over our country for years now, and people often ask me if it's really true.

I either say, "Yes," or "Most of it."

But, brothers and sisters, I'll tell you the parts that weren't true.

First, I was actually probably the best guy on the team. I scored about fifty touchdowns a game. I just didn't want it to sound like I was bragging in the story.

Second, the 'shroom thing didn't really happen until I was a senior. My hand was broken, so I couldn't have gone to practice anyway.

And my epiphany that sports were kind of bullshit (unless you were gambling on them, I would later learn) happened after high school, when I was in Santa Rosa, California, where lots more people had mushrooms. The more I took those things, the less I understood running into another person on purpose.

The reason I made myself a junior in the story was because that's the age I wanted to reach back to and say, "You can fuck all that sports shit and get into the Dead, you know. Or do any other fucking thing you want. You're gonna die in your own arms, anyway."

So, you know, have a blessed day.

—

The spring of my sophomore year in high school, we all moved to Houston, Texas. I went there for two months, discovered Hank Williams Jr.—maybe not technically "discovered," since clearly everyone else in Texas already knew about him—and developed an accent. During this time, I noticed that my family was breaking up, and it became clear that my dad was fucking his secretary. These facts were not necessarily disconnected.

So my dad was taking a trip out to Portland by car. He said he had to finish up some business out there. I rode with him, and then when it was time to go back to Houston, I said, "I'm not going to go back." A family called the Satys took me in after that. I think they felt sorry for me, and I think my parents started sending them a couple hundred bucks a month. After I left home, my grade point average went from a 1.4 to a 3.2, if that tells you anything about our house.

When I was first in high school, my family was pretty well off. When I came back to Portland, I realized how much having money adds to your looks and popularity, and how much not having money detracts from those things. The girls didn't like me as much, now that we didn't have a pool.

I loved my dad. He was funny as shit. I thought so, his friends thought so, and his secretary probably thought so, too. But he was really into the sports thing, and I was getting less into it. When I was ten and started to play football, the doctors said my scoliosis was so bad that I shouldn't play. So after that, my dad started paying off different doctors, so they'd say that I could play. He thought he was doing me a favor. To this day, I have enormous back pain.

After high school, my dad talked me into going to Santa Rosa to play football at the junior college. A kid from a town called Tigard gave me a ride. That guy had a plan, and I didn't, so I had him drop me off at the football coach's office when we got to Santa Rosa, at four in the morning. I fell asleep on the floor, in front of the coach's office. When the coach got there, he woke me up and helped me start to get a plan to-gether. My dad had said that when I got to Santa Rosa I should call him, and he'd send the money so I could get admitted to college. I called his number from the coach's office, and his number was disconnected. I couldn't find him. I called my un-cle, and he sent the money.

After my uncle paid for me to get into the junior college, I was on the football team. And, by a mile, I was the worst player and the least ambitious. They were giving me a chance just by letting me on the team, and I wasn't really taking ad-vantage. I was obsessed with poetry by then, and I was starting to find pot and was way more into The Doors than into foot-ball. I was damn near the mascot of the team; nobody wanted me in the game, but everybody wanted me at the party.

We had great parties. One time, we had a party and we played a song called "Oh Sheila" for the entire time. Everybody was dancing crazy. Then two guys beat each other almost to death. They got taken away in an ambulance. Good times.

Before football practice, everybody would get high. One day in practice, the coach switched me to quarterback, so then I became the fourth-string quarterback instead of the fourth-string linebacker. As quarterback, I threw to the wrong guy in practice, and the coach asked me if I was stoned.

Before I thought about it, I said, "Yes."

That was the end of my football career.

There I was in Santa Rosa. I was off the team. I'd never ac-tually been to a class at the school. I was staying on the couch of three guys whose parents had gotten them an apartment. Then their parents came, saw I was living for free at the apart-ment they'd paid for, and didn't like that.

The parents said I had to leave the next day.

That night, I took a bottle of vodka and a harmonica and climbed on the roof of the apartment building. I think I'd seen this in a movie called *St. Elmo's Fire*. I was gonna go up there and have a Rob Lowe meltdown, but somebody called the police. I was four or five stories up, and they thought I was going to kill myself.

I wasn't going to kill myself.

On that roof, in that moment, it occurred to me that no one was really watching me. I mean, there were police watching and yelling and shining a light, but the thing that occurred to me was that no one that I cared about—no family or friends—was paying much attention to me at all. I was happy about this. It meant that I could open up the menu to anything I wanted. I was not going to embarrass myself in front of my old high school friends if I decided my goal was to go to the moon, and then I didn't make it. They might not even know. No one was watching me fail, so I could fail at anything I wanted.

I thought about what I wanted, knowing that I'd probably fail to get it. And I decided that I wanted most to fail at being a singer in a band. I was going to be a singer, period, and write the lyrics.

That's what I wanted to fail at in this life.

And, oh brother, have I. Over and over again. Spectacularly. Unaware of my private epiphany, the police were worried that I was going to jump. I told them I wasn't going to jump, that I was just having fun.

They said, "Well, go back in and have fun."

I did.

The next day, I didn't get to stay with my buddies. My brother, who was working construction in Austin, said he'd send me a plane ticket, so I could stay with him in the place where he was crashing on a friend's couch, and where he thought they'd let me stay on another one of their couches.

I had a night to stay in Santa Rosa before my plane took off. I found a house that wasn't finished being built, in a subdivision under construction. I slept there, out of the wind. The next day, I hitchhiked to the San Francisco airport. This was a new experience for me: hitchhiking. I was a suburban rich kid, turned suburban less-rich kid, turned stoner wannabe poet. I was trying on my Woody Guthrie pants for the first time.

My flight was an inexpensive one, where you could only have one bag.

I had a bag with my records and a bag with my clothes. My brother and I are the same size. So I figured I could wear some of his clothes.

———

I landed in Austin in late November. When I walked out of the airport, my brother wasn't there. Instead, there was a guy named Bonehead, with a fucked up old car.

He yelled, "Are you Todd?"

I said, "Yeah."

He said, "Get in. I'll take you to your brother."

He had a joint lit up—for himself, not for me—and he drove me from Austin to San Marcos, to an apartment where there were six guys taking bong hits and playing guitar.

None of these guys were my brother, but this was the place he was staying on a sofa. Then they took me to a party where he was supposed to be, and he wasn't there either.

At that party, I met a guy named Trog. I have mentioned him before, as well, though I am not sure I have stressed how huge he was. Let me check. I have stressed it. In fact, it was all I stressed, mostly. I will stress it again. He was six feet, eight inches tall, and weighed more than three hundred pounds. Well shit, I don't know if that's true for sure, but he was a Wookie if there ever was one. He was also a Deadhead, and he lived in a crappy apartment filled with guys who liked to get high and play rugby. Those guys would gather around Trog and laugh at his stories. They were always so funny. I went over there and started laughing, too.

Trog let me stay at his apartment, on the extra couch, for three months. He introduced me to music I didn't know and showed me the way to a job, which involved busing tables at a place called Pepper's. It seemed like everybody around me played guitar, at least a little, and I learned two or three chords pretty soon. I could play "Can't You See" by The Marshall Tucker Band, and "Pink Houses" by John Cougar Mellencamp, whom we called John Puma Melonfield. I wasn't having any luck getting in a band, though. Turns out the hardest way to get into a band is to call yourself a lyricist. Robert Hunter couldn't even get into the Grateful Dead, and he wrote lines like, "Lately it occurs to me what a long, strange trip it's been."

Then came Luckenbach, Texas. Or rather, then I came to learn the odd, compelling legend of Luckenbach, Texas. Here it is, in short form. An eccentric old guy who had been a swimmer at the University of Texas saw an ad in the paper that said a town was for sale, and he couldn't resist. The guy's name was

Hondo Crouch. He bought the town and created a universe that to this day is absolutely magical. You get to Luckenbach, and your inhibitions lower and your inner child comes out. Hondo created the place and made it so distinctive that it required words of its own: "plike," for example, which means "to play like." It's easy to use. You can say "We're gonna put on badges and plike we're police officers," or "Let's walk across the field, say we discovered something, and plike we're Lewis and Clark." There is a sense of discovery and of carrying the wonder of childhood into adulthood, not to mention the fun of making up words. Hondo was into "unlearning" the things the machine teaches you. The machine says there's no such word as "plike?" Bullshit. I just used it four times. In a book.

Hondo could get wild animals to come up to him. People would stop him on the street and ask to have their picture taken with him, not even knowing who he was. He just looked like some sort of weird thing. He was a Gandhi-like, Santa Claus character for Texans, and the town he owned had a population of three, with a dance hall, a bar, a post office, a store, and a parking meter. They called him "The Grand Imagineer," and Jerry Jeff and Willie Nelson idolized him the way I idolize Jerry Jeff and Willie Nelson. Their goal in life was to free their spirit as much as this guy, Hondo, had freed his. I think they did a really good job of that.

Hondo was already dead by the time I heard the legend of Luckenbach. I found out about it from Kent Finlay and from finding out about Jerry Jeff Walker, who had recorded an album there. Supposedly, Jerry Jeff's record label wanted to get him into the studio, but they couldn't get him out of the bar in Luckenbach. So they trucked over some microphones and a mixing board, brought the studio to the bar, and got a record on Jerry Jeff by recording him in his native habitat instead of making him go to theirs.

As soon as I heard about it, I wanted to go there and play there, at a place called Luckenbach Dance Hall. Kent Finlay, the owner of Cheatham Street Warehouse, made me a demo tape of three of my tunes, and I sent that tape to Luckenbach Dance Hall, and for a long time nobody called me back. But one day, we were watching *WKRP in Cincinnati* at Trog's place, taking bong hits. *WKRP* was a 1980s sitcom about a radio station. Don't know it? Look up a four-and-a-half-minute excerpt called "As God is my witness, I thought turkeys could fly." We loved *WKRP in Cincinnati*. We had a dance we made up to the theme song, with moves like The Temptations. When the show came on, we'd stand up from our bong hitting and do that dance—me, Trog, Brown-Eyed Brad, Turtle Leather Neck. Yes, I will admit, we might as well have been a frat. So we were watching *WKRP* when the phone rang, and it was Large Marge from Luckenbach Dance Hall. Turns out her opening act for the next night, Steve Fromholz, had canceled, and she wanted to know if I could cover it.

Fuck.

Yes.

After I related the news, everybody in our room was happy. The big plans started to materialize. I had an old Toyota Celica that I got for $700 from some girl at Pepper's. It had no tags and no license. I eventually drove that car off a cliff and left it there. The next night after Large Marge called, though, I got in that car and led a caravan of misfits up to Luckenbach. Well, not all the way up to Luckenbach. See, Luckenbach is hard to find. There were no real signs directing tourists and/or aspiring musicians. Later, I learned that people stole the signs, 'cause that's how cool Luckenbach is. But at the time, we were frustrated, plain and simple. We couldn't find Luckenbach. But we saw this place called The Devil's Backbone Tavern, which is right off The Devil's Backbone Highway, which you don't believe is a real thing but actually, for sure, is a real thing.

The tavern was rough looking. And the guys told me that since this was my gig, I had to go in and ask the people there how to get to Luckenbach. I went in and encountered what can only be described as a pretty serious Texas bar. There were about twenty people and seventeen teeth. The old woman tending bar seemed like the least frightening person in there. So I asked her where Luckenbach was.

"Fuck Luckenbach," she said. "Drink with us."

I went outside and told my friends about this genius idea my new friend had. And we went with it. Our rationale was airtight: we were gonna be late for Luckenbach anyway, so we shit-canned our big plans.

At The Devil's Backbone Tavern, there was a devil's head carved into a rock on the wall. There was a magician who stuck a cigarette through his hand and did something else with a coin that freaked us out. And there were people who asked if I would sing for them. I sang, and they loved it. I had a song called "You Bring the Condoms and I'll Bring the Wine," and that one went over great. Everybody got fucked up and started singing along, and at the end the bartender—Miss Virgy was her name—told me I didn't have to pay her any money for my beers, 'cause I'd entertained all night.

I never said that I'd do it again the next week, but I did it again the next week. Me and Trog and the guys started going out there on Fridays, because we liked it. Miss Virgy made me feel like I had some talent, and her belief in me meant a lot to me. Then there was also a guy who was mean to me, who used to tell me that I was a crappy guitar player. I tried to make the criticism not so much a big deal as the praise. I mostly succeeded when I noticed that no one was really paying attention to my failures, except for maybe that guy. I also noticed that the people at The Devil's Backbone Tavern were more hung up on what they did, instead of being hung up on what they got for what they did. I got the idea that I should write a song about that place: a song mostly about how Virgy had encouraged me and a little about how that guy was mean to me. And I got the idea that there should be a preamble, like the one in "Alice's Restaurant" by Arlo Guthrie. So I wrote a song with the exact chord changes to "Alice's Restaurant," which were really the only chord changes in the world that I definitely should not have used. Those were the ones I picked, though. Sorry, Arlo. I owe you about $86.

I didn't finish the song until years later, and by that time it was a postcard from a place that no longer existed. But that place and those people, especially Miss Virgy, helped me a lot when I was in Texas, and it still helps me to sing the words to the song I wrote about them. It was a lesson several people taught me, either by word or by example: if you're trying to work on a song for profit, you should think again, because there are a million better ways to get what you're wanting to get. Work in an office, and you'll definitely get money for what you do. As a songwriter, I'd say I get money for about 9 percent of the work I do.

Of course, I don't work very hard. So there's that. Here's the song I wrote.

THE DEVIL'S BACKBONE TAVERN
By Todd Snider

Old Miss Virgy tended bar at this shack out in the hills
It never made her any money boys but it paid up all her
*   bills*
Now she must have been 80 years old but her heart was
*   warm*
And her beer was cold
She gave away more than she ever sold
Smiling all the time
I used to sing off in the corner every Friday night
To a loud crowd of cowboys, bikers and bar room fights
They were drinking beer, carrying on, not a one of them
*   listening to one of my songs*
But old Miss Virgy sang along
She said she knew 'em all by heart
And then one night after closing she poured me another beer
She said "Come on over and sit down you little shit
I got something you need to hear"
She said "Life ain't easy getting through everybody's gonna
*   make things tough on you*
But I can tell you right now if you dig what you do, they will
*   never get you down"*

She said life's too short to worry
Life's too long to wait
Too short not to love everybody
Life's too long to hate
I meet a lot of men who haggle and finagle all the time
Trying to save a nickel or make a dime
Not me, no sirree, I ain't got the time

Now I ain't seen Ol' Virgy in must have been about ten years
I've been bumming around this country singing my songs for
* tips and beers*
Now the nights are long
The driving's tough
Hotels stink, and the pay sucks
But I can't dig what I do enough, so it never gets me down

I told you I played there every Friday night for the rest of the summer. There was this one guy that used to sit there every Friday and listen to me play. He'd sit there drinking beer, hogging three or four teeth all to himself. One night at the end of the summer, he came up to me and said, "Boy, I've been watching you."

I said, "You know, I've noticed that. I wanted to thank you."

He said, "No, don't thank me. I think you suck."

I understood what he meant when he said I sucked. But he wanted to go on and on about it.

So he did.

He said him and his brothers were big fans of Eddie Van Halen and the Eddie Van Halen Band.

He said, "Last summer, we drove into Austin to see Eddie Van Halen and the Eddie Van Halen Band. Whole damn concert Eddie V. was on the top of his guitar, playing all these notes way up high."

He said, "You play the same three chords the whole damn night. It sucks."

So when I came up with this song I thought of old Jerry Jeff, of course. I thought of Trog and Miss Vergy and of Eddie Van Halen and the Eddie Van Halen Band. But most of all I thought about that guy and his brothers. And I thought, "Eat your heart out, you inbred son of a bitch."

I say life's too short to worry
Life's too long to wait
Too short not to love everybody
Life's too long to hate
I meet a lot of men who haggle and finagle all the time
Trying to save a nickel or make a dime
Not me, no sirree, I ain't got the time

I had a girlfriend in Austin, but then she dumped me. Right around that dumping time, I got a call from my dad. By then, he was living in Memphis.

"You know that guy Keith Sykes?" he asked on the phone.

"I love Keith Sykes," I said.

And I did.

And I do.

Keith Sykes has written more than a hundred songs that other people have recorded. He's written with John Prine and Guy Clark and Jimmy Buffett. His own albums are filled with brilliant stuff. He writes songs that make you cry and smile at the same time.

"Well, I'm at a bar," Dad said.

Not a surprise.

"And the bartender is Keith Sykes's wife's sister."

Surprise.

My dad got Keith Sykes's address from the bartender, and I used that address to send Keith Sykes a tape with three of my songs on it.

It was a long time, at least long to a twenty-year-old, before I heard anything back. In my mind, I'd sent a tape to Keith Sykes, and he didn't like it. But one day, my mind changed. The phone rang, and it was Keith Sykes, and he said he thought the tape had shown promise, and that I could send him some more songs.

That call was enough to get me to move to Memphis.

I had a Buick LeSabre that I'd gotten for $800, and I figured it would get me to Memphis. I figured wrong. It broke down in Waxahachie, Texas, about thirty miles south of Dallas. So I called Trog from a pay phone and talked him into a road trip. "Do you want to go to Graceland?" I said.

My dad said I could stay with him for two weeks, and only two weeks. Trog wound up getting a job working for my dad, and he started living with my sister. I didn't want a job working for my dad, because I was going to be a singer. I mean, I was already close friends with Keith Sykes, right?

I think the main reason my dad didn't give me any money was that he didn't have any money. And I think the main reason my dad didn't let me stay with him longer than two weeks was because having a twenty-year-old hippie kid around wasn't conducive to his idea of having a good time. But the way he kicked me out of his house was actually helpful. He said, "You're never, ever gonna make it in music if I help you. You need to find a shitty apartment downtown and try and get something going. Go be poor, tough guy."

He was mocking me, like, "You think you're Springsteen?"

"Go get yourself hungry and see what happens," he said. "You'll be back here, looking for a construction job in a month."

I was not back in a month, looking for anything. Starving didn't seem like a big deal to me. I don't have a wide food palate anyway. To this day, I like Taco Bell.

I called Keith Sykes and told him I was in Memphis now. He said, "Great. If you get new songs, stick them in my mailbox."

I found an open mike at a place called the Daily Planet. When I got there, there was a British guy singing James Taylor songs. Not like "Fire and Rain" or "Carolina in My Mind" or anything else on James Taylor's greatest hits albums. He was singing deep album tracks that most people wouldn't recognize. And come to think of it, he never actually credited James Taylor as the writer of those songs. But I had the albums, and I knew.

This guy, Hank, was one of the most fascinating people I'd ever met. He'd become an American citizen, though he kept his cool British accent. He'd fought in Nicaragua and lost a ball there. He'd been to Harvard after that and was now teaching literature. He was also the concierge at the nicest hotel in Memphis. He was a stand-up comic. His great sorrow in life was that his beloved parents were dead, and his great joy was his wife and two kids.

Hank and I became fast friends. When we'd go to other bars, he'd create new personas for us, as a game. We weren't the British guy and the hippie kid from Oregon; we were roadies on a break from a Jackson Browne tour. I thought, "This guy and I go around bullshitting people, and it's hilarious." I never thought, "I wonder if this guy is bullshitting me."

Hank let me stay on his couch, at a house with his wife and kids. He told his wife he was going to help me make it and was going to be my manager. He bought me a P.A. system, on credit.

Then his wife left him and took his kids with her. Bummer for Hank, but now there was room for my new girlfriend of three weeks to stay there with us. I remember my girlfriend and I would sit and listen to Nanci Griffith records for hours.

One sunny day, the power at Hank's went out. This was not because of a downed line, it was because Hank hadn't paid the power bill. We didn't really give a shit, though. We just sat around for a month without power, singing Nanci Griffith songs ourselves instead of listening to her sing them on records.

Then we found out that Hank was in trouble, that he hadn't actually been to Harvard, that he was losing his teaching job, and that all this was probably going to get him fired by the hotel people, too.

I knew that the teaching dismissal was going to be the hardest for Hank to take. He loved that job. He'd taken me to work one day, sat in his office, and talked.

But then we found out that he wasn't technically being fired from the school, because he didn't actually work at the school.

The office he'd taken me to? I think that was just an office some other professor had left open.

While I was processing this, the phone rang.

It was Hank's mother, from Arkansas.

Arkansas, not London.

Alive and talking on the phone. Not tragically dead.

I got to talking with his mother, who informed me that Hank had never served in the military. I looked up at the wall at the photos of Hank in his military uniform.

Elaborate guy.

So Hank's entire life was a lie, and that's why his wife left. Massive debt. No job.

But Hank had helped me a lot, and I liked him. And, while I may not be a very good friend in terms of picking up dinner tabs, coming up with baseball tickets, or babysitting your kids,

I'm a good guy to have in your corner when your whole life turns out to be a lie. I won't ever hold that sort of thing against you, and I might respect you more for coming up with a grand grift like that.

So my girlfriend and I told Hank that we knew what was going on, but that we liked him anyway. We told him we should all put our heads together and figure out what to do.

We rallied around him.

And he picked up his gun and chased us down the street.

I was scared to death. A guy's life falls apart, he loses everything, and now he's chasing you with a gun, I figure that story rarely ends with, "And then everything was okay again."

Hank didn't kill us, though. We escaped, and then my girlfriend's friend gave us a ride to a nearby college, and we moved in there.

It was in that dorm room that I made up the ballad of The Devil's Backbone Tavern.

I didn't talk to Hank again.

That's not true. I talked to him for a few minutes, three years later, when I saw him in a bar with a new girlfriend. He introduced me to her, they seemed deeply in love, and no one mentioned the stuff about teaching and Harvard and the hotel and the military and the parents and the chasing me with a gun.

I never did find out whether the thing was true about him only having one ball, and we didn't talk about that, either.

I didn't hear from Hank again until 2005. I got a letter from him that said, "I'll bet you know where I'm at. Be out in about a year. Hope you're good."

Now I hear that Hank is still playing open mike nights. These days, he plays my old songs and tells people they're his.

To that, I say, "Godspeed, brother." If you're gonna lie, I'm gonna swear to it. The old days are still here for me, too, man.

—

The Daily Planet held about eighty-five people. There were Superman cartoon murals on the wall, and there was a pool table and a table for shuffleboard. The Planet had a decent stage and P.A. system. In the back was a kitchen you could use for a dressing room, but probably not for a kitchen.

At an open mike, I told the Planet's manager that I wanted a night to play there for myself.

"I'll play some songs tonight," I said. "And if you like it, tomorrow I'll do two sets, for nothing. You don't have to give me any money."

Sounded like a deal to him, and I started playing there every Thursday. My first gig, there was one person in the audience—her name was Sandy Hiess, and she bought me a rose, and we're still friends—but it slowly started to grow. Two months in, I'd easily quadrupled my original crowd.

I had plenty of songs, at least a hundred by that point, but only one of them that I'd consider playing now. Everybody except John Prine has to write a lot of bad songs before they start getting somewhere. The tide turned for me when I made up a song called "My Generation, Part II," which talked about all the good things people my age were contributing: "Here's to drum machines, stonewashed jeans, credit cards, fax machines / Big bow-headed chicks and frat guys wearing forty dollar tie-dyed T-shirts," was part of it.

See, I was being sarcastic.

But people liked that song, and they started filling up the nine-table area near the stage. So now there'd be forty people there. Before that song, the Planet was a bar gig. After that, it was a listening room where people would come and pay attention and sometimes leave tips for me.

My dad left tips, as well.

"You'll still be doing the Planet when you're eighty," he said. And I was thinking, "God, if I could only be so lucky." So many of the people I admired were folksingers who made careers out of singing in places the size of the Daily Planet. I was big into folk music. My favorite rock band at the time was even fronted by a guy who made folk music. The band was Drivin' N Cryin', from Georgia, and they were big on rock radio at the time. But they had acoustic guitars, and their lead singer, Kevn Kinney—just like "team," there's no "i" in Kevn—had put out a solo folk record called *McDougal Blues*. I listened to all of the band's records, a lot, but *McDougal Blues* was the record I spent the most time with. It sounded to me like Kevn had listened to a whole lot of John Prine, but he had a different spin on things, with songs like "Meatloaf and Fishsticks" and "The House Above Tina's Grocery."

Back then, anytime I thought of a new song, I would make a tape and leave it at Keith Sykes's door. One of those tapes had a song on it called "Nobody Wonders, Nobody Knows," and Keith thought that was good enough that someone might record it. He became my publisher, which meant that he'd try to get other singers interested in my songs, in the hopes that they'd record them, and then he and I would split whatever money we made from those other people's versions. I didn't really understand how all that worked, and I'm not sure I understand it now, but the gist of the deal was that Keith Sykes—who had had songs recorded by Jimmy Buffett and Rosanne Cash and a bunch of other people I loved—was officially interested in me and my music. I thought then and think now that it was a great deal.

To get other singers interested in "Nobody Wonders, Nobody Knows," Keith wanted me to make a better quality demo (short for "demonstration") tape, in a Memphis studio called Kiva Studios. I got there on a Thursday morning, and at some point I went to the kitchen to get some water and there was a long-haired guy there, microwaving a sandwich. I asked if he was recording at Kiva that day, and he said, "Yeah, my band's here today."

"What's your band?"

"We're Drivin' N Cryin'."

I said, "That's my favorite." Which it was. And then I went on and on about the band, about Kevn and especially about *McDougal Blues*.

I could see this guy I was talking with—he was the drummer, Jeff Sullivan—kind of smiling past me, in a way that made me realize there was someone behind me. I turned around, and there was Kevn. He'd just heard all this nice shit I'd said about him.

We got to talking, and he said he'd heard there was a folksinger people were listening to, somebody someone had told him about at the studio. I told him maybe that folksinger was me, and that I had a gig every Thursday at a place called the Daily Planet.

That night, I went down there to the Planet for my gig. About an hour before I was supposed to play, there were maybe four people there. Then Kevn and Drivin' N Cryin' walked in. Then the four kids who had been there before immediately ran outside to the pay phones to call their friends.

By the time I went on, you could not move inside that building. It was elbow to elbow, and for the first time, I was playing to what seemed like a whole lot of people. Kevn played during my set and talked to everyone there about how we were best friends.

We'd just met that day, but he was right. We were best friends, and still are.

To be clear, most of the people who jammed into the Planet that night were there because of Kevn and Drivin' N Cryin', not because of me. But most of them also wound up having a good time. After that, a lot of those people came to see me on a lot of Thursdays. It was a turning point.

That night, we were all heading back to my apartment to get drunk and high. Kevn and I stopped at a convenience store to get beer, and Kevn got recognized by some kids. They wanted his autograph, but they didn't have anything to sign. He told them they should buy some baseball cards, and he'd sign those. When the kids came back with the cards, one of them looked at me and said, "Aren't you Kurt Cobain, from Nirvana?" Before I could answer, honestly, that I wasn't, and that I'd never heard of Kurt Cobain or of Nirvana, Kevn answered, "Shit, yeah."

The kids handed us those cards. He signed "Kevn Kinney." I signed "Kurt Cobane."

First autograph I ever signed.

I didn't know who Cobain was then. Now, I know. He was, by a mile, the comet songwriter of my generation. He knew more about music at the age of twenty-five than I know now at forty-six, and he made the world a better place than it was. He was one bad motherfucker.

Later, I wrote a song called "Talkin' Seattle Grunge Rock Blues," about a band from Seattle that was too cool to even be bothered to play music. The song was kind of funny, and people thought I might have been making fun of Kurt. I wasn't. In my mind, I was crowning him as the guy that all the douche bags from my generation were going to copy, and I was determined not to be one of those guys. When I heard his music, I knew it was great, and I knew I'd never measure up to him by attempting to do what he was doing. He was influenced most of all by a rock band called The Pixies. Well, Jerry Jeff Walker was my Pixies, and I wasn't switching, and I still haven't.

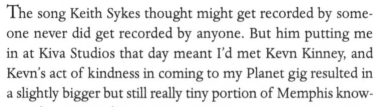

The song Keith Sykes thought might get recorded by someone never did get recorded by anyone. But him putting me in at Kiva Studios that day meant I'd met Kevn Kinney, and Kevn's act of kindness in coming to my Planet gig resulted in a slightly bigger but still really tiny portion of Memphis knowing who I was and enjoying my songs.

Keith started taking me to Nashville, because that's where you go to pitch songs now that Elvis is dead. The first time I went to Nashville was to hang out with Keith and to try to write a song with Susanna Clark. Susanna was known to many people as the wife of Guy Clark, but she was much more than that. She was a muse to Rodney Crowell and Townes Van Zandt, and she was a great painter. She was also the person who caused me to be lying to you earlier when I said everybody except John Prine has to write a bunch of songs before they get good at it.

One time in the mid-1970s, Susanna was having to play hostess to Guy, Rodney, and some other songwriters while they were drinking and talking about their art. At some point she asked what was so hard and fascinating about songwriting, and she got an answer something like, "If you think it's so easy, try it."

So she went off by herself and wrote a song called "I'll Be Your San Antone Rose," then walked it down to Music Row and got it recorded by a hit country artist of the day named Dotsy. After that, Emmylou Harris recorded it. And then Emmylou recorded one that Susanna wrote with Carlene Carter, called "Easy from Now On." That last song became the first track on Emmylou's famous *Quarter Moon in a Ten Cent Town* album, and, get this, Susanna's painting was the cover art for that album.

Smart gal, then, Susanna. She died in 2012, after spending the last ten years of her life mostly in bed, taking pills to numb something that was bugging her. I don't know what was bugging her, but I do know that you've got to crack your heart open repeatedly to be a songwriter, and I do know what it's like to want to numb up.

That first trip to Nashville, Keith dropped me at Susanna's apartment. She and Guy were split up at the time, so he wasn't around. I was supposed to meet back up with Keith at a four-star-minus-three hotel called the Shoney's Inn later that night.

Susanna and I finished the song and got drunk. I fell asleep on her outdoor patio and got sunburned. Then I woke up and stumbled to the Shoney's Inn. I didn't know Keith's room number, though, and I couldn't find him. But then, while I was wandering around that shitty place, I heard someone singing a Dean Martin song. It sounded really good, and I could quickly tell that it was Keith.

I got to the room and the door was open. I walked in. Keith was alone with a bottle of Jack Daniel's. He was standing on his bed, singing as loud as he could, pretending to be Dean Martin.

He was not embarrassed that I saw him doing this. He was kind of proud. Might have been for my benefit.

And, again, it was really good.

I hung around for a while, and then Bob Livingston, Jerry Jeff Walker's bass player, came in. I thought I was gonna shit myself to be around royalty like Bob and Keith, though I did not for the record shit myself. Royalty that night was partying long and hard, and I was already sunburned from my first party. I went to the parking lot and slept in Keith's car. The next day, we went back to Memphis.

Sometime around 1991, things were going good. I was getting gigs opening for people much bigger than me at halls that were much nicer than the small places I could fill. I was having a ball playing the Planet, and some record people were coming to shows. Keith was trying to help me get a record deal, but a lot of the time he was frustrated with me. I'd turn in a batch of songs, and he'd say none of them were any good. He'd say sometimes that he didn't understand why I wanted to be a singer. He'd say I had terrible rhythm and I didn't know the chords very well on the guitar. With hindsight, I can tell you that he said those last things mostly because I had terrible rhythm and didn't know the chords very well on the guitar.

I think Keith thought it would be in my best interest to get molded into the typical kind of singer who is successful in the mainstream, but also frustrated that I didn't have the material from which he could mold such a creature. He was frustrated with his own singing career, because he felt like he'd been screwed around by record label people and because the great albums he'd made for big record companies had not resulted in the kind of success experienced by the people who'd recorded his songs.

Keith's wife, Jerene, sometimes told me the opposite things from what Keith said. She was the one going, "Just be you. Don't let anybody change you." And Keith was the one trying to change me.

Jerene was tough, man. She threw Keith out one time, 'cause of a record he'd made. He made a puss-ass record, and she threw his shit in the yard because it sounded like he was chasing the fucking rainbow instead of singing his poems.

Keith got most mad when I screwed up an opportunity he'd created for me. Like the time he'd convinced someone from a record company in Nashville to drive three hours to Memphis to see me. I was drunk and weird that night, and the record company guy said I reminded him of Charles Manson. The young, handsome Charles Manson, I'm sure.

Keith said, "I thought we were in this together. That guy drove a long way. And I told you to open with 'My Generation, Part II.'"

But I knew then and I know now that Keith was helping.

He wanted to help.

He knew how to help.

He helped.

And he didn't have to.

Or maybe he did. Maybe he kind of needed to. Keith Sykes is a problem solver by nature, and I'm a problem by nature.

I was also a fan. A big fan. When I was twenty, I walked into my favorite record store. There was a guy who worked there, and I'd just give him money and tell him to find me something I would love. He knew I was obsessed with Jerry Jeff Walker, and Keith was a pal of Jerry Jeff's. The record store guy pulled Keith's *123* album off the rack for me and told me it was something I would love. He told me right. The whole record was spooky, and beautiful. I wore it out. I didn't learn the songs, because I couldn't. Keith Sykes is a virtuoso guitar player and a composer and an arranger. I'm none of those things even now, so you can imagine what the case was when I was twenty.

I came to Keith as a pleaser and a yes-person and a nonentity and a project. That's the way we established our relationship. He was the sage, and I was the orphan. Keith thought he knew better than me, because I told him every five seconds that he did.

And he did.

And he probably still does.

He had lots of contacts in Nashville, and he told them all about me. He got a guy named Buzz Stone from Liberty Records to come see me play, and then that guy started calling all the time. He wanted me to play The Bluebird Cafe in Nashville for the head of Liberty, Jimmy Bowen. I went up and played, and Jimmy Bowen said, "I want to sign you to my label. I'm not exactly sure what you do yet, but before you even started singing you reached down and did something to your shoe and I was interested and captivated and wanted to know what you were doing to your shoe."

So, kids, that's my advice, plain and simple: if you're looking to sign up with a record company, try doing something to your shoe. I play barefoot now, except when I'm looking for a record deal. Then I wear penny loafers, and when the show starts I stuff quarters into them.

Looking back, I think Jimmy Bowen was trying to be nice and tell me that I had charisma.

And looking back, I think Jimmy Bowen got stoned just before he walked into The Bluebird.

Good for me, right?

Bowen was a funny guy. We were at his mansion one day, and I asked him if he believed in God. He looked around his place, opened his arms, and said, "He sure seems to like me."

—

So now I had a record deal, and I didn't think there was anybody who signed to a record company who wasn't a star six months later.

They sent Keith a check for me, for $10,000, and he gave it to me, and I had to get a bank account. I had my money in a coffee can in my $250 a month apartment, and now I had $10,000. I thought it would last a long time. I used that money to live off of, and I started a band and started splitting my gig money with them.

Then it came time to do my first recording sessions, with Keith Sykes as producer. On that first session, we came to Nashville and pretended we were country. And it came out terrible.

When I played it for my friends, they said, "Oh, that's terrible."

When Keith played it for the label, the label agreed with my friends.

Then another producer came in, and we got drunk and tried to be a full-blown rock band, and that was worse than the country one.

Then I got dropped from Liberty Records.

Dropped didn't mean I had to give back the ten grand, but I was still pretty sad. Keith was angry. His position was that Liberty Records were assholes, and that we'd been screwed.

Screwed by assholes. Don't ask me how that works, but Keith was sure of it.

Here's a theory on the music business I began to develop around that time: I think the reason people think everybody in the music business is a weasel and a jerk and only out for their own gain is that when somebody gets a record deal and they go on the road and have fans and get famous, you don't really see them around town anymore. You don't have much access to them, ever again.

If you had access and asked them about their record company, they'd talk about their "record company family" and how great everyone was.

But you don't have access to them. You have access to singers who used to hang out at your favorite bar, and then they get a deal, and then that record deal fails, and then they're back at the bar, and you ask them, "Shit, I thought you were gonna be famous. You got fired. What happened?"

Ten out of ten singers don't say, "My music wasn't good enough."

Ten out of ten singers say that they were screwed by assholes who made them do something they didn't want to do.

Anytime I hear an artist say that now they're finally making the record they want to, I dismiss every inch of everything they ever do, forever.

Hey, you lied to me three years ago. You told me that record was your heart. Now you're telling me it was somebody else's heart? I have a feeling it's still somebody else's heart, just being sung by a new person.

They didn't make Kurt Cobain do shit-all.

They didn't make me do shit-all, even when they maybe should have.

Every label I've ever been on gave me all the rope in the world, and it was my job to not hang.

This time, I hung.

And I got fired. And when I was asked why I got fired by a paper called the *Memphis Star*, I gave the classic lines of bullshit that everybody who gets fired and has to come back to town says. I said, "I didn't want to do what they wanted me to."

I played the card that I dismiss people for playing now.

And I played it well.

The whole town was like, "Hey, way to be a rebel."

Yeah, right?

Jimmy Buffett, who had stood on a thousand stages with Keith and recorded Keith's songs, saw that article and was amused.

And Jimmy Buffett had his very own plane, and his very own boat, and his very own record label. You see where I'm going with this?

———

Keith arranged for me to play a festival in Nashville called Diamonds in the Rough. After I played that show, Mike Utley and Bob Mercer introduced themselves to me.

I didn't know Bob Mercer, though I learned later that he was the guy who signed the Sex Pistols to a record deal, the guy who managed Paul McCartney from The Beatles and Roger Waters from Pink Floyd, and the guy who helped Jimmy Buffett establish his record label, Margaritaville Records.

I didn't know Mike Utley personally, but I knew that he'd played organ for Jimmy Buffett's Coral Reefer Band. In Jimmy's song, "Volcano," just before the instrumental break, Jimmy calls out, "Mr. Utley!" That's Mike Utley.

And who wrote "Volcano"?

Keith Sykes wrote "Volcano."

Turns out Mike Utley ran the day-to-day operations of Margaritaville Records. And he and Bob Mercer both said they loved my show and they were interested in me and they thought Jimmy would like me.

Then Bob and Mike came to Memphis to see a show at the Planet. And from that show, they called Jimmy Buffett and said, "We've seen this guy twice. We want you to see him."

Jimmy was, again, amused. He said, "Bring him to me."

They brought me to him and let me open for him at the Greek Theater in Los Angeles. He stood on the side of the stage with Clint Black and Joe Walsh. And as I was walking off, he offered me a record deal.

Hello, second chance.

But first, I needed to make demands.

I wanted complete artistic control, in writing. Now, keep in mind, I had no idea what I was going to do with complete artistic control. But, damn it, I wanted it. I demanded it. In writing.

Jimmy and Bob and Mike were kind of "meh" about that demand. But Bob and Mike came to a thing I did in Memphis, and at that thing I opened with a song I'd just written. It's the one I told you about earlier, called "Talkin' Seattle Grunge Rock Blues." Brand new song. And it killed.

Backstage, Bob Mercer said, "This album you have in your head, does it include this song I just heard about the band from Seattle?"

In fact it did. Hypothetically but assuredly.

"Do you intend to record that song just exactly the way I heard it? With just your guitar and harmonica and voice?"

Sounded like a fine idea.

"In that case, my son, you can come to Margaritaville and do whatever you want with the other twelve songs."

That night, my friend Joe Mariencheck and I stayed up all night looking at each other, saying, "Now how did we do this?"

We didn't answer each other, "It sure had a lot to do with Keith Sykes."

Though that was true.

———

One day soon, it was official.

Keith said, "You can tell your friends you have a record deal. And if they don't put out your records, they're gonna have to give you a fuckload of dough."

All I'd ever wanted was to travel and have it be because of my art. And it looked now like that was on. And it looked like no one could take it away.

Time to call my dad. I was going to let him know who the baddest motherfucker in the world was: not him.

My dad was a developer. He developed land for drug dealer types in different places. He'd build neighborhoods for those guys to put their hookers in, and he reveled in that. When his construction friends asked about me, he'd say, "He doesn't do real songs. He makes up songs."

I called. "I've got some interesting news for you, Dad."

"Me too. I should go first."

Okay. I let him. I figured that would only make my revelation bigger and better. The baddest motherfucker in the world was letting someone else go first.

"I have lung cancer. I've only got about nine months to live. What was your thing?"

My dad came to a recording session. He met Jimmy Buffett. He saw me play at a show to celebrate my signing the record deal and saw me sweating through my shirt when I was done. He said, "I didn't realize how hard you were working."

That show was in February or March 1994.

He died in May.

The record came out in October.

Bob Mercer said the next step for me was to come to Nashville and meet with Tony Brown. He said it wasn't an audition, but that if it went well, that was better than it not going well.

He said, "Tony wants to meet you."

I knew who Tony Brown was, because he'd produced Steve Earle and Lyle Lovett and Nanci Griffith. I loved him before I knew him, and once I knew him I loved him more. I would help this guy hide a body. I don't know you, but I would help Tony Brown hide your body, and I would never think about it again.

I borrowed a car from Mark Marchetti and drove from Memphis to Tony Brown's office at MCA Records. Huge office. Bunch of cute secretaries. Big screen television with Country Music Television on it, playing with the sound down while we talked. Lots of trophies.

Tony said, "Hey, Jimmy's excited about you. I think the next step is for me to hear all your songs. How many are there?"

There were a bunch, but I didn't want to show him a bunch. I told him I had the whole record in my head, in sequence. He said to play him the first song, and I played "My Generation, Part II." He asked for the second song. I played him one called "Easy Money," written about my mom and dad hooking up. It was not a sweet song. It was about people using each other. I played him the whole album. And he said, "You in the mood to do that again?"

Sure.

He called other people, including cute secretaries, into his office. And I did it again, and then it was done: MCA in Nashville would work to promote my album, in conjunction with Jimmy Buffett's Margaritaville Records. And Keith Sykes would produce. Or at least coproduce.

What does a producer do? I didn't really even know at the time. But the producer hires the musicians, decides the way things will get recorded, and makes about a thousand artistic decisions that dictate the way the music sounds. He's like the director of a movie. He's into everything, all the time. He makes the trains run on time.

And Keith would be my producer. Because I loved and admired him, and because I owed him. And because I had complete creative control, in writing.

Keith had a long and complicated history with Jimmy Buffett, and he was well known to Tony Brown and Bob Mercer, and Tony and Bob (probably at Jimmy's bidding) started saying that maybe Keith should have a coproducer. And they started saying that the coproducer should be Mike Utley. And as soon as he heard this, Keith decided he was mad at Jimmy and that all these assholes were fucking him, and that this would be just like the thing at Liberty, where he was supposed to be producer but got fired after his first try.

I thought Mike Utley was a great guy, and that he and Keith would work well together.

And, it should be noted, I didn't know anything about making records. I'd never made one. At present, I've made a bunch of them and I still wouldn't tell you that I know a bunch about making them.

With my complete creative control, I agreed that Mike would be a great addition to our recording. Keith was immediately angry. We went to record in Key West, and Keith said he knew that nobody was going to listen to him. He was pissed off, and he started drinking the first thing on the first morning.

At the end of the first day, Bob Mercer said, "This isn't going well. You didn't finish anything today."

He said that because it wasn't going well, and because we hadn't finished anything the first day.

He said that because he thought, correctly, that Keith had the musical talent to do the job, but that he probably shouldn't be drinking in the morning.

The next day, Margaritaville shut the sessions down.

I was confused. I had no idea how any of this was supposed to work. And I came from a family of alcoholics, so Keith's work process didn't seem weird to me. But clearly, we had spent two days in the studio and had recorded nothing worthwhile. And by nothing worthwhile, I mean nothing at all.

The phone rang in my five-hundred-square-foot apartment. I picked it up, and Jimmy Buffett was on the other end of the line.

I recorded the conversation, because I was paranoid. I wish I could say because I was smoking pot, which I was. Anyway, I was paranoid. And I was angry, because my mentor Keith Sykes was angry. And because I had complete creative control, in writing, and things were happening that didn't seem like I was completely in control.

Jimmy Buffett said that Keith had been fired.

I said, "My contract says Keith is my coproducer, no matter what."

Jimmy laughed his ass off.

He said, "That was cute how you got all that in your contract."

Then he explained that contracts can also be used to wipe your ass.

Then he explained that I could sit in my apartment if I wanted, and that I don't have to make an album. But that Keith was fired.

And I said, "I could go to another label."

And he said, "Well, that's where it gets a little tricky."

He was giggling. He thought it was funny.

I said, "You're telling me that you're a jerk?"

He said, "Yes, we're clear on that."

And his tone of voice wasn't mean. It was more like flirty. He did this with charm. And he never lost his temper.

I made up a song later that night called, "When It Comes to Being Cool, Jimmy Buffett Missed the Boat."

That one didn't make the album.

In hindsight, I'd rewrite that to say, "When It Comes to Being Cool, Jimmy Buffett Built the Boat." I was glad to be on that boat. Though once I rewrote that song, I'd still shred it and make sure you never heard it.

As soon as I got off the phone with Jimmy, I drove to see Bob Mercer. And Bob said I should talk to Tony Brown.

Tony said, "I'm gonna be really frank with you. Keith is not going to produce your record. Mike Utley is going to produce your record. You can do that, or you can not do that and I'll give you a really small amount of money every year for another nine years and that'll be it for you, because by that time you'll be too old to get a record deal."

And then he said, "You're gonna thank me someday for doing this to you. You're at the wall, and you're going to lose. And the wall is right, and you are wrong."

Tony Brown wound up coproducing the album with Mike Utley. They gave Keith some money and told him to go away, and he kept 100 percent of the publishing, on every song on the album. And he sat at home, feeling screwed and blaming me and Buffett and everybody else.

By the time the record came out, Keith seemed to have forgiven everyone. And that lasted a month or two.

I never felt good about any of it. Keith and I kind of settled at, "I screwed him and I was sorry." I carried guilt. My rationale, and my friend Joe Mariencheck helped me with this, was that this was my second chance. Are we going to tell the record company people to get bent again? We've got people who get paid good money to produce records telling us that this guy, my mentor Keith, can't produce this record.

I just wanted everybody to like each other.

But they don't, really.

My record was not a hit.

All the record company people tried, and I tried some my-self. I did a radio tour, where you go to all these stations and play songs for them.

I can't for the life of me remember what the people from the label did that I didn't appreciate, but I do remember going AWOL to teach everybody a lesson.

I got home from the radio tour, and the real tour was sup-posed to crank up in three or four days. I decided that I wasn't going back out on tour until all of whatever it was that was bothering me got resolved to my satisfaction.

I went to my friend Shamus's apartment and crashed out there for about three days without telling anyone where I was. We sat around and listened to John Denver, because John Den-ver songs always made Shamus cry. I'm standing up to every-body, by hiding and listening to "Leavin' on a Jet Plane," over and over again.

We were drinking beers, and maybe even smoking some dope, and the hour was getting a little bit late. And it was brought to my attention that I was supposed to go to St. Louis and play a show, and that some people would be happy if I missed that show and some people would be mad if I missed that show.

I was thinking, "Yeah, that's my point. You will see that this is what I am going to do."

Whatever that was.

The phone rang at Shamus's house, and it was Tony Brown.

How did he find out where I was? Deep down, we all knew Mark Marchietti gave him the number, but it was more fun to pretend that he'd tracked us down in some kind of evil spy way.

Tony said, "I can't be clearer about this. As an older person talking to a younger person, you absolutely, positively, for sure want to be getting in your van right now and driving up to St. Louis to do your show. Your record is not hot enough to bargain with. I don't even know if I'd use the word 'hot.' Not failing ain't success, and I'm not saying you're not failing. I'm just saying not failing ain't success."

We got in the van, immediately.

You know, having proven our point. I wish I could remember what it was.

We hauled ass toward St. Louis, six hours away. And it started pouring down snow. Somewhere in Missouri, it was pounding snow, and we got the word from the radio that we just could not go on anymore and that we'd have to pull over. We realized we were going to have to get a room and that we were not going to play the gig Tony Brown said we had to play.

But it was okay. It wasn't my fault. It was the snow.

We walked to a little diner to get some breakfast that next morning, and the lady who waited on us said, "You guys look like you're in a band or something."

We were in a band or something, and this diner was attached to a little honky-tonk that had a small bandstand. And outside there was a trailer that said "Nick Nixon Band" on it.

Somebody in our group said, "Yeah, we have an album out. It's on MCA Records."

The lady said, "No shit. Our cook used to be on MCA Records. Let me go get him."

And she did.

The cook and I were dressed almost identically.

My outfit was a costume.

The cook brought his MCA Record out and showed it to us. It was handy. He also brought us articles about himself, articles that said he'd punched out Elvis Presley.

You can look this up; I did. It was true. The cook used to be on MCA Records. And I could not, would not, and still can't, cook.

I thought, "From now on, I'm going to try to make it to all the shows, without any drama."

Which, to be clear, I have not.

$\sim$

So, let me recap. Keith Sykes tried time and again to solve my problems.

And that's where we differ.

I like my problems.

I have a song that says, "I wouldn't trade my troubles for anybody's troubles / I've gotten used to my own."

Keith and I became friends again, even after he got me my record contract, and even after he got knocked out of something that meant a lot to him and that continued to mean a lot to him.

Behind almost every record deal is a Keith Sykes. There's always a guy thinking, "I fucking did that, goddammit, and I'm not a part of it anymore." And they're right. They did fucking do that, goddammit. And they're not a part of it anymore.

Our relationship has always been tumultuous.

$\sim$

Many years after my first album, I decided to produce an album on Keith with my friend Peter Cooper. My manager told me I could afford it if I wanted to put somebody on a label of my own. So we took Peter and his microphones and his mixing board and our friend Stacie Huckaba and her cameras, and we made something I feel is a masterpiece. You've never heard it. You can't hear it. It's not available.

We went to Keith's house in Memphis, and he sat on his couch with his Martin guitar, and he told us stories and he sang us songs. He played his heart out, and he sounded like a two-thousand-year-old guy. The best kind of two-thousand-year-old guy. Sam Phillips heard Howlin' Wolf and said, "That's where the soul of man never dies." I felt that way about hearing Keith play songs on that couch. The plan was to put out that album on my label, the same way I'd been putting out mine.

Maybe this was me trying to solve Keith's problems, an uncomfortable scenario for both of us. It was a tricky thing. And the further plan was for my mentor to go out on the road with me, in my bus, and open shows for me and sell this CD at the shows.

I was trying to give him something I thought he wanted, which is what made me angry at him whenever he tried to do that for me. Circle of life, my ass.

The tour was starting, but first we had a conversation. I said, "Please, when we're out there, I ask you one favor: I don't want to hear ideas about how to be more famous or how to be more rich. Go through any article ever written about me, and you'll never find me complaining about my lot in music." Except, of course, that Memphis article where I blamed Jimmy Bowen, and it helped me get a sweet and fine record deal. But I never did that again, so forget I said anything.

I said to Keith, "Let's go out there and be happy and satisfied and excited about the shows we're doing. Let's not be about trying to get into some bigger room."

But Keith and my relationship had always been about him helping me. And the conversation invariably turned to how I wasn't where I was supposed to be, or doing what I was supposed to be doing.

Three dates into the tour that was supposed to promote Keith's brilliant album that I'd coproduced, we had just played somewhere where I felt absolutely fulfilled. We were on the bus and drinking wine, and he said, "This is crazy insane that you don't have a special on HBO. There's gotta be somebody we can call."

Then he said he knew somebody at HBO, and then he said I wasn't taking him seriously about knowing somebody at HBO. And then he said other things.

If I had it to do over again, and if there was enough wine, I suppose it wouldn't hurt me any to sit up all night and talk about trying to get on HBO. Someday, I hope to fix that. It's not fixed right now. It's really the only unfixed thing I've got, besides some family. And it's the only unfixed thing I've got that I want to fix.

At the time, I had a panic attack. I was breathing into a bag, and I knew that we had booked thirty more days of this. I talked to my wife on the phone and she supported me doing anything I could to end the bag-breathing episodes, even if it meant kicking Keith off the bus.

"You know I can't kick Keith off the bus. You're asking me to punch the person I'm perceiving to be the bully."

But I could have Keith kicked off the bus. And I didn't have to have his brilliant record come out on my label.

Today, I'm not sure who was the bully, or if we both were or if neither of us was. All I know is that I could not personally kick Keith off the bus, so I had my tour manager, Elvis Hicks, do it. Elvis told him he was going home, and Elvis told him that this was not the place to be working on our relationship. Keith said, "We don't have one." Keith, my mentor, was wrong. We do have a relationship. It's irrevocable, and it's as old as my relationship with my dad, and maybe as important. And I wish it were better, and maybe it will be. I love him and he helped me.

Maybe you know somebody like that.

I fear you know somebody like that.

I hope you know somebody like that.

CHAPTER 7

WHO WEARS
A WAISTLET?

After I started making records, I started going to New York and Los Angeles a lot, often for some reason other than gigs.

One time, not that long ago, I was in LA for some kind of meeting. I wasn't supposed to sing or anything at the meeting. It was all that other shit we have to sit around and talk about if we want to travel and drink free and be applauded for our pointless observations and chord progressions.

This trip was probably going to involve eating with strangers. I knew that, since I'd been to a ton of these things.

And with the same breath, I can tell you that I've met some of my closest friends at these things. I can also tell you that most of these things are root canals. No offense to root canals, which are helpful and often necessary.

My point is, I was not looking forward to it.

The good news was, as is often the case in my line of work, I wasn't paying for anything. Some people used to say that I would pay eventually, but I knew I wouldn't. And I didn't. So there.

I was staying, for what (as I just knew) turned out to be free, at some cool yellow hotel off the Sunset Strip. And whatever mess I wanted to make of myself in the bar was cool, I was told.

The meeting was for lunch, at noon. So my idea was that I would go to the yellow hotel bar around 10:30 and have a few drinks, to take the edge off.

The bar was nice and warm and dark and black and red and leathery, and I knew right away it was about my speed. As I made my way up to a stool and took in the surroundings, I could see that there was nobody in the bar but myself, the bartender, and Slash from Guns N' Roses.

Right, Slash. Lead guitar. Nose ring. Born in England but doesn't talk that way. He was about six stools over to my right, but around a bar corner, so that we were kind of facing each other.

He was drinking vodka and smoking cigs, with a velvety black Metallica baseball cap on backwards, big Jim Morrison-style mirrored shades, and no shoes.

Around both of his wrists he had at least a dozen bracelets, and probably more. Bracelets of every manner and fashion. Pukka, friendship, conch, leather, silver, gold. All that shit. Slash was a bracelet guy. He made Mr. T. look like a lunch money pimp.

Around his neck, he had roughly the same gamut of stuff. A neckless guy, too.

But, also, around both ankles he had tons of what they call anklets.

He had anklets of all manner and fashion. Pukka, friendship, conch, leather, silver, gold, link.

Bracelets, check. Anklets, check. But I'll go you one further. Around his waist he had all the same shit. What is that? Is that a waistlet? You ever see a guy wearing an assortment of waistlets? I had not, and have not since. Nor do I expect to. Slash had on more than a dozen waistlets.

But, wait. There is more. You know those shorts people wore in the early '80s? Those shorts that Nike made and people wore to jog in? Those silky, revealing short shorts that Richard Simmons wore so well? Those kind of shorts that if you're wearing them today and you're not Richard Simmons. Well, man, you know. Those shorts.

Well, Slash had those fucking shorts on.

And nothing else.

Shirt?

Fuck no. He's Slash. He doesn't need some fucking shirt.

Shorts, cap, shades, necklaces, bracelets, anklets, waistlets, cigs, vodka.

That's it. Slash, of Guns N' Fucking Roses.

I was awestruck, terrified. I didn't so much as nod at the guy. I wanted to ask him a million questions and decided to ask him none. I wanted to at least tell him that I knew he was Slash. Though, to be sure, this was not a secret he was trying to keep.

I never got the nerve to tell him anything. My hope, though, was to be cool. And my decision was to leave him alone. Which I did.

About an hour later, when I noticed on the clock that I had about twenty minutes to get to the meeting, I paid my tab and got up to head out.

And as I got up to head out, Slash looked over at me and said, "Take it easy, man."

And I did.

Totally did.

Still do.

CHAPTER 8

FEAR AND LOATHING IN THE GREEN ROOM

Seventh grade, and I was up late, and *Where the Buffalo Roam* came on the TV. That's a movie starring Bill Murray as the writer Hunter S. Thompson. I thought the movie was fictitious, and I didn't understand what the drug jokes were about. But I loved the movie, and I loved the character of Hunter. He seemed so unconcerned.

I told my friend Morgan Butler at school about *Where the Buffalo Roam* and he explained to me that Hunter was real. Then he told me about a Hunter book called *Fear and Loathing in Las Vegas*, and I got it and thought it was priceless. I hadn't done any drugs yet, but I quickly knew I was going to be doing them soon. And I was writing for the school paper at the time, so I already identified with Hunter, a writer who happily subverted reality. I thought I wanted to be Hunter, and then I found Jim Morrison of The Doors and I thought I wanted to be a singer. Later, I found Jerry Jeff Walker, who was not only a perfect combination of Hunter and Morrison, but who was also a friend of Hunter's. Finding Jerry Jeff was it for me. It solidified everything.

As I moved toward that point, though, as I moved through my teens and twenties, I was always watching *Where the Buffalo Roam*. I still watch it a few times a year. I'd read all of Hunter's books by the time I was out of high school. I liked the books, but mostly I liked the crazy behavior and the speeding and the drugs and raising hell in hotels and being a degenerate. Hunter was a degenerate who seemed to never get in trouble and who actually got praised for his bad behavior. He was very Keith Richards–like in that way. I thought he was funny and irreverent and nonsensical and absurd, and I wanted to be a part of all that. I thought, "What a hilarious way to plant your flag in life." From Hunter, I was inspired.

Years after that, as I have mentioned, Jimmy Buffett signed me to his label. I was in New Orleans playing Jimmy's club, Storyville. After the show, we moved the guitars and amps into the van, and then in came Jimmy. He came into the dressing room with Ed Bradley from *60 Minutes* and another guy I didn't recognize right away. Jimmy said, "This is my friend, Ed Bradley, and my friend, Dr. Thompson."

I said, "Hunter Thompson?" and I just lit up.

Hunter lit up, too. He said, "Yeah, I think so."

They were clearly, all three, fucked up. They'd seen the show, but maybe not close up. It wasn't like, "You're Todd, Jimmy's told me all about you." It was like, "You were in the band we just saw?"

Hunter said, "Well, get your guitar. Shit. Let's hear some more."

I said, "It's already buried in the van."

He said, "What kind of singer are you? You don't even sing?"

I was being challenged by a man I'd loved since I was twelve.

"Who packs the guitar up right away?" he said. "We're here to hear you sing. What the fuck? Go get your goddamn guitar and let's do this." And then Hunter S. Thompson, the great Gonzo journalist, shoved me. Menacingly. "I'm through dicking around!" he said. "I want you to sing. Get your guitar out of the van! Jimmy, you said he was a singer!"

For some reason, once he started pushing me, I felt threatened and bullied. It was instinct. He pushed me over a little coffee table, and I landed on a couch. Jimmy was laughing. Will Kimbrough, who played guitar in The Nervous Wrecks, saw this. And Shamus, our sound guy, saw this and started crying. That was unusual. Shamus never cried. Then Jimmy and Ed Bradley and Hunter S. Thompson went off into the night. I later regretted not going with them, but I just didn't see that I belonged there.

When I look back on it, they were fully prepared for me to take the world on. They'd seen lots of people do it, and it wasn't a big deal to them. I think they thought I'd be very famous a short time later. I definitely think Jimmy thought that. But as much as I looked up to them, it was a relief when they were gone. For one thing, no one shoved me after that. For another, I was glad to be back in the bubble with my band.

Those guys who came backstage that night—Jimmy and Ed Bradley and Hunter—were alpha guys. They were loud, boisterous, aggressive people who took what they wanted, like pirates. They were '60s and '70s guys. By the time I came along, fame and ambition were things you were supposed to be a little embarrassed about. I think it was in the '80s, when Guns N' Roses came along, that the decadent shit got taken to its problematic finish in debauchery and waistlets and the rest. I think watching my dad be a sucker for money and glory and success, and watching it gut him so deeply, was a big turnoff for me. I watched him spend beyond his means so his neighbors would think he was more important. This is not to put down Jimmy or Ed Bradley or Hunter S. Thompson, by the way. They were all great, and they were motivated toward art and freedom and against conformity. But they were aggressive in a way that I was neither willing nor able to be.

And I will admit, upon reflection, that there was something off-putting to me about Hunter screaming at me and shoving me in anger. It didn't seem as fun as when he was on TV, doing that to other people. But I still loved him. New Orleans was the only time I ever saw him, but I still watch *Where the Buffalo Roam* all the time. Everywhere I go, the first thing I think is, "This is the old Babyface Nelson place, right?" That's a line from the movie that became a line from my life, and it even helped me when I met John Cougar Mellencamp.

But enough about him, until much later in our epic adventure.

CHAPTER 9

PLAY A
TRAIN SONG

Most people don't yell in the early hours after sunrise. Yelling is usually for the part of the morning that's technically still part of the night. A neighbor's fight interrupts your sleeping, not your breakfast or the reading of your morning paper.

But here was a guy yelling at me while I was doing my little morning walk, with a foghorn voice that sounded like one of those old Muppets from the balcony had been drinking lots of bourbon.

This startled me a little. When I'm home in East Nashville, I rise pretty early, blaze one or two, and then take a right turn outside of my door and go around a two-block area, five times. It's not so much exercise as it is walking. Sometimes I go by

myself, sometimes with my wife. And here was a man yelling—
and not just yelling, but yelling about my walking. "All that
walking's gonna kill you!" he said.

I looked up to where the voice was coming from, to the
porch of a house in my neighborhood. We call the neighborhood "Little Hollywood," but I've been to the actual Hollywood and it's pretty different. Calling where I live "Little
Hollywood" is like calling Scranton "Little New York." The
voice was coming from the mouth of a tough-looking, biker-
type guy. I looked at him and smiled and kept walking.

Next time around the block, he yelled again. "Where are
you going?' he said. "Need directions?' The time after that it
was, "Want a cigarette?" I did, but I walked on.

A week later, my wife and I were doing that same walk.
We went by the biker-looking guy's house and didn't see him
the first time around. But on the next time, as we approached
the house we could hear rock 'n' roll. And I recognized the
song. "There's a truck turned over on the highway, flares burning out of the snow," were the words. "Freezing rain in the
passing lane, I got 45 miles to go."

I had a thought about the song. This was it: I've got a song
that says that exact same thing, but it's on an album that isn't
coming out for another month.

But it was, in fact, my song, and here it was, coming right
out of the biker guy's window, loud. A premiere screening,
right there in Little Hollywood.

By the time we got to his house, he was standing in his
doorway, grinning. I said, "Where'd you get that?"

He said, "I could tell you, but then I'd have to kill you."

This is a throwaway line for a lot of people. But there was
some amount of gravity behind him when he said it. It was not
like hearing it from the guy at your office party, I promise.

He said his name was Skip, and he invited us into his house for some pot.

Don't mind if I do. That's usually how you get to me if you want to get to me. On our bus, we call that a backstage pass. Skip came up with that term. Let me clarify. Someone else apparently came up with the term "backstage pass," but Skip applied it to weed.

We walked into his house, which was actually the downstairs apartment of someone else's house. One wall of his house was completely signed: everybody that came there signed the wall, and it turned out everybody had come there. His wall was like Willie Nelson's guitar, where the only place there wasn't a signature was the place where there was a hole. His whole house was the closest I'd seen a house get to the dressing rooms they create for us in the backs of these places we play. There was a bunch of used furniture, a table, a jam box, and a toilet that worked sometimes.

He was always having parties down there, which I knew because I'd heard them from down the street.

We started smoking and listening to my album that he wasn't supposed to have, and talking. We never really finished that conversation, not that day or the next or the day after that. I spent two hours a day with Skip Litz for the rest of his life.

Skip was insane, in the best ways anybody has ever been insane. He was a drug dealer, first and foremost. He had been a roadie, and he worked sound at a place called The Radio Cafe. He knew every person in Nashville who could make a note. If you knew how to touch something or blow into something and make it sound like music, he knew you.

And he heckled you.

Heckling involved yelling, as I had learned on my walks. And the main heckle involved yelling, "Play a fucking train song!" at the top of his lungs. Everybody knew him for that, and almost everybody would do it when he yelled it. He could yell that at any club, with impunity. There was an occasion when a band from Texas was playing at a place in East Nashville called The French Quarter (I think it was probably named that by the same guy who named us Little Hollywood), and Skip started yelling for them to play a fucking train song. The band wasn't happy about it. A standoff ensued, as they say, with the owner. Someone said "Either that guy goes or we go." That guy stayed. The band went. At least that's what that guy said. I never bothered to verify. It doesn't really matter. Around here, Skip's word was gospel. We believed in him. This belief grew stronger at happy hour, when he'd go by every single East Nashville bar and drop off a huge bud of pot to whoever was tending bar. As a result, I never saw Skip pay a dime or dollar for whiskey, and we all saw him drink whiskey a lot.

At night, before going back to his house, he'd drive past all his friend's houses and honk. I think he was watching to make sure everybody was okay, and he was honking to let us know that he was watching.

Once Skip and I stole a Christmas tree from the Kroger's grocery. There's no great story behind that event other than the event itself. We just drove up and he took it. He acted like it was his, and then it was.

Skip's actions were not always unnoticed by the authorities. One night, he was driving his motorcycle real fast. Skip didn't have a license plate or a driver's license, and his idea was that he should go fast because of that, until the cops caught up with him, and then it was time to go really slow.

So on this night, a cop got mad at him for going fast, so he started going slow, but didn't stop. That cop called another cop, and soon there were seven patrol cars, lights and sirens going, in a parade behind a guy wearing a broken moped helmet, riding a Harley at four miles per hour. Skip led this low-speed chase past all the bars, honking and waving at everyone like he was heading up a parade. It was the stuff of instant legend. Skip led the cops to a party that was already going on at his house. He pulled up, put the bike down, and was promptly beaten to shit by the cops. They took both his shoulders out of socket. That last part always got left out when Skip told that story.

In spite of what the police thought, we all knew Skip was the unofficial mayor of East Nashville. As there is no official mayor of East Nashville, this made Skip the main mayor.

One time at a club in East Nashville, Skip yelled for some guy to play a fucking train song, and the guy said he didn't know a train song, but that he'd had one of his songs cut by Garth Brooks and George Jones.

Then he went into a song he said he wrote, a song called "Beer Run." I had a song called that, too, that was not cut by either of those gentlemen. Without ever mentioning my name, Skip got onstage and made the guy stop. "I saw some barefoot kid in Memphis play that song ten years ago, you fucking thief!" he said. "If you actually lived out your songs you wouldn't have to steal them."

Skip knew I didn't think that song was stolen from me or from the guy I made it up with, Keith Christopher. Skip himself was not being truthful about having heard the song in Memphis. I personally thought Skip was probably wrong to bother the guy. But somehow all that made it seem funnier.

The singer didn't think it was funnier, or even funny. He went into another song. And Skip sat back down and started singing my version of "Beer Run" at the top of his lungs.

Skip had a million sayings, or slogans. He said them all the time.

He said, "I want to die peacefully in my sleep like my grandfather, and not screaming and whining like everybody else in the car."

He said, "Dying is the best part of living. That's why I saved it for last."

He said, "Never go straight, always go forward."

He said, "Don't apologize to me, I don't care enough."

And when he answered the phone, he said, "I'll play your silly little game."

The mayor of East Nashville had a diverse constituent base and was quite popular with both men and women. So popular with the men that they didn't question him hitting on the women.

"You're hotter than the hinges on the gates of hell," is what he told my wife. He was right, of course, but if anyone else had said that to her I'd be jealous and angry. When Skip said it, I laughed, and so did she.

Certainty was big with Skip. He knew that being tentative is almost never helpful. And he could smell tentativeness in other people. After he started going on the road with me as the world's least manageable road manager, I saw him repeatedly sniff out tentativeness and exploit it.

One time in Atlanta, we had our little pigeon rat dog named Lulu with us when we were checking into a hotel that didn't keep dogs. Skip carried Lulu in his arms, right through the lobby, and the guy behind the hotel desk saw Skip and nervously said, "Is that a dog?"

He did not say, "The rules are that you can't have a dog, and that's clearly a dog." He said, "Is that a dog?" and "Is that a dog?" is a question.

And Skip had the balls to answer, "No." Rather, he stopped, turned to face the guy so the guy got a good, full view of Skip and of Lulu, and then he said, "No." And then he turned around and walked to the elevator, and nobody said another word about it.

Skip was a veteran, and it was veterans who started motorcycle gangs. Skip was real happy when the motorcycle gang thing came along, and he joined up real fast. Kids like Skip who went to Vietnam were told to go camp for their lives, sleep out there, and shoot back if anybody shoots at them. Then they got back here, went to a movie, and some usher told them to pipe down. Uh, no. Not completely interested in piping down. And this is not a dog.

He was unbelievably confrontational with strangers. One time we were in Milwaukee, and there were five guys in this bar. They were older businessmen watching George W. Bush on the CNN feed, with reverence. One of them said something nice about George W. Bush. And Skip, loudly, said, "They ought to fucking hang him for war crimes, right, guy?"

They didn't answer. They tried to do the same thing I'd done when Skip first yelled at me about walking. But they were sitting there, not moving, and Skip's voice got considerably louder. "DON'T YOU THINK THEY OUGHT TO HANG THIS GUY FOR FUCKING WAR CRIMES?" he said. Now they were scared. "ANY OF Y'ALL EVER KILL ANYBODY?" And they hadn't. "I HAVE. FOR OUR COUNTRY!"

They bought him a drink. I mean, of course. Bartender, get that hero a drink. Anything he wants.

He wants Southern Comfort.

Now, if those guys had been saying, "George W. Bush is an idiot," he'd have come at them with something else, equally loud: "HE'S THE FUCKING PRESIDENT OF OUR COUNTRY. WHO THE FUCK ARE YOU GUYS?" But the ultimate outcome would have been the same. Skip would be sitting there with a free Southern Comfort in his hand and a smile on his face.

On the rare occasion when someone got real mad at Skip, he'd get a hangdog look on his face. "Jesus," he'd say. "I'm a fifty-year-old veteran with a pacemaker. I'm a drug addict. I'm not well. You ready to kill a guy?" And it would all turn to laughter, every time. I don't know why everyone always thought that last bit was so funny. It was the God's honest truth.

Skip was a nice guy, but he had been in a biker gang and had been in a war and had killed somebody in that war. And he had shot someone and gone to jail for it earlier in his life, and he spoke of a past that sounded pretty violent. When everybody was freaking out about the end of the millennium, Skip told me he had a shotgun and a bunch of bullets. He said as soon as the whole world went kaput, he was going to sit around and get high, then take that shotgun and walk around until he heard a generator.

I think he was kind of disappointed when the first part of the new millennium turned out to be a whole lot like the last part of the old one.

Skip was from Maryland. His dad beat the shit out of him and his brothers, and his dad would get drunk and make them play Russian roulette. It was the kind of house where going to Vietnam seemed like a pretty good plan, and Skip did three tours of duty there.

One night in Maryland, after the war, he was sitting in the basement of a house he was renting when he heard a noise that drew him to the window.

Outside the window, he saw a man dressed all in black, holding a rifle and crawling across Skip's yard. Instinctively, like our country had taught him to do, Skip reached for his gun and fired.

He said he yelled, "Fuck you, motherfucker!" first, then shot.

Then there were cops everywhere. I don't mean in minutes, I mean in seconds. It seems the cops were getting ready to raid Skip's coke-dealing neighbor and hadn't told anyone.

The guy didn't die, but they arrested Skip, even though the guy was crawling with a gun on Skip's property.

Skip thought he was being railroaded and thought no judge would believe him, so he decided to escape, right then and there.

He said he used cardboard to pad the barbed wire, but that the cardboard didn't really pad too good. And then he ran through some woods. They shot at him, and he thought he was hit, but he kept running through the dark until the ground under him dropped about ten feet to a small river, and he waded downriver until he got to where he could make it to a friend's house.

He said the cops searched his friend's house with him in it, but didn't find him. And then he went to check on his girlfriend and stay at her house, until they got into some kind of fight a couple days later, and she turned him in.

Later, he went to trial for the shooting and was found innocent.

He also went to trial for the escape and was found guilty and sentenced to a year in prison.

After prison, he joined back with his motorcycle gang. Then he had a heart attack, and nobody from the gang came to see him in the hospital, and that pissed him off. So when he was healthy again, he just took his bike and rode away, first to Michigan and then to Ohio and then to some homeless shelters, and finally to Nashville. He took a job running sound at The Radio Cafe, but he mainly became known as the guy who knew everyone and who knew how to get everyone everything they needed.

Need a ride? Call Skip. Need jumper cables? Bootleg tapes? Pills? Christmas lights? Cigs? A fake ID? Guns? A fake community service letter? Call Skip.

He told me he'd tour-managed a band before.

A band called Red Bud Thunder.

He also told the hotel clerk he wasn't holding a dog.

But Skip was my best friend, and he wasn't well. He was dying to some degree. This was the part he had saved for last. He had a tumor in his stomach that you could see if he laid down on his back. He called it "The Alien." He had it the whole time we knew each other.

We only knew each other three or four years.

Skip had been given eight months to live, and he was supposed to have a surgery at the VA hospital. He called me from the hospital and told me to get his leather jacket from his apartment and to bring $40. I got that jacket and that $40 and brought it all to him. The doctors had told him he had a 50/50 shot at making it through the surgery to get rid of The Alien. I walked into his room, looked at him, and he had plastic spoons taped all over his face. I looked at him weird, the way you'd look at someone with plastic spoons taped all over their face, and he said, "Oh, no, did they fuck up my plastic surgery?"

Then he got out of bed and went into some other guy's room and did the plastic surgery bit again. The nurses were telling him to get out of the guy's room, but the guy was laughing and didn't want Skip to leave. It was so obvious that he was helping, but they kept making him stop helping.

At the hospital that night, Skip took the tubes and shit out of his arms and said, "Me and my friend are going to get a couple of drinks."

The nurse lady looked at me like I was supposed to do something about this. But I'd already done something about it: I'd brought the jacket and the $40. Skip put his leather jacket on over his hospital gown, and then he put his jeans on. There was a tube sticking out the bottom of his jacket sleeve, and you could still see his hospital tag.

"We're gonna get something to drink, and then some cigarettes," he said.

They tried to lay it on him, like that would be a bad thing to have a drink and a smoke as death waited in the wings. We got out of that hospital and went to the bar and had a bunch of drinks. He was telling all the girls that he was going to die the next day and asking them if they could show him their tits.

They could.

He drove back to the hospital in his own car, and we said good-bye like it was no big deal. But after he went away, my wife started crying. I called Skip in his car, and we had a little moment. And then I had to fly to Philadelphia for a gig. When I got to Philly, I found out that Skip had made it through the surgery.

"I'm going to be your tour manager," is what he told me when I talked to him. "Fuck, man, I haven't felt this good in years. I'm ready to travel with you."

And he was.

And he did.

We never even had to do a benefit show for him to pay for his time in the hospital.

The hospital sent him a bill for something like $35,000, and he wrote "Deceased" on it and sent it back and never heard another word.

Skip was a natural tour manager. He kept everything safe and kept everything fun. We went to a Brewers game in Milwaukee; saw Bob Dylan's childhood home in Hibbing, Minnesota; saw the last place Buddy Holly ever played; and drank Southern Comfort on the beach in Santa Cruz. I kept telling him how great Santa Cruz was, and he claimed not to be impressed when I finally got him out there.

"Isn't this great?" I said.

"Nah, I don't see the big deal about it," he said.

Then we went to Palm Beach in 2003, and we swam in the ocean and roared and had a blast.

"Now, this is how you go to the beach, man," he said, and then said some untrue shit about Santa Cruz.

One time, we'd been paid in $100 bills, and we were both hungry after the show. Skip took the money to a Taco Bell and went through the drive-in there.

"Can you break a $100 bill?" he asked, and they said, "No."

"Then give me $100 worth of tacos," he said. And they did, and that's a lot of tacos.

In 2003, we were supposed to go to play a show in Virginia, where Skip's daughter and grandchildren lived. By this time, Skip had moved to a place about twelve blocks away from my house, so I walked over less and called more. The day before we were leaving for Virginia, I called in the morning to see if he wanted to drive over and read the newspaper like we'd been doing since he moved.

Skip didn't answer the phone, but I didn't think anything of it. But then I kept calling through the day, and he kept not answering, and Melita and I started to worry. By happy hour, we were out on the porch, and our friend Libby decided to make a beer and cig run. She said she'd swing by Skip's, and then five minutes later she called, saying, "Come quick."

So we came quick, and when we got there Libby was on the porch, yelling into her phone to 911, "Just fucking hurry!" They did, but it didn't matter.

We walked inside and saw Skip the way I'd seen him many times before: on the sofa, with his hands under his head like a pillow. In that same second, I noticed that his face had a smile on it.

He died laughing.

⌁

A couple days later, Skip's brothers came to Nashville, and a bunch of us went over to Skip's house to meet them. At first, we all sat around looking at each other, but that only lasted about a beer. By the top of the third, the house was filled again with laughter. Skip's brothers decided to bury him in his "Your Favorite Band Sucks" T-shirt, and they decided I should make the call to the newspaper about the obituary. Just before the lady at the paper picked up, Skip's brother Norman said something and everybody laughed. The first thing that lady heard was a room full of laughing. Then she asked if she could help me.

Still laughing, I said, "Yeah, I need to ask about obituaries."

At that, the room erupted even louder in laughter, and I thought, "Skip would like this."

Later, Peter Cooper from the newspaper came over to ask some questions about Skip for a story. That was the first time

I met Peter, who wound up being a good friend and a guy I make up songs with. Him and me and Mac Hill, who ran The Radio Cafe, wound up going on the most unsuccessful beer run ever. I didn't have ID and got carded, so they wouldn't sell to me. Mac went in, and they wouldn't sell to him, because they knew he was with me. Finally, we found beer at another store, and then, walking into the house too many minutes later, I dropped a case of Budweiser and shattered five or six cold beers.

Skip's brother Doug said, "You're not going for beer anymore," and then there was more laughter.

Peter knew Skip from the neighborhood, but he didn't know much about his history. So he started interviewing Skip's brothers.

"Was Skip drafted, or did he volunteer for Vietnam?"

"Neither . . . he went to avoid jail."

Laughter.

"How come he was in jail?"

"He stole the mayor's car."

Louder laughter, more and more, into the night.

—

Skip's funeral was a turning point for our neighborhood. Skip and a guy named Michael Grimes had been pushing this thing about East Nashville, pretending we were all living in some chaotic, artistic scene that was simultaneously hilarious and deep. They pretended it was Paris in the '20s, but with more Lortabs. Skip always liked to sing a children's song he made up that went, "Sunshine, lollypops and Lortabs, tra la la la la la la la."

Anyway, Skip and Grimey kind of pretended East Nashville into existence. At Skip's funeral, we all looked around and realized we were in the middle of some chaotic, artistic scene that was simultaneously hilarious and deep. It was really happening, and we were all in it together. Over the next ten years, travel magazines and music magazines would have stuff in them about East Nashville, like it was something more than a place with low rent and lots of places to buy discount cigarettes. That's because it's become something more, and Skip was able to see that before it even really existed.

Almost immediately after Skip died, I started working on an album I called *East Nashville Skyline*. In reality, our skyline just looks like the sky, because we don't have any tall buildings like they do on the other side of the river in Nashville proper. But I don't live in reality, remember? I live in the middle of some chaotic, artistic scene that's simultaneously hilarious and deep. And I wanted to make this album without leaving that scene. Eric McConnell, a guy I met through Skip, had a house in East Nashville where he'd recorded a famous album by Loretta Lynn, one called *Van Lear Rose*, that won Grammy Awards.

I walked over to Eric's house with a new song I'd made up about all the things I've been writing about in this chapter. Eric started playing drums, and I started playing electric guitar, and then we called a bunch of other people who knew Skip. That wasn't hard; everyone knew Skip.

"Play a Train Song" was more given to me than written by me. I was depressed because my friend had died and depressed for a bunch of other perfectly good reasons, and my depression started to rhyme.

PLAY A TRAIN SONG
By Todd Snider

Smokin', long black Cadillac, the engine's winding down
He parked it up on the sidewalk like he owned the whole
damn town
I'd hear him talking to some chick through a thick ghost
of smoke,
Through a thicker haze of Southern Comfort and coke.

He'd say, "Girl you're hotter than the hinges hanging off the
gates of hell
Don't be afraid to turn to me babe if he don't treat you well."
And by he, he meant me, so I laughed and I shook his hand
He laughed a little bit louder as he'd yell up at the band

Play a train song, pour me one more round
Make 'em leave my boots on when they lay me into the
ground
I am a runaway locomotive, out of my one-track mind
And I'm looking for any kind of trouble that I can find

I got this old black leather jacket, got this pack of Marlboro
reds.
Got this stash here in my pocket, got these thoughts in my
own head.
The right to run until I've got to walk, or until I have to crawl
This moment that I'm in right now and nothing else at all

Play a train song, pour me one more round
Make 'em leave my boots on when they lay me into the ground
I am a runaway locomotive, out of my one-track mind

In the television blizzard lights, we looked around his place
We found him cold there on the sofa, a little smile across
*   his face*
And though I tried with all of my sadness, somehow I just
*   could not weep*
For a man who looked to me like he died laughin' in his sleep

Singing a train song, drinking one last round
We made them leave his boots on on the day they laid him
*   down*
He was a runaway locomotive, out of his one-track mind.
Play a train song, play a train song
Play a train song

CHAPTER 10

IS THIS REALLY GARTH BROOKS?

In 1999, I'd just moved into my house in East Nashville, and the only person who knew the phone number was the singer Mark Marchetti. Mark liked to call and pretend to be other people, and I always played along. It was fun for him, and for me; it was a great way to pretend to talk to Keith Richards, Hank Williams Jr., or Margaret Thatcher.

On this day, it was Garth Brooks, the biggest selling solo artist in the history of music.

"Yeah, shit man, what's up, Garth?" I said.

Then he said a couple of other things, and I said, "Seriously, what's up, man? Stop fucking around." I didn't want to play anymore. I wanted to know why Mark was calling me.

But Mark didn't catch my drift. Because, as it turns out, Mark wasn't on the line. "Mark?" I said.

"No," not-Mark said. "Garth."

Garth Brooks was talking to me and had been doing so for a couple of minutes. I gracefully shifted the conversation in light of this new information. "Goddamn," I said. "I thought you were fucking around, and I wasn't listening to any of the shit you said. Can you start over?"

Without complaint or any hint of irritation, he started over. He told me he was making a movie, and he wanted to put my song, "Alright Guy," in the sound track. He told me the story of this character he was playing in the movie, a pop singer called Chris Gaines, and how he'd created an entire history for this character, and he wanted "Alright Guy" to be a song that Chris Gaines sang in the 1970s. Since the song had a few lines that were specific to the 1990s, he wanted to work with me to change some of the words, but he made it very clear that he was not going to take any credit or money for making those changes. In Nashville, when a singer tells you he wants to change some words, he usually means he wants to cowrite a song that you've already written and take half the dough. This wasn't the case here, though, and everything Garth told me about the movie and the sound track—which was going to come out before the movie was even made— sounded brave and cool. Most of the time, singers play movie characters that are just like themselves—Prince in *Purple Rain* or George Strait in *Pure Country*—but Garth was going out on a limb, creating a new persona and finding songs that didn't sound anything like the hits he'd recorded. The closest thing I could think of to what he was talking about was Kris Kristofferson in *A Star Is Born*, and I love that movie.

Also, I loved Garth Brooks. I was, and am, a very big fan. I think Garth Brooks fucked up country music for a while, through no fault of his own: he made music so good and so successful that tons of people came along after him trying to imitate what he did. Garth fucked up country music like Kurt Cobain fucked up rock.

Garth was a fascinating, comet-like figure. He hasn't made a record in a decade now, but he's interesting enough that people to this day ask me about my brief time knowing him a little. It's a great story to tell. He has a powerful, Michael Jackson–like presence. I should tell the story sometime about how he called me up and I thought he was my friend Mark.

Because of Garth's massive success, there's a bit of a push and pull in Nashville about him. When you sell more records than anyone has ever sold, you tend to make more people jealous than have ever been jealous of a singer. You don't have to be in town for long before you'll hear somebody say something jealous about Garth Brooks, and then you'll find that there's somebody within earshot of the jealous person saying something nice about him. The stories of Garth helping people are unbelievable, though he won't tell them himself. I know for a fact that he's bought homes for people and paid off hospital bills for family members of people he cares about. He's one of those rare people whose capacity to help is equaled by his willingness to help. He's concerned about other people, and he demonstrates that concern in ways that make those people's lives easier.

I didn't know Garth when he called, but I knew all his songs, and I knew his reputation. And I was thrilled that he was considering recording one of my songs. Over the next few weeks, we batted lyric ideas around three or four times, and we settled on some stuff that worked. We'd send the song back and forth on fax machines. I had a fax machine, but still didn't have a computer. Then one Saturday, he called and said, "What are you doing?" I wasn't doing anything, and he said, "We're recording 'Alright Guy' tonight. Can you come by the studio?"

Could and did. The studio was in a mansion out in Franklin. When I got there, everyone was eating Chinese food. Tommy Sims—a great bass player who wrote a song called "Change the World" for Eric Clapton—was there. And I was mesmerized by the producer, whom I immediately recognized as Don Was, because Don Was had produced . . . wait for it . . . The Rolling Stones. I was already starstruck before Garth walked up and introduced himself. He said, "I thought you had red hair," because he'd seen me on the *Austin City Limits* television show, and I'd dyed my hair red for that show. It wasn't supposed to be red. It was supposed to be dark brown. My plan was to look like John Fogerty, but instead I ended up looking like the guy from the movie *Dumb and Dumber*. "You look like that guy from *Dumb and Dumber*," people would tell me, and I would insist on Fogerty. So now that the red had worn off, Garth Brooks and Don Was thought I'd died my hair blonde.

Garth took me aside and said, "C'mon, I'll show you what we're doing." He and I went into the control room while everybody else ate their Chinese food.

He said, "I don't know if you like commercial music at all. You ever listen to any commercial stuff?"

Like it? Listen, I know I'm not the most commercial artist in the world, but I didn't think I was so uncommercial that Garth Brooks would suspect that perhaps I had never listened to the radio. I mean, my God, sometimes it's not so much the heat as it is the humility.

Garth showed me some of the songs they were working on, and I thought they sounded cool. I really liked one called "It Don't Matter to the Sun," and I noticed that this stuff was a long way away from the country songs he sang on the radio. Then everybody got done with their Chinese food, and we recorded "Alright Guy," with Garth singing and me playing guitar and harmonica. We recorded several takes, and at the end of one of the takes, Garth was ad-libbing at the end, and he said, "I think I'm alright, fuck you."

When we got done, Garth let me take a mix of the song home. I said, "Can I have the one where you say 'Fuck you'?" He said, "Yes, but if I ever hear that version somewhere else, it will hurt my feelings and that will be the end of our friendship." He was serious enough about the way he presented himself to the public that it would really bother him to have that "fuck you" out in the world, and I promised him I'd keep that version to myself. He was a nice, kind person, and I didn't want to do anything to hurt his feelings or his image. He listened closely to everyone in the room and had a way of directing his attention to you that was free of distraction. I remember thinking that he reminded me of what I imagined Bill Clinton was like.

Garth was a lot less music business–oriented toward me and a lot gentler and more poetic toward me than some of my supposedly art-first songwriter friends. My television and my magazines had told me that "alternative country" people were altruistic and art oriented, and that commercially successful country music people were money-grubbers. But as it turned out, I didn't come away from that studio disappointed with Garth; I came away from it disappointed with my television.

Word started to get out that Garth Brooks had cut my song, and my friend base doubled pretty quickly, while I started thinking of what I should buy with the money that would come from Garth recording the song. Should I buy something stupid? Isn't that what you do? Maybe an animal or something? Tom T. Hall has peacocks. Should I get one? Or maybe a monkey? I've never trusted monkeys, but maybe I could learn.

Time went by, and Garth's people got all my publishing information, and I kept debating the merits of monkeys versus peacocks. And then Garth's mother got sick, and Garth made a decision that he was not going to do anything to even remotely challenge his mother, whom he loved very much. One thing that his mother was uncomfortable with was a line in "Alright Guy" about smoking dope. So Garth called me, told me "Alright Guy" wasn't going to be on the record, and told me why. And he apologized. He did not have to do any of that. He had nothing to be sorry about. He had every right to put any song on his record and to leave any song off. Singers don't have to even communicate with writers. I wrote a Top 20 hit for a singer named Mark Chesnutt, and I've never even met him. Nobody called to tell me he'd recorded it. I heard it on the radio. Garth had given me a once-in-a-lifetime experience of being in the studio with him, Don Was, and all the others. I was grateful, and I told him that.

A week later, there was a check in my mailbox for $10,000, with a note from Garth that said, "Sorry, man."

If you're reading this and thinking, "Well, that was the decent thing to do," I'm telling you that you're wrong. I've been in this thing for twenty years, and this was ten thousand times more than the decent thing to do. This was unheard of. He owed me nothing but paid me $10,000, and apologized for that. The ten grand was on top of the thousands he'd already spent recording the song in a world-class studio with world-class musicians.

So if we're pondering the decent thing to do, the decent thing would have been for me to rip up that check, send his mother a "get well" card, and spend the next few days walking around the neighborhood telling everyone what a swell guy Garth Brooks is.

Instead, I cashed the check and wondered what to name my monkey.

In late 1999, Garth's Chris Gaines album came out and failed. By "failed," I mean sold more than two million copies, charted as the second best-selling album in America, and spawned a Top 10 single.

Garth took a bad beating for this. He became a punch line for doing something way more successful than anyone I've ever met has ever done. People made fun of him, and the lost momentum meant that he never even got to make the Chris Gaines movie.

The last time I'd been around a failure as popular as Chris Gaines, it was my friend Darius Rucker, who fronted a band called Hootie & The Blowfish. I opened a show for Hootie in front of four hundred people at a little club in Atlanta in early 1994, and by that summer I was opening for them in front of ten thousand people in Colorado. It got bigger from there. Their first album sold more than ten million copies. Everybody had it. And then in 1995, the year Hootie outsold everybody, even Garth Brooks, Darius came to my show in South Carolina.

Afterward, he came up on the bus with me, Jack Ingram, and Will Kimbrough and told us there was a party going on at his house, and we were all invited. He wanted to show us Hootie's next record, which they'd just finished.

The house wasn't a mansion, but it was a nice-sized place in a nice neighborhood. We walked in, and the first thing I noticed was that the party seemed a little out of control. Two girls went dashing by as we were walking through the foyer. I was struck by the chaotic nature of the whole thing, and I noticed there was a security guy in the kitchen who didn't seem to be taking an active interest in calming things down.

I asked Darius if the party was for any particular reason, thinking it might have been his birthday or something. He said that it was actually a party they'd had the previous weekend and that they were having trouble winding it down.

We went down to Darius's room to listen to the new record, and he had a big walk-in closet there. He and Hootie had made a famous music video where he was wearing a Dan Marino football jersey, and I said, "Is that closet where you keep the Marino shirts?" He laughed and said, "Actually, yes." And as he went to show them to me, we could see four feet behind his clothing.

Darius ordered the feet to come out, and they were attached to two college boys who were in his closet. Darius said, "Go upstairs," and they did.

We went further into his room, and there were candles everywhere. And there were two girls in his bed, and he didn't know either one of them. They were asleep. He told them to wake up, but they didn't. We just left them there, sleeping.

And then we sat on the floor, by the edge of the bed these girls were sleeping in, and we rolled a joint and put on the follow-up to the biggest-selling album of 1995, *Cracked Rear View*. We listened to the whole record, and liked it, and then when we got up to leave Darius called for the security guy to get the girls out of his bed so he could go to sleep himself. He wasn't wrapping up the weeklong party, just putting someone in front of his door so he could be by himself for awhile. For all I know, he got up in the morning, grabbed his golf clubs, and marched through that same party.

How do you end a party like that? How did he get those people out? They were like rats, scurrying everywhere. But he didn't seem bothered by it.

The album he played for us that night, *Fairweather Johnson*, was a colossal failure because it only sold four million copies. Darius and his band had to spend the second tour of their lives dodging people who were telling them something was going wrong. That's when the party started to dwindle, and all those kids were gone by the third album, which only sold a million.

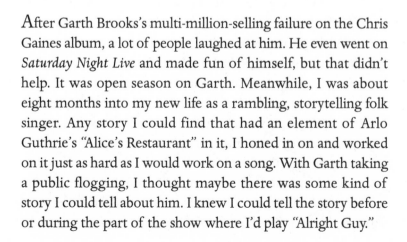

After Garth Brooks's multi-million-selling failure on the Chris Gaines album, a lot of people laughed at him. He even went on *Saturday Night Live* and made fun of himself, but that didn't help. It was open season on Garth. Meanwhile, I was about eight months into my new life as a rambling, storytelling folk singer. Any story I could find that had an element of Arlo Guthrie's "Alice's Restaurant" in it, I honed in on and worked on it just as hard as I would work on a song. With Garth taking a public flogging, I thought maybe there was some kind of story I could tell about him. I knew I could tell the story before or during the part of the show where I'd play "Alright Guy."

And so I made up a story that started with the phone call from Garth. And most of the story is pretty true. But at some point, I realized it would be beneficial for me, in my attempt to get laughs at my show, to pretend I knew in real time what a disastrous idea this Chris Gaines thing was. In the story, I played along and told Garth that it was a great, smart idea, knowing that he was going to fall on his ass.

That was not in fact anywhere near true.

The truth was that I thought it was going to be successful, and thought it was cool, and had hopes that it was going to do well.

In fact, I still don't think it was stupid. I think it was smart of Garth Brooks to make a creative choice that resulted in selling millions of albums. Sign me up for that kind of stupid.

No matter the truth, though, I decided to exploit the idea that not everybody likes Garth Brooks to my own end. And I told myself that Garth wouldn't be hurt by something like that, because he was so successful.

That's a crock.

It's a crock that I think prevails in this country: we bully the people who entertain us. We get on the computer and bully them. We buy magazines with pictures of them where they look fat or drunk or imperfect. And we suppose that those people's success excuses our meanness.

I say this as somebody that this is, for sure, not happening to; I'm not popular enough to get bullied in this way. I'm just unpopular enough to mostly get encouragement.

In my young life, Garth and Jimmy Buffett were the people I got to be around who were so powerful that other people didn't treat them like people. They got treated like a television show, or like a football team or a wrestler. And I got caught up in that and wound up telling a story that took the piss out of a guy who had shown me kindness and graciousness, and who gave me—with no strings, no contracts, with an apology, even—ten thousand dollars.

That's embarrassing. It's a shame wisdom comes so slow. It's what makes life hard to look back on. It's the downside to giving everything in your life to this idea of suspended adolescence: you find yourself doing immature things at awkward ages. In my case, it involved being a douche to someone who was cool to me, just to look cool in front of other people. I did this when I was in my thirties, and in truth I probably already had the wisdom to know better. I just chose to ignore it.

A couple of years ago, I saw Garth at a Country Music Hall of Fame thing, and he called out to me by name, immediately. Then his wife, Trisha Yearwood, started telling me how much Garth liked me. I assumed he hadn't heard my little stage story, or that if he had he wasn't bothered by it. It doesn't matter whether he heard it or whether he was offended by it. A bully is a bully. Putting negative energy into the universe is just what it is, and it isn't art and it isn't funny. It's a crock of shit, and it's mean.

By the way, every time I've told someone the story of Garth remembering my name and giving me money, it's been topped. Somebody's got a better one. There aren't a lot of stories out there about me remembering names and giving away money, but I'm going to try to get better at that.

CHAPTER 11

IT GETS HARDER TO
LISTEN ALL THE TIME

I walked onstage at the Whisky a Go Go on the Sunset Strip in Los Angeles.

The Whisky is where Jim Morrison got his break. Jim Morrison was lead singer for The Doors, and he managed to get arrested for whipping his dick out onstage. Now that's rock 'n' roll. These punk kids today, with their water bottles and their parents in the wings, they can suck Jim Morrison's dick.

But enough about Jim Morrison's dick.

At the time, which was 1998, I thought that if you wanted to go where they have art for art's sake, you should go to New York. And if you wanted to go where they have art for glory's sake, you went to LA. I walked out there at the Whisky and looked out at a bunch of people that I decided immediately, for a variety of wobbly reasons, were in the glory business. They didn't feel like my kind of people. And that takes a lot, 'cause when you're stoned almost everybody is your kind of people.

And, to be sure, I was stoned. And drunk. I was also getting sick of the "you're gonna be a rock star" talk that was lingering around. The people who were my heroes were not—no offense to Jim Morrison—rock stars. They were people like John Prine and Nanci Griffith: People who weren't on the radio, but who let their hearts bleed into every note they sang, and even into the spaces where they didn't sing.

Prine wrote lines like, "Just give me one extra season, so I can figure out the other four," and "Broken hearts and dirty windows make life difficult to see / That's why last night and this morning always look the same to me."

John Prine has been interviewed by the poet laureate of the United States, because the poet laureate guy wanted to learn some stuff. I'm not an expert on much, but I can tell you every word Prine ever rhymed, and I know most of the "why and how" stories, too. John Prine is a Mount Rushmore type for me.

By "Mount Rushmore type," I don't mean John Prine would desecrate a sacred Native American burial ground by carving four white presidents' faces into it. I mean, if I was desecrating a sacred burial ground by carving people's faces into it, I'd carve Prine's.

He's definitely not someone you can copy, because he didn't copy anyone himself. Trying to copy Prine is like knowing someone who got hit by lightning and saying, "I'm going to stand out in the yard and get hit, too." You just stand there for the rest of your life. You can't learn to copy John Prine, but

John can teach you not to copy, and that's the kind of thing I wanted to learn.

John Prine was not there at the Whisky that night with me. If he had been, he might have told me to calm down.

I'd just made a record that was supposed to be all about Memphis, but sounded a lot more like somebody who might sound enough like Tom Petty to land a song on the radio. The record was a direct reaction to being in a group that went on at 11 at night, and that played to people who wanted to stay up until 2 in the morning.

None of the people in the crowd at the Whisky were against the record I'd made, or at fault for it. Anything that was a mistake was my mistake. I was the one telling everybody what to do. But that night I played two songs and then looked out at a group of people who I thought were looking down on me while they were looking up at me. I don't know what it was that made me feel that way, but I felt that way.

There were about two hundred people there that night. And over the last fifteen years, I've met all seven hundred of them.

I looked at them and told them that I had a better car than theirs.

Way better.

I didn't even have a car at the time.

I said, "You should see it. It's amazing."

I pointed at some women and said, "I bet you girls were prettier when your lips were the normal ones." I've heard sarcasm is the lowest form of humor. But whoever said that never heard lip augmentation humor. For the record, I have no problem with lip augmentation. That was the booze and drugs talking. Then I said, "We're gonna play this one more song, and then fuck y'all."

The "y'all" there included a healthy chunk of people employed by the major record company that employed me, at least until that night. Some of them had nice cars, and others of them had beautiful, full lips.

The band and I played the song, and when the song got over there was pin-drop silence. I jumped off in front of the stage, and people looked shocked or afraid or both, and they just parted. I walked past them, out the front door. And when I pushed that front door to go out of there, you could hear the click echo through the whole place.

I walked out and then down the Sunset Strip, past the Viper Room to a little Chinese joint that looked like it might have beer.

The Viper Room was a place where an actor and singer named River Phoenix was supposed to have performed on October 30, 1993. Instead, Phoenix convulsed on the sidewalk and died in the early Halloween hours. They said it was cocaine and heroin. I believe they said right.

At the Chinese place, a man—I guess he was the owner—came out and saw a sweaty, wet-haired, shell-shocked guy waiting on his beer. That guy was me. In broken-ish English, the man shouted, "No, no River Phoenix!" and pointed at me.

That meant it was probably time for me to leave.

So I found a bar down the street, had another beer or two, got a cab to my hotel, went to my room, and trashed that.

Trashed it, like a dick. I wound up having to pay for the room.

The next day, I had to see the guys in the band, and it became clear to me that I'd lost sight of the fact that there were more people than me who had given our lives to this thing that I'd just given away. I hadn't been thinking of it as a long-term job. I never thought of anything in my life like that. My dad died at fifty-four. No such thing as long term for me, was my train of thought.

After Jerry Jeff Walker heard about my LA show, he called me and said, "You know what you ought to do? You ought to set up some Christmas lights on your roof, to spell out 'SORRY.' And then when you get home from a long night of drinking, you just flip on the lights and go to bed." He said he'd seriously considered the idea back in the '70s, when it would have been most useful to him.

Prine told me later that he'd seen a video of that show.

"I thought you gave a great speech," he said. "But it went on about three minutes too long. Had you cut it by three minutes, it would have been epic. They'd still be talking about it, and not in the way they're talking about it now."

The rest of us watch a car accident and see a car accident. John Prine watches a car accident and thinks, "Well, there's too many verses."

The day after my triumphant show at the Whisky, I was dropped from the record company. Which means we were all dropped from the record company. Maybe the people at the company said they wanted me to go back to rehab, and maybe I said I wasn't going to do that.

At the time, part of me thought all this was funny. I didn't like the people who thought I was going to be a rock star, mostly because they didn't understand that I didn't want to be a rock star at all. I wanted to be with John Prine—to open shows for him, to learn from him, and to be around him—and I was doing anything to make that possible. I'd studied under Jimmy Buffett, and that was cool, but I'd ended up learning things I didn't want to know, like about security and merchandising. John didn't care about those kinds of things.

Half the reason I'd been so mad is because my record didn't sound anything like anything Prine had done, or anything like anything he'd ever do.

The night I walked offstage at the Whisky, I had seventeen songs that hadn't been recorded, or even heard by anyone. After I was fired from the record company, I made a cassette tape of all of those songs and gave it to Al Bunetta, who was John Prine's manager and best friend, and who was one of the very few people willing to help me at that point in my life.

Somehow, some other people had gotten the idea that I was "difficult" or "hard to work with," or, and this is just crazy, "not a team player."

Al told me he'd play those songs for John, on the very day I gave them to Al.

The next day, I went to Al's office, on Music Row in Nashville. And Al said, "John thinks that one of these songs, 'Missing You,' is really, really good. And he says there's another one, 'D.B. Cooper,' that's not done and that needs an ending."

Okay, so that's two of the seventeen.

"And then the rest," Al said, leaning toward me. "The rest is shit."

Al Bunetta wasn't saying that he interpreted my songs as being shit. That would have been too easy on me. Al was saying he'd shown the songs to John Prine, and John Prine said they were shit.

He said that John said they were, and I quote, "invulnerable crap."

I asked for an example. That was probably my mistake, because he gave me an example. I had a song called "It Gets Harder to Listen All the Time," about a girl who went to Alcoholics Anonymous and didn't like it and ended up not going anymore. At a certain point, that girl in the song said, "I never did like the 12-Step Crowd."

Al said, "See, in that song you're saying it's about a girl and it's actually about you. And then you're saying you don't like someone, but actually it's someone you're afraid of."

Well, yes. And yes.

This information hurt like crazy. I wanted John to think I was good, like him. I wanted to be better than I was.

That night, me and my wife and Al went out to dinner, and Al told my wife how he and John had rejected fifteen of my seventeen songs. He said, "Hey, Melita, today we told Todd that fifteen of his songs sucked! You should have seen the look on his face! It was hilarious!"

Brutal.

And she didn't have to have seen the look on my face, because it was the look that was still on my face.

Again, brutal. But if he'd treated me like a wounded bird, or like I had cancer, and not made fun of me, I probably would have gone all the way down. By making fun of me, he made it like it wasn't that big of a deal. His approach was more like, "You've got to make it better, like John does."

I didn't try to make anything up for a month, at least. But after I spent some time drinking enough to make the 12-Step Crowd just as afraid of me as I was of them, I realized that I was learning something.

If you want the job where you open your heart for people and then they cheer you for it, that's really what you have to do. When they say that the greatest singers are brokenhearted, there's a reason: You are going to be breaking your heart. You can't just make up a song about some car you saw when you were driving down a road; it'll be like carrying a piano up a mountain when you have to sing it live, and no one will give a shit.

I'd be lying if I said that I wasn't enticed by the idea of playing music in order to get wasted, have a cool scarf, and have chicks tell me I was deep, even if I wasn't. But the thing I was wanting to be, which was what you might call a lifer, wasn't going to be about coming up with a cute melody once. It was going to be about daring to be humiliated, over and over again. And when your heart finally starts to heal up, that's when you're in trouble. Contentment, not rejection, is the enemy.

I think rejection is supposed to be fuel for art, and I'm not trying to brag, but I've been rejected a ton.

I'm not saying I don't get hurt, because I do, and I think everyone does. But from the beginning, I just kept moving forward.

The rejections came from worthy sources. First, it was Kent Finlay, a Texas songwriting guru. Then it was Keith Sykes in Memphis. Now, John Prine was tearing me up.

Not long after this happened, I saw John and he said, "Did you talk to Al?"

Yes, I remembered the conversation quite vividly.

I fixed that song about the girl. I made it about me, changing the names to incriminate the guilty. "She came in off a dead-end street" became "I came in off a dead-end street." And in the chorus, where the girl had said, "It gets harder to listen to people all the time," it was me saying, "It's been a long, long year." I went from pretending to admitting, from not liking people to being afraid of them.

When John heard the song after it lost the girl and became "Long Year," he just said, "There ya go."

So then I made up "Lonely Girl," which was about meeting my wife in rehab. Two months before, I would have written metaphorical bullshit about a girl I didn't know, thinking of some cool-sounding name to sing over some great chords, not realizing that Mick Jagger was breaking his heart open all the time.

When I had enough songs that John didn't hate, I made a record called *Happy to Be Here*, for John and Al's label. On the first day, I got to the studio, and the producer had the band already there, and they sounded just like The Nervous Wrecks, the band I'd made the last record with.

I told the producer, a genius-level artist named Ray Kennedy, that what we were doing sounded just like the last album to me. And I walked out of the studio and went home, which is a good way to waste John Prine and Al Bunetta's money, but for some reason it seemed less inappropriate at the time than it seems to me now.

When I got back to the studio the next day (hey, no hard feelings, right?), I told Ray that I wanted to track the songs by myself and then add other instruments later. I wasn't afraid of having a song on the radio, but I wanted it to be my song and not my version of a Tom Petty song.

The last album sounded an awful lot like it wanted to sound an awful lot like Tom Petty. And I love Tom Petty: top to bottom, every song. But I was trying to be a lifer, not an impressionist.

When I got my first record contract, I'd been playing music onstage by myself, most every night, and I had it pretty well dialed in. I remember telling my first producer, Tony Brown, that I wanted to start with a band and then go solo later, instead of going solo and adding a band. Starting solo and adding a band is what makes people mad at folk singers, for some reason. They got pissed at Bob Dylan for that, from what I understand.

So Tony Brown let me get a band, and I quickly realized I didn't know anything about being in tempo or being in tune. That stuff matters more when others are involved. It took me a long time to learn how to do that, and right about the time we got dropped—okay, the time that I got us dropped with my Whisky a Go Go stunt—we'd all gotten really good together.

Then that went away, and I had to get back on my feet playing solo, and it took about a year to find my footing again and not just be banging on that guitar in perfect time and singing really loud. That doesn't work when you're playing shows with John Prine, which is what he let me do in 2003 and 2004, and in some fine times since then.

When I wasn't opening for Prine, I was doing my own shows, solo, and it was proving more difficult than I'd thought it would be. But a buddy and tour manager named Sam Knight and Al "John Says You Suck" Bunetta—it's not his real nickname, but it is to me—helped me to figure out a few things that are real simple but that help an awful lot.

I'd always thought that a night of live music was about the songs and the singer, nothing more, but there's more to it than that. Some of what happens is in between the songs, and some is before the songs even begin. Sam, who is the nephew of the great Bob Mercer, helped a lot with the between-songs part. We were in Iowa City, and I was getting ready to play a solo show. It occurred to Sam and me that we were getting ready to go around the country for the second time with the solo thing, and that I couldn't just tell the same stories I'd told the first time around. We decided we needed a new story.

There was a little lake in the middle of town, and it took probably twenty-five minutes to walk around that lake. We decided to walk around, and since it gets awkward just walking around in silence, we started to talk about the times Sam had been with me to Moondawg's Tavern in Frazier, Tennessee. Sam said he thought I should tell the story of Moondawg's Tavern when I played a song I'd written called "Moondawg's Tavern."

I said, "Okay, let's try that."

We walked around that lake, and I'd tell him the story, and he'd tell it back to me, and I'd tell it back again, and it kept getting longer and more fun. We kept adding more things, and then connecting it to other songs, and then telling the stories of how those things and those songs connected. Sam started calling what we came up with "The Trilogy," and if you want to read "The Trilogy," I've included it for your enjoyment elsewhere in these very pages.

It took us about four hours of storytelling and lake walking before we could remember it all and had everything we wanted to say in it, and after that, Sam helped me with a lot of my stories. Later, Elvis Hicks returned as my tour manager, and he seemed to understand early on that the telling and keeping of stories was as important as or more important than the checking-in-to-hotels part of tour managing. Elvis is a big help to me now, and I will later illustrate why with a story about him.

Al Bunetta didn't help me tell stories, but he did help me set up the room so that people were ready to hear them. When I worked with Al, he told the people who ran the places where I was booked, "No television sets on, no beer lights, no lights headed in any direction other than at the stage." He said the room was supposed to be as dark as a movie theater, with all the chairs facing the stage.

Turns out, Al was right. And those small things seemed to change things and to make it a better show for everybody. People listen differently when they are seated and when they can see the performer but can't see each other.

—

I don't think that when I got done with my fourth album, *Happy to Be Here*, that John thought it was great. But I think he thought it was a step in the right direction. And he said, "You know, once you make five you'll never get out."

And this was good news, because it's what I wanted. I wanted to be a lifer. John's famous for saying, "Everyone talks about how hard it is to get into the music business, but no one talks about how hard it is to get out of it."

So off I went on tour with John Prine. I toured with him a ton, until I was big enough in those towns we played that I had to go up there myself and get all the money. John is the most gracious person you could ever play with. He hands his audience to you. If you're a John Prine fan, you know that whoever is opening for him is up there because John thinks you'll like that person's music. And he usually calls you up during his encore, to sing his songs with him. He shows the people who came to see him that you've got his approval, which is a lot better than having him tell them that your songs are shit.

Twice a week, to this day, people ask me what John Prine's like. I can tell you exactly what he's like. In 2004, him and I and his band and his tour manager went to Europe. We got on a plane and flew eight hours, through the night. We had a layover somewhere, and then finally got to wherever it was we were supposed to be landing. I think it was London. Anyway, long trip. We got our bags and met the kid the promoter had sent. He was supposed to drive us in a van to the town we were playing, which was going to be another two and a half hours from London.

When we got in the van, me and the tour manager and the band got in the back, and John got up front. The kid took off, and John started reading a newspaper. But in a few minutes, John said, "If I remember right from the last time, we were supposed to go that way," and he pointed in the opposite direction from the way we were actually going.

The kid said, "No, we're going the right way." And John said, "Okay."

We drove about two hours, and the kid said, "Oh, shit, you were right. We were supposed to have gone that other way."

In the back seats, between the band and the tour manager and me, you could feel anger start taking over. It was intense.

You could smell the venom.

Except from John Prine, who never even looked up from his paper.

When we were all ready to tell the kid, "Fuck, don't you know how long we've traveled?" John just said, "No big deal. It's fun to drive around in Europe. Don't sweat it."

He wasn't a guy in a negative situation working hard at being positive. He was being real, and this was easy for him to do. This wasn't something he did because of some self-help book he'd read. This was his natural state.

You don't knock John Prine off his square. It just doesn't happen. His compassion isn't something he has to access. I've never met another human being like that, but I think they say that about the Dalai Lama.

On that same trip, we were driving around in Ireland. We drove to a house on a cliff. It was beautiful. And it slowly dawned on me that it was John's. I knew he got away in the winter months to Ireland, but I hadn't processed that he was getting away to this paradise.

I said, "Holy shit, is this your house?"

He smiled and said, "Got it for a song."

I once had a tour manager named Spike, and it took awhile to figure out that she wasn't a guy. She looked like a nineteen-year-old boy, but she was a twenty-one-year-old woman.

One day, on a Prine tour when Spike wasn't with us, someone started talking about her, and someone else said, "I think she might be gay."

I said, "I was asking her about that the other day."

John said, "You asked her? What did she say?"

I said, "I dunno, I never listen to that bitch."

John spit up his soda, laughing.

And that made me so happy. I think about that when I'm down sometimes.

CHAPTER 12

EAST NASHVILLE CAR WASH

After playing a weekend's worth of shows that were way better attended than we expected, my wife agreed to let me buy an old car.

Not one of those "antique" cars, with the cool license plates and all that. She said I could buy an old car. I looked in the paper and found a 1964 convertible Rocket 88. They weren't asking much, but the car was in great shape.

It isn't anymore, but it was back then, a couple of years ago. I can't really have nice things. These days, the top won't go up, so I should clarify that it's no longer actually a convertible since it won't convert. But one of my favorite things in the world to do is wash that car. When I come home from a road trip, the first thing I do is roll a joint and head for the East Nashville car wash.

One beautiful day, I was down at the car wash. I was power-hosing the car, which I find very relaxing. The radio was on the Mexican station, which makes me cross-cultural.

And right then, in that lovely and solitary moment, this guy comes walking toward me, across the car wash, sweat soaking through his clothes and beading off his face. He was clearly high on crack and without sleep, and either homeless or at least prone to sleeping outdoors on occasion.

In a mildly intimidating manner, he said, "Hey man, how 'bout you give me a couple of bucks and I help you wash your car?"

There was a small sense of threat in his tone. But I really enjoy washing the car for myself, so I screwed up a little nerve and said, "Listen, man, I really find this relaxing to do alone, you know. So, how 'bout if I give you a few bucks and you don't help me wash my car?"

And, no shit, he says, "No, man, I think I'm gonna help you wash your car."

Is that legal? That's like demanding to mow someone's lawn. Can't be legal. But I didn't know what to do, and I was scared, so I screwed down the nerve I'd screwed up and said, "Okay."

He picked up the broom brush and said, "You squirt the soap water, and I'll scrub."

Yes sir.

We pretty much did the whole car that way.

And as we did, we got to talking about ourselves and our lives, and the different places we'd been and the different people we'd been and the troubles we'd been in and the girls we knew and the times we had money.

We even talked some about the Tennessee Titans football team. They aren't very good, usually, but you can see the stadium from the East Nashville car wash.

Then he said, "Okay, now I'll rinse."

Sure, you're the boss.

As he did, we kept talking. And I've got to tell you that by the time we finished, not only did I like him, but the car was quite clearly cleaner and better off for having been washed by two guys rather than just one.

I had some dollar bills on the car seat, so I picked those up and as I handed them to him I very honestly said, "Hey man, thank-you. I really enjoyed that."

He said he did, too, and that he liked my car. He said he'd never washed a convertible while the top was down before. I didn't have the heart to tell him it's not technically a convertible, but I thanked him for doing a really good job keeping the water out of the car.

He said he'd keep an eye out for me, and then as he was about to walk off, I said, "Hey man, one more thing, honestly. . . . When you first came over here, were you thinking about robbing me?"

To which he laughed out the word, "Yeeeeeaaaaaahhhhaaa ahhhhaahhhhaaa."

I laughed too, but also kind of panicked. And in what I guess I'd call a fit of fight or flight, I decided to reach out my hand toward his like I wasn't rattled at all, and say, "What's your name, man?"

Without even blinking, this fucking guy says, "I'm Tony Bennett."

And, without blinking more than three or four times, I said, "Oh, okay. I see. Well, I'm Bing Crosby. Nice to meet you."

Well, this really pissed him off. And with his eyes widening and voice rising, he said, "Are you fucking with me, man?"

So I said, "Are you kidding me? You started it."

"Started what?"

"Bullshitting. You said your name is Tony Bennett."

And with that, he reached into his pocket and pulled out a single plastic piece of some sort of identification that definitely was not a driver's license or a passport or anything that I recognized at all, but it had his picture and the name Tony Bennett on it.

Well, fuck.

I didn't know whether to shit or wind my watch. So I did neither.

And I said, "No shit, Tony Bennett. I'm sorry. You're right. I was fucking with you. I'm not Bing Crosby."

He laughed at that. And we hugged each other good-bye, and he walked off and that was that.

I thought.

But I'm pretty sure—as in 100 percent positive—that it was in that good-bye hug that Tony Bennett managed to remove three twenties and a fiver from my jacket pocket.

I can't prove it, but I know it.

And he knows it.

And I'll bet he's pretty sure I know it.

When we see each other again some day, we're gonna have it to discuss.

So that, friends and neighbors, is the story of how Tony Bennett stole $65 from me.

I should add that when I say to my friends, "I'm going to tell you about the time Tony Bennett stole $65 from me," when I get to the end, they usually say, "Well, shit, Todd. When you said you were going to tell us about the time Tony Bennett stole $65 from you, we thought you meant the famous one who sang 'I Left My Heart in San Francisco'."

So, I should clarify that I'm not talking about the Tony Bennett that left his heart in San Francisco.

I'm talking about the Tony Bennett who hangs around the East Nashville car wash.

Sorry if there was any confusion.

CHAPTER 13

THE
GROUPIE WAY

When I was first getting into the music business, every single person I met told me what the music business was like, even though few of those people had been in it.

Everybody knew what the music business was like, and everybody told me this: the people who aren't onstage are weasels, and the girls who hang around to meet the guys who go onstage are sluts.

I've found both things to be as far from the truth as you can imagine. Some of the most soulful people I've met in my life were big wheels at record companies. Tony Brown has more soul in his pinkie than I have in the best verse of my best song. He oozes soul and wouldn't be a big wheel if he didn't. Bob

Mercer never wrote a song, but he was probably my favorite songwriter. By a mile, he was my favorite artist, and he would never have called himself an artist. He was more than an artist. He was art.

The groupie truism is equally untrue. "Groupies are sluts" could not be more unrepresentative of the people I have met and been privileged to know. If you're looking for a sad girl who gives her body away because she doesn't feel that her father loves her, you might find her around the football team, but you won't find her with the band. The girl who ends up with the band might like to fuck, but she definitely doesn't care what you think about that. She's not fucking people to fill something inside of herself that is empty. She's fucking people because she has filled that thing inside her, and she's no longer worried what people might think of her. She likes to be around people who are exotic and interesting, and she's not interested in getting with someone who can get her a house and a fence.

Girls who like bands—and by "girls" I mean "women"—tend to make sure the bands have what they need. Sometimes that's soup, and sometimes it's sex. Sometimes it's a shrink. Sometimes it's someone to help decide on an album cover, and sometimes it's someone to say that the song needs another verse. From the outside looking in, those girls might look like an insignificant part of what is happening onstage, but that couldn't be further from the truth.

There are people who get called "groupies," but I have never met one I wouldn't introduce to my mom.

The first time I met one was in Oxford, Mississippi. She presented herself as "the girl" from Oxford, and she explained a little bit about what that entailed. Maybe that seems to people outside of music like it's some kind of debauched, crazy thing. It's not crazy. It's just different. We are travelers, and our friendships develop over minutes. The third time I see somebody on the road, they're like a brother or a sister to me. It all happens a little quicker. We don't get to stay in town a few weeks and court.

And let's not overstate the sex part of it. The whole time my band, The Nervous Wrecks, were together, I never saw one person cheat on a wife or a girlfriend, and there were groupies everywhere. We'd bum their weed. They'd bring us the local magazines. They weren't there to get laid. They were there to help.

A few years after I started making records, someone told me that Pamela Des Barres wanted to meet me. Pamela is the most famous groupie there's ever been. She's written four books, and I'd seen her on *Oprah*. She documented her life around Bob Dylan, Jim Morrison, Jimmy Page, Mick Jagger, and a bunch of other greats, and she did so in a way that was empathetic and sweet, not tawdry. Mick Jagger was a big part of my life, and anytime I get a chance to be around someone who has contributed to his life, I perk up. But I was clear on what it involved. When I heard she wanted to meet me, I didn't think I was going to be getting ready to have sex with somebody, and I was right—we never had sex, which was not offered or proposed. I thought I was getting ready to meet someone who knew Bob Dylan and Jim Morrison and Jimmy Page and Mick Jagger, and to get a chance to talk to her about those things, and I was right.

I met her in Texas and liked her right away. Then she wrote the bio for my third record and a piece on me for *Playgirl* magazine. We became good friends. Her house became the place the Wrecks and I often went when we were in Los Angeles.

We'd watch movies, smoke dope, and listen to Dylan. At the time I met her, I was struggling with my relationship to Christianity. I was starting to read books about the Book I'd been told was the only book. She gave me *The Bible According to Christ* to read, and then a bunch of others, and she helped me to recover from Catholicism. I would not have gotten out from under that burden without Pamela Des Barres—and as I have said, I don't mean that in any illicit way. When she comes to town, she always comes to see me and my wife, and we see her every time we're in Los Angeles.

One time I met Robert Plant from Led Zeppelin, and he said, "Boy, they used to call Pamela a groupie, but she's also an author." She's also a musician who was in a band Frank Zappa produced. I consider her a sexual pioneer, somebody who has been good for the universe and good for women. There's a documentary where Pamela finds all these groupies from all around the country and helps them to see that they're providing something beautiful. A lot of that Jimi Hendrix stuff you and I love so much was made with people like her. Take the groupies out of the control room, and you've got a different record. It's the same with the drugs you think are awful. *Electric Ladyland* was made on drugs and cool chicks.

Pamela played a big role in a lot of bands and in a lot of albums, including some of mine. She's been in the studio for a bunch of them, and she brought along her friends, who are really cool. I get along with all of them. I have also known Sweet Connie from Little Rock. I met her the first time I played Little Rock, opening for Keith Sykes. That chick's got soul. She's the one in the Grand Funk Railroad song, "We're an American Band": "Sweet, sweet Connie, doin' her act / She had the whole show and that's a natural fact." So without her, we wouldn't have "We're an American Band." Or at least we'd be missing a verse. That's a natural fact.

I have stayed friends with Pamela over the years. She's one of the most moral people I know. She's very honest and straightforward about who she is and what she will do. I remember once telling her that I used to think Jim Morrison of The Doors was a great poet, but that eventually I thought his words were crap. "How old are you?" she said. I told her I was thirty-two.

"Jim was twenty-six, and he died," she said. Her point was that everything I've heard from Jim Morrison was written when he was twenty-six or younger, and I think her further point was that I wouldn't want to be judged by what I wrote when I was that age. I proudly showed her a song I wrote when I was less than twenty-six, one called "Bus Tub Stew." Turns out there's no "break on through to the other side" anywhere near "Bus Tub Stew."

Another time, we were talking about a session musician great named Waddy Wachtel. Somebody around us said, "Waddy's playing with Weird Al Yankovic now." Weird Al is a guy who parodies popular songs. He turned Michael Jackson's "Beat It" into "Eat It," famously. I said, "Too bad he's with Weird Al," and she said, "Fuck you, Weird Al Yankovic is a genius and a friend of mine." She was right on both counts. And Waddy Wachtel doesn't join bands he doesn't want to be in, but dumb young guys sit around all the time and say stupid shit about people they don't know.

Pamela believes in rock 'n' roll. And rock 'n' roll for her is a revolution for love and positivity. She's right about that, too. People say rock 'n' roll changes, but it does not. It is antihatred, antiwar, prolove, and profreedom—not democracy, necessarily, but freedom. Pamela Des Barres is the embodiment of rock 'n' roll. And she's less a groupie than a sexual pioneer, even though she proudly calls herself a groupie.

She is an artist, and that's not because of the books she's written. Some people's art doesn't take place on a stage or in a picture hanging on a wall. Some people's art is just being themselves, like Hondo Crouch or Skip Litz. Pamela allowed herself to be whomever she wanted to be, to such a degree that she couldn't help but draw attention. How's that different from Hendrix? It's not. Hendrix had a guitar, but what difference does that make? Figuring out how to work a prop doesn't mean you're radiating more creativity into the world than somebody else.

CHAPTER 14

WAYLON JENNINGS SUCKS

One night, a long while back, I was playing a gig in Detroit, on top of a building that had grass on it. (Like most of the sidewalks do in Detroit, only this was a building and not a sidewalk.)

The gig was a festival that was sponsored by a radio station called WDET, where there was a DJ named Ann Delisi. And the deal with the gig was that you'd play, and then you'd go over to talk to Ann at this DJ booth. As I was talking to Ann, I saw out of the corner of my eye that security was starting to circle some guy who didn't have the right passes and the right stickers on his legs and shit.

I was trying to answer Ann's questions and watch this guy at the same time, and at a certain point he maybe saw me watching him, and I saw him point to me and say something to a security guy. After that, one of the security guys came over to where I was, with Ann, and he said, "This guy here says he's part of your crew and he just doesn't have his pass yet."

I looked over at the guy, and if there was a way someone could make their face say, "C'mon, man, please," that was the face this guy made.

I said to the security guard, "Yeah, he's with us. You'd better get him some stickers and shit."

So they hooked this guy up, and he ate the food from catering and maybe got a massage from the table they had backstage for the bands and crew. After I was done talking to Ann, he came over and thanked me, and I asked him if he had any pot. He answered in the affirmative, and then I said, "Can you roll a joint, man?"

He said, "On the head of a pin, in a hurricane, I can roll a joint."

That's exactly what he said.

He's been with me fifteen years now.

When he came over to me, he had a shirt on that had a picture on it of a guy who looked like Juan Epstein from *Welcome Back, Kotter.* The closer you looked at the shirt, the easier it was to realize that it was the guy wearing the shirt whose picture it was on the shirt. Just way younger. 'Cause this guy no longer looked like Juan Epstein, who had a big Afro.

This guy was bald and pretty small.

I said, "Holy shit, that's you on the T-shirt."

He said, "Yeah, everybody says I look like Elvis."

That night, he helped me and the band get some weed, and then we told him we'd see him around sometime. Turns out that sometime was six days later, when he showed up in

Cincinnati. Then the night after that, he was in Dayton. Then a couple of nights after that, he was driving.

His real name is Dave Hicks, but everyone calls him Elvis. The resemblance is uncanny.

Maybe you've heard the thing that old musicians sometimes say: "The gig is free. They pay me to travel."

In other words, the miles are the hard part. That's wrong. They're not. The miles are almost as good as the gig. What Elvis and I do is to come around some corner in Montana, where one minute you're staring at the side of some beautiful mountain and the next minute it looks like a John Wayne movie expanse. And then we go to Alaska. Are you kidding me? Man, oh man, if you ever get a chance to go to Homer, Alaska, I mean, fuck, take that chance.

When Elvis and I started up together, he would take a Greyhound bus to meet up with me and the band. And then we'd get in the van and go somewhere. Right before I was about to get fired from a big record company, we were on tour in Virginia Beach, and the van broke down. Soon as it did, me and the band and the two other roadies scattered in different directions. We all went to the beach or to the bar. I think I went to the bar. And hours later, when I got back, Elvis was covered in oil. He'd somehow gone and gotten a water pump and changed out the old one for the new one, so that the van worked. Everyone else was trying to numb the wrong. Elvis found a way to make it right.

We all knew the "everybody says I look like Elvis" joke. It was the joke that kept on joking. But he didn't want it to be a joke. Dave is obsessed with Elvis and has been since he was four years old. He knows everything about Elvis. At first, though, we didn't know that he could sing just like the other Elvis. He'd been with us for almost a year when we all went to a lake house and were drinking and having fun and singing. Dave wasn't singing, because nobody knew he could sing. Maybe to make fun of him, someone said, "You sing an Elvis song." He stood up and nailed it. He sounded just like Elvis and did all the moves.

That night Shamus, our tour manager and sound guy, cried. That was strange. Shamus never cried. As a result, we were all moved. Here was a guy who had learned every trick in the Elvis book. He idolized Elvis to the point that he became Elvis. And now that Elvis was gone, nobody could be Elvis like Dave Hicks. He was bald, bearded, elfin Elvis. And for us, it was, "If you can't see his pompadour, we feel sorry for you."

When we decided Elvis was going to come on, be official, and get money and be a part of our crew, rather than just riding with us and eating leftovers, the deal was that he was going to officially be Shamus's assistant. Not just the joint-roller, the assistant.

Though, come to think of it, I shouldn't say "just" the joint-roller. That's quite a skill, especially in a hurricane, on the head of a pin. I sure don't mean to make that sound like a put-down, like "elfin."

Just after making Elvis an assistant, we were in LA at the Chez Poo Poo hotel. Something like that. Shamus knew he had to teach Elvis the tricks of the trade, so he said, "Okay, Elvis, today I'm going to start your training."

Elvis said, "Okay."

Shamus said, "You know those whiffle bats?"

"Yeah."

"Well, they have little thin ones and big, thick ones. I need you to go to Walmart or Walgreens or someplace with Wal in it and find a thick one."

Couple hours later, Elvis comes back with a big, fat, pink whiffle bat.

"It's the biggest one they had," he said, proudly.

Then he handed it to Shamus. And Shamus took it and hit him on the head with it, as hard as he could. I think he got him right on the ear, with this one-handed, neck-jarring swing.

Then Shamus said, "When you fuck up, I'm gonna do that. Consider yourself trained."

———

Shamus and his whiffle bat wound up working for other, more popular bands, and Elvis became my main highway companion. For fifteen years, he's kept me from having to know what time it is or from having to check into a hotel for myself. I'm not in awe of people who can check into a hotel for themselves. I pity those people, whoever they are. Hail, hail, rock 'n' roll.

Elvis reminds me of Jerry Jeff Walker a little bit, in that he invented himself. I don't know what day it was, but one day he decided he was going to be something else other than what other people had told him he was supposed to.

And he understands me and encourages me. People will tell you to be normal, and it's hard to find somebody who will tell you to be anything but that. The tour managers I'd had before, they didn't want me to run into the sun as fast as I could, and that really is the job. My version of the way this all works is that it's got to be insanity all the time. I don't want to be grounded. I'm not looking for that. It doesn't help.

I had one tour manager before Elvis who told me I had to stop smoking pot in the van. Seriously, can you imagine the nerve? But she was right. That tour manager was an employee of mine. And, by technical law, you can't really subject an employee to breathing in illegal drugs. You can't make your employee drive around while you smoke pot in the van. It's against the law. But you can leave an employee at a truck stop in Phoenix.

I didn't sign up for this to be a professional. When I feel like leaving, I leave, and then my free-spirit buddy Elvis has to turn his free-spirit vibe off and go back and get the guitars. I sometimes really kick it into the trees, and then Elvis takes me to the hotel, and I go to my room to watch Piers Morgan, and he goes back and collects everything. I create some emotional mess under the guise of being true to myself, and Elvis goes back and cleans it up.

———

I was playing a gig in Texas, which was fine with me. I wasn't nervous, except for the truth of it is that I'm always so nervous that I don't eat before I play or after I play. Sometimes people, trying to be nice, will say, "Would you like me to take you to dinner?" and I'll say, "No, I'm too nervous. Can't eat." Before or after the show, my blood's hauling through my veins. Not hungry.

At this Texas gig, Elvis had to go out and deal with a situation. When he came back, he let me in on it. He said, "This woman who is promoting the show thought you'd want dinner, and she's prepared dinner for you, and she's now gone from 'I made you this dinner' to anger after I told her you didn't eat dinner before the show."

She wanted me to have dinner with her and her family. I thought, "Oh my God, I can't eat food and talk to somebody's family and then jump out there and sing. I'll throw up. I need to be someplace getting drunk with somebody I know really good, or some bartender I just met, but I sure as fuck am not supposed to be eating dinner with somebody's kid and shit."

Am I right?

Of course I am.

So I did the gig, and people clapped, and it was time for us to go. I got in the truck with Elvis, and he said, "She still hasn't paid us."

I told him to go back to her, and he went back to her, and he came back to me and said, "She's not going to pay us until we eat dinner with her."

I said, "I'm not going to do that."

I told Elvis that we'd just go home and get our people in Nashville to make her give them, and us, the money.

So we got in the van to go home. And just as we decided to do that, we noticed a couple of big ol' Texan guys standing in front of the van, so that we couldn't leave. And then another big ol' Texan guy came up to us and said, "Hey, man, you're low-class. That's a good woman you just offended."

Elvis said, "Look, man, he said he'd sing. He didn't say he was going to have dinner. You can check the contract."

The Texan said, "A lot of big stars have had dinner with her."

Elvis said, "Name one."

The Texan said, "Waylon Jennings."

And then Elvis said something no one had ever said before, and no one has said since. He said something that won't ever be said again. He said something that no one has even thought. He said, "Yeah, well, Waylon Jennings sucks." And then he hit the gas, and those guys had to clear out.

—

You ever have one of those times in life when you're driving down the highway, doing nothing wrong, listening to the radio, loud, with your seat belt fastened, obeying the speed limit, and then up ahead on the highway you see the lights atop a patrol car tucked behind some highway bushes, and before you can stop to think that you have done nothing wrong, you stab your foot down hard on the brake for no real reason other than your brain deciding it needed to tell your foot to do something to acknowledge that your brain had seen something? And you know that had you not made that mistake, you would have passed by the officer unnoticed? But now, because you did make that mistake, he thinks you might have a tied-up kid in your car, and he decides to tail you?

Well, that's what happened to Elvis and me not long ago in a small town called Greencastle, Indiana.

We did not have a tied-up kid in the car.

But we were pulling a joint back and forth at the time, and that joint plays a big factor in this story later on.

So, Elvis shoved what was left of our stash in the side gulley to his left, and he lit a cigarette. Then he opened the window, and I sprayed a quarter-bottle of spray shit everywhere, and we pulled over.

"Do you know why I pulled you over?" the officer asked.

" 'Cuz I'm young and I'm black and my hat's hung low? Do I look like a mind reader? I don't know." Did we say that, or was it Jay-Z? That was all so long ago. Upon reflection, I think all we said was "No."

And he said, "Well, you boys seem to be a bit nervous. You up to no good?"

"Not at all," we answered.

So he said, "Do you boys have drugs on your person?"

"No," we said, honestly again. They weren't on our person. They were in the car.

The officer then asked Elvis to step out of the car, which he did.

From the passenger side, I heard him questioning Elvis by asking him every possible leading question he could, without being direct. I do not know why this was his tack.

"Are you a drug smuggler? Have you been drinking? Can I search your car?" Here, grammar matters. You can answer that last question truthfully by saying "Yes," and you're still not consenting to a search. You're just acknowledging that this man is indeed capable of searching a car. Dig?

Anyway, as this was happening, more police cars showed up to circle our car. The first officer questioned Elvis for five or more minutes and got nothing but the truth, and yet still got nothing to pin on us because he kept asking the wrong questions.

Finally, he came over to me and said, "Sir, are there drugs in this car?"

"Yes," I said.

"What kind?"

"Pot."

"Where?"

"In the gulley."

"Why did you lie to me before?"

"I didn't."

"You didn't tell me you had drugs in your car," he said.

"You didn't ask," I said.

———

From there, it was on to being arrested. But I wasn't worried, because while we at that point had never been arrested for possession of marijuana, we had been driving up and down the road for twenty years possessing marijuana, and also smoking it and planning for an event just such as this. We were ready. We had a plan.

In fact, we didn't just have one plan, we had two: Plan A and Plan B. But here's the thing: I can't tell you the specifics of either plan. Because we don't want other people using them to the point that the law catches on.

But I can and will tell you this: Plan A didn't work. And neither did Plan B.

So I wound up sitting in a little jail in Greencastle, Indiana. But as I mentioned before, I've been a legal dissenter in many ways for many years, so I knew the drill and was not afraid of it.

Plus, I had a pretty good buzz going.

In jail, before they put people in the cell, they line them up on a bench with others, to be printed, processed, and photographed.

As I was sitting on the bench, the oldest guy in the room by ten or more years (older than the cops and the cons), the shame was setting in. And by that I mean the shame of getting caught at my age. Not the shame of smoking pot at my age.

So as the shame was setting in and my broken give-a-shit gypsy side was settling in beside it, I heard a faint waft of music coming out of a door from around the corner.

When I hear music, I can't ever help but kick into a game of "Name That Tune." I know a lot of tunes, and I knew I knew this tune. The guitar riff was familiar. Then I heard a wisp of the words: "Helicopters over the house again."

Hold on, I thought. Here it comes. I know that song. Oh, right, that's me. I have a song called "The Devil You Know," about how helicopters are always flying over my house in East Nashville, with police inside those helicopters looking to take somebody on the run and put them off the run. In the song, that somebody runs into my house, and I wind up helping him escape by giving him the keys to my car. Not one of my cop-friendliest tunes.

And so I said nothing. Being a singer—of my stature, at least—had never helped me in jail before, and don't think I hadn't tried. It just didn't work. Sometimes it had made things worse. So I just sat there, taking in the situation, silently assessing my life as a Greencastle prisoner.

By the time I had been processed, photographed, and fingerprinted, my buddy Elvis had paid my bail, which meant that if the judge wasn't too backed up I would be out pretty quick.

I had taken the fall for Elvis, of course. That's part of Plan B. I'd tell you more, but I can't. Both plans are back in the shop.

The whole thing took seven or eight hours, and I never left the drunk tank. It was pretty easy, really. I was never too worried, because I knew it was less than an ounce of possession, and I even made up a new song in there that ended up on a record. That song was, and is, called "Greencastle Blues." Here's the words part:

GREENCASTLE BLUES
By Todd Snider

There was a time when I was handsome
There was a time when I had money to burn
There was a time when where I landed
Was the least of my, the least of my concern
But it hurts to lean back in these handcuffs
Like nine kinds of shame turned to rage
As a younger man I might have put up a fight
But I feel like such a fool at my age
Most of this trouble just finds me, you know
No matter where I turn

How do you know when it's too late?
How do you know when it's too late?
How do you know when it's too late to learn?

You know the number one symptom of heart disease?
The number one symptom of heart disease is sudden death
It's like time stands still forever until it starts shaking
*   around on you*
Shaking around like some kind of crazy old hooker on meth
And you know me, I can't take no preaching
Not on Sunday or any other day
But I feel like I ought to be praying or something
And I have no idea what to say
Some of this trouble just finds me
But most of this trouble I earn

How do you know when it's too late?
How do you know when it's too late?
How do you know when it's too late to learn?

I've learned nothing out here on this highway
But I've been passed by and I've passed by more than my
* share of cars*
And I do remember my younger days when I was so certain
That driving even faster was going to get me far
So there's nothing for me to learn here
Just this half-full or half-empty cup
Less than an ounce of possession?
Man, I could do that kind of time standing up

Most of this trouble just finds me, you know
No matter where I turn

How do you know when it's too late?
How do you know when it's too late?
How do you know when it's too late to learn?

After Elvis bailed me out, we headed down the road, to
the gig in Bloomington, which was about an hour away. Elvis's phone rang, and it was the sheriff of Greencastle, Mark
Frisbie. He said he was going over some paperwork and saw
a Todd Snider and wanted to know if it was Todd Snider, the
singer. Elvis said it was. The sheriff said he'd been listening to
me all day in his office, and that if he'd known I was there he
could have gotten me off.

Elvis told him I was straight and married. The sheriff said
he meant he could have gotten me off on the charges. Like,
helped me get away with it. Damn, I should have said something. Oh, well. Live and don't learn.

That night in Bloomington, Sheriff Frisbie came to the
show with his wife and kid, and he brought some other cops,
too. They told me that the guy who got us was the local Bar-

ney Fife, and that had I gotten any other cop I probably would not have been pulled over and definitely wouldn't have been arrested for such a small amount of dope.

The sheriff—I call him "The Frizz" now, and he's my brother for life—also said the kid who busted me was the son of the sheriff before The Frizz, and that it was an ugly feud. He said he wished he could fire the guy, but couldn't under the circumstances.

Eventually, this Fife kid and his ex-sheriff dad figured out that The Frizz had spent about seven grand of the city's money taking his family to Mexico, a move I still consider wise, to this day.

They came down hard on Frizz, though, and he had to spend two months in jail. Though it was not a prison, it was a jail, and a fairly white-collar one at that. It was the kind of place where if you were asked on a game show, "Would you spend two months here in exchange for a $7,000 family vacation to Mexico?" you'd say, "Oh, fuck yeah, no problem."

And, now that I think about it, that day as Elvis and I were pulling that joint, if he'd have said, "Would you trade eight hours in jail for this buzz we're catching?" I'd have said, "Oh, fuck yeah, no problem."

Me and Elvis were walking up and down Something to Do Street one day in Iowa, when my phone rang. Elvis always holds my phone. We still had about ten days to go on tour, but this phone call came from his wife, and it turned into a minor argument that turned into her saying she didn't love him anymore. I gave Elvis the keys to the van, and he drove back home to

Michigan, where he got his wife to agree to go with him into couples counseling.

Then he flew to meet me in Oregon, where he got a bad feeling and I told him he should go back to Michigan and see if his bad feeling was bullshit or not. He got back to his house, and everything was gone. Not a fork in the place. She didn't even say where she'd gone with his children; he had to figure it out for himself.

So now Elvis was in counseling, just not couples counseling. His presence is a big thrill for the counseling community. It's cool for them to talk to a star like that. Seriously, he's one of the most famous tour managers in the world. Of course, there's only one other famous tour manager in the world. His name is Phil Kaufman, and he got famous for taking his main client's dead body out into the desert and burning it. That client's name was Gram Parsons. Perhaps you've heard of him. Elvis and Phil are friends now, and I'm a little nervous. After all that happened with Elvis's old lady, Kaufman called him and said, "Now you're one of us: a lifer."

As I have said, Elvis and I first met when he was being hassled by security. Since then, he's been covered in motor oil in Virginia Beach and been in a hospital in northern California, when he was dehydrated and we thought he was going to die but he didn't. He's been in a jail cell in Birmingham, which is where he wrote the classic treatise, "Letter from a Birmingham Jail." Wait, that was somebody else. Never mind. Back to Elvis.

He's also been onstage with Jerry Jeff Walker, dancing around in front of twelve thousand people at a festival at Golden Gate Park in San Francisco. He's surfed in Santa Cruz and been to London and France and in the green room at *The Tonight Show*. He's become personal friends with Larry Geller, who was Elvis Presley's hairdresser and spiritual advisor. You think there's a sick and ironic joke there, right? There's not. Elvis Presley won his only Grammy for a gospel record, and his hair looked great when he died. It wasn't Larry Geller who let him down.

CHAPTER 15

THE SILVER-TONGUED DEVIL AND I

My first night at Kent Finlay's house, he showed me records from a bunch of songwriters, and he made it very clear to me that the best one was Kris Kristofferson.

He said Kristofferson would be taught in schools someday. He said the others were really good, but that they too knew the best one was Kristofferson, and they too knew Kristofferson would be taught in schools.

The first Kris song he put on was called "The Pilgrim, Chapter 33."

"He's a poet, he's a picker, he's a prophet, he's a pusher," Kris sang. "He's a pilgrim and a preacher and a problem when he's stoned / He's a walkin' contradiction, partly truth and partly fiction / Takin' every wrong direction on his lonely walk back home."

When that song was over, I felt like I knew what I was going to do with the rest of the years I had on this ball. I felt totally connected to that song, in my soul. When somebody who really likes to make up songs hears "The Pilgrim, Chapter 33" for the first time, they come away from it a different person.

Then Kent played me "The Silver Tongued Devil and I" and then every other song from Kristofferson's first two albums, all the way through.

Kent told me the story of how Kristofferson was a high achiever as a kid. He was a Golden Gloves boxer, a college football player, a great student, a Rhodes scholar, and a writer who had short stories published in the *Atlantic Monthly* while he was still in school. He went into the army, and they thought so much of him that they kept him out of Vietnam. He wanted to go to Vietnam, but the army said he was too important to the future of the country. He was on a track to at least be secretary of state or something. The army gave him a job as a teacher at West Point, but then he came down to Nashville in 1965 on what was supposed to be a little vacation. Right away, still wearing his military dress uniform, he met Cowboy Jack and Johnny Cash, and he figured that Nashville was the place where wild and smart people convene. He threw away his military career and moved to Nashville to become a songwriting bum, and he took a job as a janitor at Columbia studios. It's not like he had a bagful of great songs when he came to Nashville, and it sure wasn't like he had some golden voice: he says he sang kind of like a frog. Kristofferson just chucked it all on a pipe dream. Lots of people come to Nashville because they're already poor somewhere else, and they figure they can be poor here, too. But Kris had everything—bright young wife, parents, money, future—and to all that he said, "Fuck it, I'm going to write songs."

And, Lord, did he write songs. "Sunday Morning Coming Down." "Me and Bobby McGee." "Help Me Make It Through the Night." "Just the Other Side of Nowhere." "To Beat the Devil." And, as I quickly found out from Kent, the ones that weren't famous were just as good as the ones that were. Kent created for me this mythical character of Kris Kristofferson, and I would later find that the mythical character is actually just as real and truthful as he is mythical.

There was a store called Sundance Records in San Marcos, Texas, and I could go in there and the guy behind the counter would just give me records with the understanding that I would try to pay him eventually. My record-buying life got to be like the life you might have with a pot dealer. So, on a busboy's salary, I was able to quickly get every single record Kristofferson had put out, mostly on cassettes. I'd sit in my friend Trog's house and study that shit like crazy. I'd put it in the jam box, set the jam box on the floor, lie on the floor myself, and face the jam box like it was a television, like something visual was going to happen. And it was actually all quite visual. You could see every person Kristofferson sang about and feel every feeling as if it was your own. I couldn't move around or read or clean the house while this was on. I just lay there and took it all in. As I was learning to make up my own songs, I'd come up with some untrue thing that didn't have anything to do with my emotions. I'd say "baby" when there was no baby to speak of, but I'd alliterate like crazy, the way Kris did, and I'd think I was writing songs.

Much later, but before I made my first record, I was playing in Nashville at 12th & Porter, and Mike Utley brought in

Rita Coolidge, who used to be married to Kris. Rita told me I'd be perfect for her daughter, who was Kris's daughter, too. I went on tour with Jimmy Buffett, and Rita had a birthday party at her house. That night, I remember Rita took me outside and said, "Some of this that you're about to get yourself into is really, really going to hurt. Remember, they can eat you alive, but you're not going to die."

That made no sense then. Wish it didn't make sense now.

Rita's daughter, Casey, was downstairs with her punk rock friends and didn't want to come up. So Rita kind of made me go down there. I went down and sat with them and took some bong hits and flirted with her a little. A couple of days later, she came over to the hotel and we smoked pot. I didn't try to kiss her or anything, because of Kris, but she and I stayed in touch a little bit. When my first record came out, in the liner notes I thanked "Casey K. Jones," which was her. She went by Casey Jones sometimes, to avoid having to live up to her father.

After I'd made a few records, I'd decided I was going to make Al Bunetta be my manager. Al came to my house, saw my record collection, and saw that I had every Kristofferson record. He whipped out his phone and said, "Check this out," and a few seconds later I was on the phone with Kris Kristofferson. He said, "I love your song 'Easy Money,' and my daughter says that the Casey K. Jones in the thank-you's of your album is her."

I said, "I have every single record you ever made."

He said, "No you don't."

I said, "Test me," and he didn't. But we agreed we were going to get together and talk sometime.

These were the days of faxing. I faxed him how great it was to talk to him on the phone, and he faxed back. This was in the six-month period before I went into rehab for the first time, and I faxed him something like, "Hey man, I think I might need some help." I didn't hear back on that one. That's when I learned that distress notes are a little much to lay on some guy who has only talked to you on the phone.

I was kind of dating Casey while also kind of dating Jimmy Buffett's niece, Maura. That sounds terrible, but when I say "kind of dating," I mean that I was on the road the whole time. For me, having a girlfriend meant there was a girl I was going to go out with about seven nights a year. So forgive me if I wanted to have fourteen dates instead of seven. Somewhere on tour, I wrote to Casey and told her I was going into rehab. She wrote me a couple of nice letters while I was in there. When I got out of rehab, I was in love with someone I'd met there, but still in touch with Casey. I told her I was getting ready to play some shows in Reno, and she said she might try to catch one of those shows.

In Reno—actually just above Reno, on a river where you could raft—we were playing at a resort-type place, in an amphitheater that holds about three hundred people and that is connected to the hotel. I got to the hotel early in the morning, and I went out on the balcony to smoke a joint. I looked across the hotel, to the other side, and there was a guy on another balcony who looked just like Kris Kristofferson. Black T-shirt, high sleeves. Just like Kristofferson. I thought it was funny. I mean, I idolized Kristofferson, but this guy clearly had taken his Kris fixation too far.

Then I went back in, and after awhile there was a knock on the door. I opened the door, and it was the guy with the Kris

Kristofferson fixation, who happened to be Kris Kristofferson. He said he'd come up with Casey to see my shows, and he said they were in town for a couple of days. He came in, and we started talking. My show was in about three hours. I had a fuckload of pot, and we traded songs and ordered some red wine up to my room.

I played him "To Beat the Devil," a song he wrote directly to songwriters. It's about a guy sitting in a Nashville bar, holding a guitar, and how the Devil himself strolls in and tries to talk him out of his creative soul. The Devil says, "If you waste your time a-talkin' to the people who don't listen to the things that you are saying, who do you think's gonna hear?" Then the Devil talks about all the other lonely singers who came before: "Their voices have been scattered by the swirling winds of time, 'cause the truth remains that no one wants to know." In the end, the songwriter turns the Devil's words around on him, takes his melody, and says the singing is worth it whether or not anyone is listening, because the singing is what feeds his soul's hunger. "I ain't sayin' I beat the Devil, but I drank his beer for nothing," Kris wrote. "Then I stole his song."

After I played "To Beat the Devil" for Kris, he played "Easy Money" for me. How about that?

Then I played him a Kent Finlay song I knew he'd like, one called "Comfort's Just a Rifle Shot Away," and I told him about Kent just the way Kent had told me about him.

Kris loves songs. We sat and sang for those three hours, and then I went to do my show. My room was adjacent to the stage, and so when the crowd saw me come out of the door to do the show, they saw me with Kris. He walked with me for a moment, and everyone was watching both of us. Then he walked toward the crowd and I walked toward the stage, and they kept their eyes on him.

I sang "To Beat the Devil," and it looked like it was kind of emotional for Kris. And then he jumped up and did "Easy Money."

I don't remember how much money I got for the show that night, but I remember what I got paid in gratification and fulfillment. It was a hundred times more than I've been paid before or since.

The next day, as soon as I woke up I went to Kris's room. It was probably nine in the morning, and he offered me a Heineken. And he had some great pot, way better than mine, and we sat and watched the news. Ever since then, he's been my friend.

Kris is very encouraging, not just to me but to anyone who wants to jump in this strange deep pool of the songwriting life. The next time I saw him might have been when he was getting into the Country Music Hall of Fame, and I got to sing a verse of "Me and Bobby McGee." I accidentally did the verse Vince Gill was supposed to sing. Every time I'm around Vince Gill, I do something stupid. But that night, I got to sit in a room with Guy Clark, John Prine, Billy Joe Shaver, Kristofferson, and no one else. I still think about it a lot.

One time, I went to see Kris and he made fun of my haircut and my clothes. All of those guys that I came up studying have at some point mocked my haircut or my style. But I'm not some Texas songwriter. I'm a goddamn dandy from Oregon. High-five!

Anyway, one night he was playing with Prine at Wolftrap, up near Washington, DC, and he said to me, "If I ever find out that you stop, I'm gonna come fucking find you."

He is a person who radiates beauty and creativity, joy and wisdom. He has so much love for people and for art. He's such a supporter of the arts. If you're in a room with Kris, passing a guitar back and forth, he'll say, "Look at us. This is where we're supposed to be." I hope Kris knows how deeply his encouragement and his spirit impacts those of us who want to be more like him.

If a song gets played in an empty room, no one hears it but the singer. And there's an element of encouragement I'll hear sometimes that makes me feel like my song might actually go out there, get heard, and do something for me. That's not the kind of encouragement I hear from Kris. He's always said, "If you are in this for the right reasons, there is no chance that you can fail." When you're with him and he encourages you, it doesn't inspire you to want to be known like him, it inspires you to want to be a freeborn human being, to sing what you want to sing about, to wear what you want to wear (even if he makes fun of what you wear), to be an individual, and to allow yourself your eccentricities without fear of repercussions.

In our line of work, if you're going to start showing everybody the nooks of your heart, you are not only going to be perceived as eccentric, but over the years you may become exactly that. It snowballs, and Kristofferson is there to let you know that's actually good, and to enjoy the roll down the hill. When you're around him, it makes you want to go home and paint a picture no one's going to see. It makes you feel artistic and weird, makes you want to follow your bliss.

Some people get into this business because they love the idea of getting backstage. I understand that. Backstage, there are little rooms, with doors you can close or open at your own discretion. There's free food, and there are people guarding it all who make sure that everyone who comes back there has a special sticker or tag around their necks. Some people love all that. Kristofferson hates all that. I heard him say at an awards show one time, "This show is all backstage and no gig," which means there's too much glad-handing, pass checking, and celery eating, and not enough music and creativity. Kristofferson doesn't like the backstage part. None of the great ones I know do, unless it involves passing a guitar around and singing each others' songs.

Kris was the leader of a generation that followed an artistic boom that changed the world. Rock 'n' roll changed the whole deal, and once you got from Elvis to Dylan, you'd snapped up the best young minds of that generation. One of the biggest waves of all that went through Nashville, and some of the best and brightest young people, made that place there home and changed the language of American roots music. That was Kris, Tom T. Hall, Mickey Newbury, John Hartford, and some others.

That's not what it is anymore. It's a little like being in the theater now, as opposed to being there when *Romeo and Juliet* was just written. Same shirts, shoes, and hats, but different guys. I think our generation is good, but I'd imagine the Kristoffersons and Prines and Guy Clarks of my time aren't even playing guitar. They're busy at work on something on the computer that I don't understand.

The 1980s just kind of fucked everything up. There was all that *Cosby Show* shit, where everybody wanted the right sweater, and there was "Just Say No," and there were normal people who didn't go to prep school but still somehow turned into prep school douche bags.

What did Kris Kristofferson do in the '80s? He sang country songs about Jesse Jackson and Nicaragua and paid for it dearly.

Then in the early 1990s, a singer named Sinead O'Connor tore up a picture of the pope on national television and

206 | I Never Met a Story I Didn't Like

subsequently was actually booed during a Bob Dylan tribute concert. If you pay your ticket money you're allowed to do whatever you want. The booing shattered Sinead O'Connor, and she walked offstage looking sad and lost. Only one person on the show—and there were dozens of big stars—made a move to help. Before O'Connor could get all the way offstage, Kris wrapped his arms around her and whispered encouragement in her ear, saying, "Don't let the bastards get you down." For a lonely moment, it was her against the mob, with no one in her corner. Then, all of a sudden, the best one of all of them—the guy whose songs would be studied in school—was her protector. Then he wrote a song about her, called "Sister Sinead."

"When she told them her truth just as hard as she could, her message profoundly was misunderstood," he sang. "And maybe she's crazy and maybe she ain't, but so was Picasso and so were the saints."

He has gone a long, long way to make a lot of people feel valued.

One thing I've tried to emulate about Kris is his enormous attention span for other people's art. Very few people who make up songs for a living have that kind of interest in what their peers are doing. As I get older, I find the thing that's sometimes most inspiring is when I see younger people biting off as big a piece of this as they can chew. It inspires me to stay in the water and to not think. The older you get, there's more pull to think, and you've got to push back. I haven't had a bill sent to my house in twenty years. I don't know anything about that. I couldn't tell you how much I have in the bank. I don't give a fuck, never did and won't, and don't have to, because I worked hard at not having to. Kristofferson smiles at that and says, "God is happy," and then he listens to someone else's songs. I've been doing a lot of listening lately, too, and I try to be like Kris in getting past the jealousy that Justin Townes Earle or Jason Isbell or Hayes Carll or Elizabeth Cook or Amanda Shires has written something great that I didn't feel first, and to just enjoy that there's something new and wonderful in the world.

What I don't want to do is to put down anyone for not being Kris Kristofferson. Some people in my line of music have a hassle with anyone who does well enough with country music to get on the radio and sell out football stadiums. The argument is usually that the star in question has altered himself just to be famous.

I'm saying to you, and I feel like I've been close enough to some of them to say this, that if you think that, you are fucking wrong. It doesn't work that way. Maybe for a summer, but not for much longer.

If you see Kenny Chesney selling out Soldier Field in Chicago and think that's because he's being phony to be famous, you're wrong, and I'd go on to say that Kenny Chesney is being Kenny Chesney way more than you're being you. The problem with the phony to be famous thing is that it always falls flat. Nobody claps. It's like a magic trick where you don't have the rabbit in the hat; it won't work. If you think it will work, why don't you go get yourself a bunch of corny country songs and go be a star. Go tell the label you'll do anything they tell you to so you can be on TV. The label will tell you, "That's not what we're looking for."

Now, go tell the label that you want to sing country songs to country audiences about how much you like Jesse Jackson or Sinead O'Connor, or how much you detest a brutal American foreign policy decision, and they probably won't turn cart-wheels. But if it's what's in your heart, it's not going to be the thing that keeps you from being a lifer. It may help. You might wind up in the Hall of Fame. You might wind up in your seventies, still playing to houses full of people who believe everything you're saying, because they know that you believe everything you're saying.

Kent Finlay was right. They teach Kristofferson in schools now. My buddy Peter Cooper lectures about him at Vanderbilt University. And the first Kristofferson song he shows his students isn't "The Pilgrim, Chapter 33" or "Me and Bobby McGee" or "Sunday Morning Coming Down." He first shows them one of the many songs Kris wrote about the dangers of judgment: "Jesus was a Capricorn, he ate organic food / He believed in love and peace and never wore no shoes," Kris sang. "Long hair, beard and sandals and a funky bunch of friends / Reckon we'd just nail him up if he came down again."

Kris wouldn't nail him up. He'd hug his neck and whisper, "Don't let the bastards get you down." Then he'd write a song about Jesus that'd make the rest of the stuff in the hymnal seem shallow and trifling. And I'd learn it, and sing it back to Kris in a hotel room somewhere, just before I passed him the guitar so he could sing "Easy Money."

Amen. High fucking ten.

CHAPTER 16

THE MOONDAWG TRILOGY, PLUS DIGGER DAVE

Sam Knight and Todd Snider

I have said that I would provide, for readers of this book, the Moondawg Trilogy, and now the time has come.

This particular trilogy starts just outside of Memphis, where there was a bar that was famous on the radio, because a DJ named Zeke Logan would talk about it. Zeke would say that Moondawg's Tavern was in Frazier, Tennessee, the Camaro-driving, Copenhagen-spitting, "Freebird"-listening capital of the world. Zeke would say that every guy in the whole town had a washer and a dryer and an automobile—in their yard. He'd say that if your car breaks down in Frazier, the very first guy you run into can fix your car, but then he's gonna kick your ass for being such a sissy that you can't fix your own car. He'd say they sold more prosthetic limbs and eye patches per capita in Frazier than anywhere else in the state of Tennessee.

But mostly he'd talk about Moondawg's Tavern. He'd say they frisk you for a gun there, and if you don't have one, they give you one and send you on in. I thought this was like Zeke Logan's own Lake Wobegon, a place he invented in his mind. But one day I was at a bar called Hughie's, and the bartender said, "Hey, Todd, over there is that DJ, Zeke Logan."

So I walked up to that DJ, Zeke Logan, and I said, "I love that stuff you make up about Frazier."

He said, "Oh, I don't make that shit up. That's true."

I thought, "I'll keep that in mind."

Then one night not long after that, I was playing a place called The Highland Cue. During a break, I was leaning on a car out behind that pool hall, and a big guy came up, holding out a pair of shoes. The guy had a beard and a beer gut, and he looked like he might have worked for the Nitty Gritty Dirt Band in the '70s.

He said, "I want you to have my shoes, boy, 'cause you don't have no goddamn shoes of your own."

See, I don't wear shoes when I play my songs. This guy was obviously perceptive and quite giving. Or else he was fucking with me.

I told him I did have some shoes, told him they didn't fit but I still had 'em.

He said, "I'm Moondawg," and I said, "From the radio?"

He nodded. Now he had my attention.

I told him, "I want to come see your bar." He said, "Well, I'll give you my phone number, and when you want to come see the bar you call me up."

I said, "Couldn't you just tell me how to get there?"

He said, "No, I can't."

I thought, "That's an interesting program they're working over at Moondawg's Tavern."

Not long after that was the Fourth of July, and my buddy Joe and I were sitting around wanting to smoke some pot. But the town was dry that day. I got the idea to call the number Moondawg had given me, 'cause if the town was so dry that the Nitty Gritty Dirt Band roadie-looking guy didn't have anything, the town was probably gonna go up in flames.

So I called the number, and Moondawg said, "I'll send the Camaro."

Next thing we know, the Camaro had arrived, complete with Skynyrd songs blasting through an over-driven car speaker. The driver turned his "Freebird" jam down long enough to give us instructions.

Not instructions for how to find Moondawg's Tavern. Instructions for what was gonna happen next.

"I'm gonna have to blindfold you," he said, and then he put bandannas over our eyes.

It took a while to get to Frazier: "Freebird" was nearly over by the time the car stopped, and that's a long, long song. We were allowed to take off our bandannas, and when we did we were in somebody's yard, next to a washer and a dryer.

Noticing that this was not a commercial district in any way, shape, or form, I figured we were getting rolled.

I was scared, but then, just as I was trying to think of a way we could make our break out of there, I noticed that behind the main house were people milling around in the backyard. And I noticed the music that was playing. It was "Hold on Loosely" by .38 Special, another fine Southern group. I said to the blindfold/Camaro driver guy, "What's that back there?"

He pointed to a toolshed in the backyard and said, "That's Moondawg's Tavern."

I said, "No, that's a toolshed."

He said, "No, it's a bar. See, there were seven bars in Frazier, Tennessee, and Moondawg ain't allowed in any of them no more, so he built his own."

We checked it out. It really was a tavern, with a pool table and a juke box and everything. World's greatest toolshed. Beer was 10 cents cheaper than you could get it anywhere else, and Moondawg kept the fridge on the customer side of the bar, so he wouldn't have to move around so much. When you wanted a beer, you reached into the fridge and got your own.

Joe and I did a lot of reaching in that afternoon, and then we called Moondawg over.

"Hey, man," I said. "We thought you might have some pot. You know what I'm talking about?"

He said, "Hey, we don't fool with that kind of stuff out here, boy."

I said, "No problem, I was just joking." I didn't want to press it.

Then he said, "I'll sell you a newspaper, though."

I said, "I don't read so much."

He said, "Trust me," and then he handed me a newspaper and said, "That'll be $65, boy."

Two blindfolds and one Camaro ride later, Joe and I were back in Memphis, with only a newspaper and a slight beer buzz to show for our day.

We took the rubber band off that paper. And, brothers and sisters, the news was good.

After that, I started hanging out a lot at Moondawg's.

I liked the place so much I wrote a song about it. And the song went like this:

MOONDAWG'S TAVERN
By Todd Snider

> *Yeah, that's where I wanna go*
> *Moondawg's Tavern*
> *That's the only place I know*
> *Moondawg's got everything*
> *I'm ever gonna need*
> *Moondawg's Tavern out in Frazier, Tennessee*
>
> *Sit down and he'll tell you*
> *About the friends he's made*
> *'Bout the nights that he crossed the line*
> *And all the mornings that he paid*
> *How they threw him out of so many bars*
> *He finally built one in his own back yard*
> *He ain't been thrown out yet so far*
> *And his debt is always paid*
>
> *Moondawg's Tavern*
> *Yeah, that's where I'm gonna go*
> *Moondawg's Tavern*
> *That's the only place I know*
> *Moondawg's got everything*
> *I'm ever gonna need*
> *Moondawg's Tavern, that's where we buy our weed*

Then one winter, they sent me up to Alaska to play a show. Mariah Carey and Celine Dion and people like that, they seldom go to Alaska in the wintertime. That clears the way for a guy like me.

In the winter, they only have about four hours of daylight up there. To get to Homer, Alaska, you fly on a big plane into

Anchorage, and then south on a little plane until you look out the window and see a big ocean and a little plot of land that looks like a strip mall where they hung Christmas lights. And then the little plane lands, and you walk down the steps onto a tarmac, and then into a building that looks like maybe there were two 7-Elevens so close to each other that they decided to bust down a couple of walls and connect them. The result was a 14-22.

First time I went to Homer was in March. I got out, walked into the 14-22, and someone handed me my guitar and my bag, and then a guy who identified himself as a taxi driver walked up to me and said, "Hey, you must be the singer."

I said, "How did you know?"

"Well," he said. "There's only nine hundred people in town, and we haven't had anybody new in seven months, so we're all pretty excited about the show."

Then he said, "You want a ride over to the hotel?" I said, "Yeah, let me look at my little sheet that tells me where I'm supposed to go, so I can tell you which hotel."

But he said there'd be no need for that, because the hotel was the hotel. There were just two, and the other was something else.

So we walked out into the snow, and then another cab driver—the only other one in town, it turns out—comes walking across the snow to my guy and says, "You son of a bitch, you know you're not supposed to come into the airport to pick up a fare." And then he punched my guy right in the face. Then they fell down into the snow and start rolling around. I was standing there with my guitar, watching them, and I said, "Uh, I'm just gonna go with the first guy, no matter who wins."

So they got up, and I got into the cab with the first guy. He said, "My God, he hit me right in the fucking face. You saw him do it. I ought to call the police."

I said, "Yeah, he for sure hit you right in the fucking face, and you should call the police."

So he got on his cell phone and dialed 911, and when somebody answered he said, "Craig, hey listen, this is Jeff. John just hit me in the face, right in front of the fucking airport. The singer saw the whole goddamn thing."

So, they had an official discussion about all that, but mostly the 911 guy wanted to be sure that the singer had made it in okay. Then Jeff took me to the hotel, and the show promoter came and got me and said he was going to show me around. He did show me around. I saw a moose and some eagles—there are bald eagles everywhere in Homer, and they looked about the size of a five-year-old kid to me—and then we were down on the beach.

Yeah, Homer, Alaska, is right on the ocean. I didn't have any idea of that before I got there. There's a beach that curls up into it, but the water is pretty icy. You could hear it crashing into itself. And they have this stretch of sand, but you can't really get a tan or anything.

I looked down the sand and saw this little community of about seven shanty houses, kind of like cabins. Maybe some of them were busted in half and duct taped to a piece of a trailer, with a tent posted up over all that.

I said, "Who lives over there, man?" And the promoter said, "We shouldn't go down there."

I said, "Are you telling me you've got nine hundred people here, and there's a bad part of town?"

In fact, he assured me, there was. And, he assured me, he was not going down there.

So we went back to the hotel, and he dropped me off, and I walked immediately back over to the bad part of town. I had on a purple scarf my wife had given me. I was walking down Brunelle Street, snow everywhere, and a guy in a pickup truck drove by, rolled down his window and yelled, "Nice scarf, Serge."

I knocked on a door, and a guy with a beard that stuck out past his shoulders answered and said, as God is my witness, "Holy shit, it's the singer."

And his friends—there were lots and lots of friends—stood up and started saying, "Oh, it's that guy whose face is on the poster at the coffee place."

I sat down with those guys, and some of them had guitars, and we wound up playing songs together, sitting in a circle. It wasn't a "Kumbaya," peace and love scene. It was like the Manson family had never been caught, 'cause they'd found shanties in Homer, Alaska, and made their part of town so frightening that the cops wouldn't even come down there.

The "Nice scarf, Serge" guy was there, in the house. And there were two girls dressed like hookers, I think because they were hookers. And there were guns on a table, and every kind of drug. And these guys were sitting around smoking joints and playing John Prine songs and drinking moonshine.

I don't usually care much for the drinking or the drugs, but I sure do love John Prine.

Then it hit me that I actually do like the drinking and the drugs, too. And then, much later, it hit me that I had to play my own songs at some point that night. So I said, "I'm leaving, but if you guys want to see the show, come on down to wherever it is we're having the show."

And they laughed. All of them laughed.

Where we were having the show was Alice's Champagne Palace. Really. Alice's Champagne Palace, in Homer, Alaska. Check it out, sometime, but don't try to order the champagne. They'll rip your Adam's apple right out of your throat.

Anyway, all of the bearded guy's friends started laughing at me. I didn't understand. I was trying to be nice. But the friends clued me in on the fact that Alice's was one of the three bars in Homer, Alaska, that the bearded guy—turns out his name was Digger Dave—had been banned from, for life. And that's how many bars there are in Homer, Alaska: three.

Banned for life? I wondered why. They said, "We can't talk about it."

I said, "Well, maybe I can get you in, you know, since I'm the singer."

Says so right there on the poster up at the coffee shop.

I called the owner of the club. Mr. Alice's Champagne Palace. And he said, "No, c'mon man. If you want to get Digger Dave in here, you've got to call the mayor."

So, I called the mayor. And the mayor told me that if I would put a deposit down, Digger Dave could walk into Alice's Champagne Palace.

That night, I agreed to a deposit. And then I set about trying to find Alice's, walking through blinding snow. It's dark up there in March all the time, and snow doesn't come down, it goes across, and so you have to navigate by the Christmas lights that people don't ever seem to take down. Walking through all this, I saw the lights of a cab. I wondered if it was the guy who'd taken me from the airport. As he pulled up and rolled his window down, I saw that it was actually the guy who had punched the guy who'd taken me from the airport in the fucking face.

Letting bygones be bygones, I said, "Hey, do you know how to get to Alice's Champagne Palace?"

Rolling up his window, he yelled, "Yeah, practice!" and peeled off, showering me with snow.

But I finally made it, dried off, and went out onstage and started playing, just the same way I always do. We were all having fun. Them because it was their first show since November, and me because I have fun every time.

When you're a young guy, I might kick a monitor or yell at the sound guy or those types of things. Around thirty-two or thirty-three, I started to develop a deeper appreciation, and it evolves into this thing that just can't go wrong. It can go wrong in the eyes of other people, but not in my heart. Playing guitar and singing songs is fun, every time.

There's an old jam band saying, "Who let them in?" that sounds like a dig at the crowd, but it's not. It's an enormous show of respect for the audience. It translates like this: "Thank you for coming, I'm not going to kiss your ass or beg you or patronize you. I'm going to come up here, open my heart, find whatever the muse is for tonight, and I'm going to chase it. You could boo through it and it wouldn't knock me off my course."

By the way, sometimes changing course is part of my course.

I learned that from surfers. No way is there a bad day surfing. You can't get in the ocean and say, "That sucked." Just doesn't happen.

But enough about surfing.

Earlier that day, Digger Dave had told me that I'd done one song that really changed his life. He said it was the one I sang about a friend of mine who got kicked out of so many bars that he built one in his own yard. I told him I was glad that song could be such an inspiration.

About four songs into my set at Alice's, I decided to play Digger Dave's favorite song of mine, "Moondawg's Tavern," about my ne'er-do-well friend in Frazier, Tennessee. Right in the middle of that song, Digger Dave walked through the front door of Alice's Champagne Palace with his entourage.

Right in the middle of the song.

Standing. Fucking. Ovation.

The next day, Jeff and his newly purple eye picked me up to go to the airport. He had the radio on in the car. It was tuned to KBBI, which is the greatest station in the history of Homer, Alaska. I love KBBI. That station is a big part of the reason why all of Digger Dave's guys know every John Prine song. On the way to the airport, the guy on the radio said, "You should have seen the show last night down at Alice's Champagne Palace. It was so exciting."

The KBBI guy didn't mention my name or the songs that I'd played. But he said, "They let Digger Dave in. Apparently he knows the singer."

Thank God somebody liked that "Moondawg's Tavern" song, because Moondawg himself did not.

I remember the day I played it for him for the first time. I played him a song about him, and he shrugged like I'd just played him an album track off a Reba McEntire album. Moondawg hated Reba McEntire. I said, "What's wrong with your song?"

He said, "Well, for starters, most songs have more than one verse. It sounds like you made it up in the time that it took for you to drive out here."

See, by now I was so in with Moondawg that he finally told me his address and let me drive there myself, just so long as I promised never to tell anybody else. And I was busted. I had in fact made that song up on my way out there.

He said, "All the fucking characters that sit around here every day, and you don't mention any of them in that song. Ronnie Van Zant could'a written a whole concept album about this place."

Ronnie Van Zant was Lynyrd Skynyrd's lead singer and songwriter, before he and a bunch of other Skynyrd people died in a terrible plane crash. And, yes, he could have written a kick-ass album about Moondawg and his bar. If he had, I'd be listening to it right now, instead of typing this bullshit.

I tried to explain to Moondawg that I'd written the song out of love and admiration. I've always liked people who decide for themselves what they want to do and who they want to be. Moondawg used to be Michael Webb, and then he realized he didn't have to be. Moondawg used to get thrown out of bars. Now he can't be. He's a kingmaker who made himself king. King of a toolshed, but king nonetheless. And I'd rather be the king of a toolshed than the star of the puppet show. So, to recap, I admired Moondawg and wrote a song for him. A song of admiration. And he thought it sucked.

———

My buddy Joe and I only worked three nights a week for our living, so we'd go to Moondawg's most afternoons. In the afternoons, it was pretty empty, except for the guys who were in between jobs. I did notice in Frazier that a lot of people tended to stay "in between jobs" and got fired because "the boss" was "a useless cocksucker." Which, there's really no such thing. I promise, somewhere in the world, there's a taker.

Nobody messed with us much at Moondawg's. Nobody beat us up. All we had to endure was being called "midtown art fags," and we didn't mind it. We kind of liked it.

What I didn't like was that Moondawg hated the song I wrote for him. And I didn't like that his criticisms made a lot of sense to me. The tavern was, in fact, full of characters that I could have written about.

For starters, Moondawg's wife was named Moon Bitch. That's how she introduced herself. I saw Teenie Hodges, who wrote "Love and Happiness" and "Take Me to the River" for Al Green. I saw Jim Dandy of Black Oak Arkansas. I don't know if you remember that song, "Jim Dandy to the Rescue," but at Moondawg's Tavern he was never in any shape to rescue anybody. In fact, I think Moondawg had to rescue him on more than one occasion.

Who else? There was a guy that had a big snake. There was a guy named Chicago Mike, an air conditioner repairman who could also hold a candle or a match up to his hand for upwards of five minutes at a time. I watched him win money doing that, every time somebody new would come along. I saw Jesus out at Moondawg's, too, and I have a witness.

My witness is Mark Marchetti, a Vietnam veteran who wasn't much of a smoker or drinker. He was a poet, though, and he had been wanting to see what he called "Moondawg's Speakeasy." I had been bugging Moondawg for a while to let me bring out another friend, and he finally conceded that I could. So I picked Mark up in Memphis, drove him out to Frazier, took off his blindfold, and headed to the backyard to show him the bar.

That day, the bar was pretty empty. Moondawg was blankly watching wrestling with the sound down, and Zeke Logan's radio show was providing the sound track. Mark looked around and said, "Nice place." Then he turned to Moondawg and said, "Can I get a beer?"

"Sure, over there in the icebox. Grab me one, too."

The only other guy at the bar was skinny and homeless looking. Moondawg wasn't really paying any attention to him. The guy had Salvation Army shorts, shoes, and socks on, and his ankles were scratched and bleeding. They weren't scabbed: They were freshly bleeding, like he'd just run through some cactus maze or something. Like he'd been running from something that day, but nobody asked him about it at Moondawg's.

Nobody at Moondawg's ever mentioned much of anything.

They didn't mention that the bloody ankles guy with the ratty hair and beard was playing a harpsichord. He was a terrible harpsichord player, or maybe I just didn't understand the new direction he was taking the instrument.

Mark and I drank our beers. And then that guy stopped playing his harpsichord, turned to Mark, and said, "You know, we don't have to be ashamed about anything we did over there."

Mark looked at me with surprise, as if he wanted confirmation that he had not spoken to the guy. Then he looked at the guy and said, "Over where?"

The guy reached into the pocket of his stonewashed shorts and pulled out his Vietnam draft notice, and the first thing I thought about was how many pockets that notice must have passed through to end up in those stonewashed shorts.

Mark and I looked at each other like we were on the *X-Files* or some deal where Rod Sterling would come out, and then that guy said, "A bunch of rich white men in big houses with fences so high we'll never even see them, they're the ones who should feel bad about what we did over there, not us."

By this time, Mark and I were feeling like we might be witnessing something special and kind of moving. But we were also thinking that maybe we should get the fuck out of there. So we left, and we were on our way home when Mark said to me, "Did you see that guy, too?"

I said, "Yeah, and I think he might have been Jesus, man."

Mark said, "Yeah, I thought that, too. I bet it was Jesus. Let's pull over at a pay phone and call and let Moondawg know that Jesus is sitting right there in his toolshed."

I thought that was a good idea.

I got on the pay phone and called, and Moondawg picked up the line.

"Hey, Moon, it's Todd. Listen, we really think that might be Jesus out there at the bar."

Moondawg immediately said, "Thank God!"

I said, "What do you mean?"

He said, "Well, after you guys left I went inside and took a piss, and by the time I got back old Jesus had taken every last penny out of the till. I was pissed, because I thought he was gonna take that $47 and spend it on crack. At least now I know it'll go to some good use. Maybe it'll help a poor person or something."

Having taken Moondawg's songwriting advice to heart and mind, I wound up writing a song about all those characters in Frazier. The song was written to try to redeem the last song, and to this day that air conditioner repair guy who could burn blisters onto his hands without flinching, he's still pissed that he's not in the second song, which is called "Double Wide Blues."

DOUBLE WIDE BLUES
By Todd Snider

V-neck T-shirt with a mustard stain
Rolling up a hose outside in the rain
He's been my neighbor since '79
'Course he was in prison most of that time
Ever since then he ain't been right
His old lady works days, and they fight most nights
Laid off and blown off, pissed off on booze
Double wide blues

Metallica song blasting from three trailers down
It's them cut-off T-shirt and nunchuk kids coming around
Tonight they'll get drunk and try to get laid
End up in a fight out behind the arcade
You know, one of them little shits broke my window last spring
I told his mama, but she didn't do anything
She works two jobs, the boy runs loose
Double wide blues

My buddy Jimmy, his trailer's cool
He's got him a deck with one of them blue plastic pools
Works in construction, builds spec homes
His woman left him, though, so now he's down there alone
My friend, Anita, she loves him, he don't know
So busy chasing my neighbor's wife, Flo
Soap opera heaven, without all the clues
Double wide blues

Wild Bill the manager keeps to himself
The war took his smile like them pills took his health

Too old to run with the Klan anymore
Still got a big ol' U.S. flag hanging outside his door
I sit here watching all this nothing go on
I don't get out much since mama's been gone
Sometimes it's nice having nothing to lose
Double wide blues

Moondawg liked that song, and I liked that he liked it. It meant that I knew he knew I was listening and watching and thinking about the people around me. When I was in Frazier, those were also the people around Moondawg. He'd opened Moondawg's Tavern because he didn't want to drink alone, or be alone. He gave us a community and gave a lot of people a way to break through the double wide blues.

———

Moondawg died, and I don't want you to get too sad about that, because he wasn't afraid to die, and he lived a good life and had the best funeral I personally have ever been to. At Moondawg's funeral, we had wife-beater T-shirts and work shirts, and coolers of beer and a barbecue grill and people drinking coffee out of refill mugs that you get at the gas station. The guy with the snake was there, and there was a group of kids in rock band T-shirts pulling a bird apart behind a park bench. And the air conditioner/smoking hand guy was there, too. He didn't do that trick at the funeral, both because it would have been disrespectful and because everybody there already knew the trick, so they weren't willing to wager. Someone told me Jesus showed up, but, as usual, no one could prove it.

Anyway, it was a great funeral. Moondawg's sister got up and said, "Moondawg told me one day that he didn't want anyone to say anything about him at his funeral. He just wanted me to play you these three songs in this particular order."

I braced for Skynyrd, but the first song was "Please Don't Bury Me" by John Prine. That's the one where Prine gives instructions for how we should divvy up his body after he's gone: "Give my stomach to Milwaukee, if they run out of beer," Prine says. And he says to give his knees to the needy and his feet to the footloose, and that we should send his mouth way down south and kiss his ass good-bye.

The next song was "Big Time" by Keith Sykes, a great song written by a Memphis hero. And then came the last song, "Moondawg's Tavern." The song I wrote for him, that he said sucked. Hearing that song made me think that maybe Moondawg liked it more than he let on. Or maybe he just thought it was funny that everyone had to listen to it now except him, 'cause he was dead.

After my song—his song—ended, we had a long procession of cars, and everyone whose lights worked turned them on, and we headed to Moondawg's Tavern to sprinkle his ashes in the yard, just like he'd requested.

We didn't have a police escort, at least at first. But after a little trouble, we got to the tavern and spread his ashes, and then we drank beer and told stories and time started getting away. Then my friend and guitar player Will Kimbrough reminded me that we were supposed to be recording in Memphis at that moment, and that our record company had only given us half a day off for the funeral. We were already due back.

So we had to go.

And we decided to bring everyone from Moondawg's with us.

Which nobody at the studio except me thought was a good idea.

But what the hell? You choose your battles, right? That's all that phrase says. Doesn't say you have to choose them wisely. I thought we were all too drunk to get any recording done, anyway, though that proved not to be the case.

That afternoon, we recorded a song that I had just finished, called "Can't Complain." We all huddled into Ardent Studios in Memphis, where ZZ Top, U2, Stevie Ray Vaughan, John Prine, The Boxtops, and a million others have recorded. This was probably the only time, though, that Ardent had played host to a guy who could hold a lit candle to his hand for five minutes at a time. Not sure what their policy was on snakes. Somehow, somebody got everyone to be quiet for nearly as long as the air conditioner guy could smoke up his hand. And I spoke into a microphone, "I'd like to dedicate this song to my friend Michael "Moondawg" Webb, Wreck of Honor and King of Frazier." Then we played "Can't Complain."

CAN'T COMPLAIN
By Todd Snider

> A little out of place, A little out of tune
> Sort of lost in space, racing that moon
> Climbing the walls of a hurricane
> Still overall, I can't complain
>
> All I wanted was one chance to let freedom ring
> They said I had to get a permit, bunch of tags and
>   everything
> I never made it through the red tape, I got this paper hat
> Got a job working weekdays, You want fries with that?

I got nothin' to lose, there's nothin' to gain
It's like a one-way ticket to cruise in the passing lane
I can't complain

I was talking to my girlfriend, told her I was stressed
I said "I'm going off the deep end," she said, "God, for once,
   give it a rest"
We're all waiting in the dugout, thinking we should pitch
How you gonna throw a shutout, if all you do is bitch

I got nothin' to lose, nothin' to gain
It's like a one-way ticket to cruise in the passing lane
I can't complain

Now I got a brand new dance, I need one more shot
I just need one last chance, you know I won't get caught
I'm gonna make my last stand, this time I can't be bought
Then again, on the other hand, how much have you got?

I've got nothing to lose, 'cause there's nothing to gain
It's like a one-way ticket to cruise in the passing lane
I can't complain

CHAPTER 17

HUGS AND DRUGS

By now, you know I'm pretty open to drugs, and I'm not sorry about that. Plus, I don't care what happens to your children.

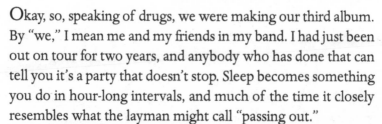

Okay, so, speaking of drugs, we were making our third album. By "we," I mean me and my friends in my band. I had just been out on tour for two years, and anybody who has done that can tell you it's a party that doesn't stop. Sleep becomes something you do in hour-long intervals, and much of the time it closely resembles what the layman might call "passing out."

It's easy to understand why. You're in your twenties. You're on the road, so your bed's about fifty feet away from you. You never sober up, so there's no hangover involved. You're with your friends, playing music and drinking all day and smoking miles of dope. The dope was our main shit, but we'd do whatever else you gave us. We just wouldn't go chasing the other stuff around.

But something was feeling funny, and not in the way that everything seems funny when you're smoking dope. I was feeling like the things I'd never dared to dream were coming true, and that things I had accepted were not going to happen to me were actually happening. That's supposed to be good, right? At the very least, it's not supposed to make you want to sort of obliterate yourself. As I look back on it, I didn't yet know what John Prine was going to show me about making up songs, so my job was still composed primarily of grabbing at things, which can make your life a little uncertain. I don't know if I had really stopped to ask myself why I was making up songs, even. Because I saw some guy sing in a bar in Texas? That didn't seem like a fully legitimate reason.

I wasn't sure about anything, except I was probably sure that our band was really good. I'm much less sure about that now, although sometimes people who come to my shows tell me that I was certainly better back then.

And there I was, making that third record, on the brink of something. I had just gotten on with Prine's manager and was starting to feel what I now know to be the weight of a choice whether to grow up or not, which is a choice you have to make every couple of years. The way I understand it now, you always have to choose "not." The older you get, the more times you make this choice, the more people will tell you that you should be responsible all the time and take everything seriously. That would—of course you know this—defeat the purpose of the whole fucking thing. I am devout about next to nothing, but I am devoutly not going to allow myself to grow up. I believe with all my soul that not growing up is going to be the best way to contribute to the world the best way I can. The alternative wasn't going to help me in any way or make any of my songs better. Even then, I think I sensed that chasing sanity or money isn't part of this shit. There's no money in chasing money in this line of work. I've seen people try it. I agree with what Aaron Allen said about being able to move all your shit in fifteen minutes: there is a flying-into-the-sun element of this.

That said, you've got to be careful. Fame has pressures, even at the lowest level. And while there was nobody in my life at this time pressuring me to reach for a brass ring, there were people who were naturally assuming that's what I was doing. And there was nothing I could say that would change that assumption. There was something about the swirl of it all that made me feel like medicating, in a big way.

When we were in Memphis, making this album called *Viva Satellite*, they put the whole band in a big house together, and I asked the guy who owned the house if he had any pot. He didn't, but suggested I try morphine.

We were scheduled to start recording on a Monday. On Sunday, I drove to Nashville and took that morphine. It hit while I was driving back to Memphis. I couldn't feel my back, which had moments before been hurting real bad. I couldn't feel anything bad. I felt everything good. At that very moment, I thought, "I should be on this all the time. I should never not be on this.'"

I went back to the guy who owned the house and bought about thirty hits of morphine. Then I went to the studio and nodded out.

That, my brothers and sisters, was that. I was on it. And when you're on it, it's a big commitment to get off it. After you've taken two, it's a pretty serious bummer to stop. The pains in your back and your heart are gone, and doing any-thing to encourage them to return seems senseless.

That's the upside of morphine. Believe it or not, there's a downside. It brings out your bullshit courage, and you find yourself arguing with someone at a grocery store over some-thing crazy, because you have no natural (and helpful) fear of confrontation.

I made that *Viva Satellite* record that way, and a couple of other records, too. We were all smoking and drinking, had built our own private bar, and were having a blast. The whole thing should have been much more fun than it really was. I was trying to make up songs and getting caught up in songs that were less linear and more complicated than the ones on the first two albums. There is a drawback to this complication: if someone asks you what a song of yours is about and you don't have an answer, you might be in possession of a song that's not really about anything. I was probably in trouble, and probably it was the creeping realization of that trouble that was making me nervous and paranoid. I mean, it certainly couldn't have been the pot and morphine.

During the recording, I got the idea that I should proba-bly go to rehab. I had only been on the morphine a couple of months, but I knew I was in over my head. Morphine isn't easy to hang onto, and you have to go further and further down into the world to get it. Also, it's not long after you come down before the itching and the throwing up start, and that triggers what I think experts call an "I don't want to do this anymore" impulse. I was dating Jimmy Buffett's niece at the time, and she helpfully suggested a rehab place she had heard about in Arizona. The day we wrapped the album, I got on a plane and flew out there to rehab.

The first night, I met this girl who had been on some kind of camping trip with her father, and they woke up to a huge fire in their camp. They were in a quick dash to try to get away from the fire, and they jumped in a raft. As they were shoving the raft into the stream, she fell out. And as her father drifted off in the raft, away from the fire, her father yelled, "You idiot!" She got burned, but the worst part was the thing where she realized her dad didn't care about her. Not everybody cares about their kids. I know I don't care about yours.

Wait, I'm sorry.

I do. Starting now.

In the rehab place, but before the actual rehab, they give you drugs to get off drugs. Then they taper you off those drugs, and that takes about seven days. You just lie there in a hospital bed. You're sick, but I've been sicker plenty of times since then.

When I got out of the bed, I got to go into the rehab part. It felt like coming back into the world, a little bit. Right away, I saw a girl whom I was instantly convinced I was going to marry. I saw her from sixty yards away. She was having lunch with her friends. I was having a cig, saw her, and thought, "Holy shit." After that, I spent less time thinking about staying off drugs and more time thinking of some way to work my way in with that chick. She was beautiful. Still is.

There comes a day pretty early on in the "back-into-the-world" phase where you sit in a circle with a bunch of people and talk about what happened to you. It's a pretty hilarious process, mostly because everybody's stories about what they did when they were fucked up are so great. It's a storyteller's paradise. "I got fucked up and ended up on a boat to Italy," some guy will say. Then he'll talk about how beautiful Italy was, and then he'll talk about how grateful he is not to be drunk anymore. "It was so depressing," he'll say. "I was with these three chicks I didn't even know. Models. It was getting crazy." No, it was getting good.

So you hold hands in this circle and talk about your family. The girl I thought I was going to marry one day was in the group. There was a sweet older woman, who was very matronly. She never said much, and we didn't even know exactly why she was in there. Another girl's father was the editor of a newspaper in Los Angeles, and she was a mess. Everybody, I guess, was a mess, on account of they were there in Arizona together. Sex addicts and drug addicts and food thrower-uppers, and all of us there in the desert with a pool and a hot tub and walking trails.

In this group of messes, there was one woman who had a really, really weird energy. She liked to make sure that everyone knew her husband was famous, and she got a kick out of not saying who he was. Then she got a secondary kick out of giving everyone a clue that no one asked for: "All I can tell you is his initials are 'P. H.'"

I tried to spend most of my energy where I was already spending most of my time, which was talking to the beautiful chick I now wanted to marry. She didn't know I was a singer, but she told me that her favorite ones were Neil Young and Bob Dylan, and I had a feeling my occupation was going to work in my favor.

Rehab wound down, though not without incident, right up to the end. On my day to get out of rehab, five of us were supposed to put our luggage in a van that would take us to the airport. We got our stuff in there, and then all of a sudden the van took off, the back doors opened, and everybody's luggage flew out. That van hauled ass. It was that old lady that never said a word: she stole the van, and then I guess went off and got fucked up. So we had to take a different car to the airport.

The day after I got home from rehab, I told my friend Joe that I was in love with a chick I'd met in rehab, at the place Jimmy Buffett's niece had found for me. That niece and I were due to go to Joe's wedding together, right after that. Joe said he thought a joint might help me relax, and he was right. It helped me relax.

I drove back home to my place in Fairview, Tennessee, and I didn't quite really break up with Jimmy Buffett's niece. That's the worst way to break up with somebody: just don't call, and don't take her calls.

Other than that, and some other awful shit I've done, I'm a pretty good guy.

But I was in love with the girl I had met in rehab. Her name was Melita. Still is. I went to New York to see her and talked her into moving to Fairview with me. Then I talked her into going out on the road with me. One day, we were flying from somewhere to Texas. Melita and I got on the plane and took our seats near the back. Just as the plane started to taxi, the baby in front of us just started screaming. We looked at each other and then walked up four seats to get away from the baby. It wasn't ours, so this didn't seem like a bad thing to do. We sat back down and buckled back up.

This guy behind me tapped me on the shoulder and said, "Hey, you're not supposed to switch seats when the plane is taxiing."

I said we knew that, but that the baby was crying and it wasn't our baby and we thought we'd move up. He repeated himself, more aggressively. "I don't think you understand. You're not supposed to do that under any circumstances."

I said, "Listen man, you don't have to take off your normal shoes and put on your clown shoes over this."

Boy, he did not like that.

Next thing I knew, a flight attendant guy said, "That man you just insulted was a pilot."

I said, "Well, I'm a singer."

He said, "Well, we're kicking you off the plane."

I thought, "No shit!" and Melita laughed.

We were the next plane to take off, or would have been if it weren't for the baby and the clown shoes and all that. They backed the plane up, took it all the way back to the terminal, and people were pissed. They didn't know why this was happening. They just knew somebody had caused some shit.

They pulled up to the terminal, and a cop walked into the plane. We were still in our seats, sort of mulling the situation over, and they said, "We're not leaving with you."

They'd pulled the little tube thing out to connect the terminal to the plane, which I was told made things official and made debate useless. So we stood up to leave with the cop, and that's when people realized we were the people who caused the plane to go back to the terminal.

That's when the booing started.

The whole fucking plane started booing. And my beautiful wife lifted both her arms, and then she lifted two middle fingers. I did, too.

We headed toward the door, saying, "Go fuck yourself" and "fuck you" to the people while they were booing.

Then we got off the plane, and I again tried to explain why it wasn't my fault. I had revenge fantasies mixed with delusion for awhile, and I might even have told somebody that my two-hundred-seat concert was going to be a two-thousand-seat concert and that I was going to tell everybody about Southwest Airlines. But by then Southwest Airlines had passed us off to airport security, and airport security said we had to get out of the airport and that the best thing we could do was rent a car.

We rented a car and drove a long time, until we got to the town where the gig was. We went straight to sound check and then checked into the hotel. Melita got in the shower, and I sat on the hotel bed and flicked on the television. The news came on, and the big story that day was that a comedian named Phil Hartman had been murdered in his home.

And after the baby and the clown shoes and the police escort and the long drive and the sound check, as soon as they said, "Phil Hartman" I immediately thought, "P. H."

Before I could even finish that thought, there was her photo. She killed him, and she killed herself. I yelled for Melita, and she hurried out of the shower, and we sat on the hotel bed and cried. This wasn't just a person on television. We'd known this girl, and it was all tremendously sad.

I remember going to the gig that night, and they were having some kind of celebration because our song had been added to some radio station. There was a cake about it. But we were raw and kind of numb at the same time. We had just experienced the horrible end to a horrible story. This woman had tried to get better, and it hadn't worked. She'd talked in rehab about her asshole husband who she said didn't care about her. And now she'd killed him, and killed herself. She never really came out the other side of her anger and her depression and her addiction.

Which is why, like I was saying earlier, I hope your kids never take morphine.

CHAPTER 18

COME ON IN,
THE WATER'S FREEZING

As may be apparent from some of the previous chapters, I don't often get asked to talk to young people. Sometimes I get told not to. And the young people who come to me for advice—me, of all people—are pretty much ruined. It's over. If they are young singers, a lot of times I can't help at all. How to make your record or how to write your songs? I have no idea. What's our goal? Why are we even doing this? I don't even want to ask those questions.

Young singers sometimes think it's about making people like you, but it's not. It's about how many people you can get to decide whether or not they like you. That's what you have to do to fill your refrigerator. Do it every day, nine to five.

You are not trying to be liked. You are trying to be judged, as often as you possibly can, so you can keep your refrigerator full.

If I was better at what I did, people would say nastier things about me.

So the most famous singers ought to be the thickest skinned, right? Nope, I think the reason these people are famous, and the reason you like to hear them sing, is 'cause they're so sensitive. They're thin skinned, and you can watch and listen right through their skin, and that's a fun thing to do. So now to do well you've got to be able to accept people judging you, and you've got to be extra-sensitive. Which is kind of like being really good at catching soup or at using chopsticks.

The truth of this is that you asked someone—everyone—to feel something. And if they do feel something, you do not get to control what that feeling is. Whether it's a fan, your mom, a journalist, or the paper boy, you sing them your song and ask them to feel. Don't be a dick and try to control what and how they feel after that. Do the world a favor and leave those people alone. They already did you the favor of listening to your whole fucking song. Now you want to tell them to do something else? Or you want to be angry because they did what you asked them to do? Jesus Christ.

When my first record came out, I saw a review of myself. The writer began with, "I hate Todd Snider." That was the first line of the review. It got me past my waist into the water. Come on in, kid, the water is freezing. "I hate Todd Snider, and I'm about to tell you why," was the full first line, in a San Diego newspaper article that was supposed to be previewing my show. When's the last time someone told you they hated you, un-ironically? Teenage girls don't count.

I wrote a letter back to the person who wrote that review. I still have the letter. I pull it out and read it when I need to feel embarrassed for myself. As it turns out, I was not—am not—the kind of person who can naturally handle being told I suck. People like me will know what I mean. We're the kind of people who can rhyme how bad we felt when we were dumped by our girlfriends. That comes easy, but the longer game, the life's journey, is to learn how to handle what the lady in the San Diego paper or anybody else says about what we rhymed about how bad we felt getting dumped, and we have to learn to handle it without rhyming our feelings about the person who judged us. More to the point: the person we asked to judge us.

Very few artists finish the song about how their critics don't understand them.

It gets uncomfortable when someone makes me feel like what I'm doing isn't worthwhile or of value. But here's the thing: they get to say whatever they want to say to us. Even the guy who threw a beer at you paid to get in. You get to keep his money, and sometimes you get to drink the rest of his beer for free. And sometimes, he actually bought the beer for you and brought it to you, and the part where he threw it at you was your imagination.

Even when that beer bottle seems to be coming at you, it's not yours to know why it's coming at you. Sing. That's yours. That's what you want to do, right? Sing. Don't be a bitch.

This is earned wisdom. You're hearing this from a guy who has walked off a stage more than any of his buddies have. You're hearing this from a guy who didn't learn this until he was in his forties. I'm not preaching or bragging; I'm just saying. You can gain wisdom from experience, sure. That's how it's supposed to work. But it shouldn't take as long as it's taken me. I should have gotten it about the seventy-seventh time. Some mornings, I'll look around until I find something shitty someone said about me. I'll do this before I start my art. I don't do this to get angry or to get motivated. I like to give somebody the freedom to think whatever they want, and that allows me to be free to do whatever I want to.

Getting knocked is sometimes, now, for me, the fuel that creates. It's not the hurt or the anger that turns into the fuel. It's accepting the knock. It's not listening to and learning from it, it's hearing it and not getting mad or thinking of things to say that would force or shame that person into thinking that they think what they think because they're not as smart as you. And then not saying it to them.

I met these surfer kids once, and they imparted some philosophy. They told me that when you surf, you don't have a goal, and it doesn't go good or bad. You just do it. You get in the water, and you don't ask the water to do anything different than it's doing. You don't ask the sun to be warmer. You just get in the water, because you want to be in the water. You surf. It doesn't go well, or go poorly. It goes.

Riding one is no less fun than falling off one at the top. And if you don't think so, go do something else. If being booed isn't as fun as being cheered, find another gig.

I got booed once opening for Hootie & The Blowfish. It was exhilarating. Then there was a show in Carbondale, Illinois, when I left because people were grabbing at me, and not in a teen idol way. I was terrified, and it was exhilarating. I'm excited that my life took me into a fight or flight situation (I chose flight), and I try not to judge what happened. It was fun and exciting, and better than when I was busing tables.

Making up songs, critics will tell people that you've done well or poorly. Again, these are the critics that you have asked—begged, really—to have an opinion. And then they give you one, if you're lucky. A bad review is a good review. The worst review they can give you is no review at all, and that's the one they give almost everybody.

I have just written many things right here about how to handle reviews philosophically. That said, I sure am hoping people like this book. For one-star reviews, revenge will be swift. Because writing a book is way, way different than making up songs. I can totally see how authors go off the hook and get pissed. We're kind of a cut above the rest of y'all, and sometimes we get sick of listening to your drivel.

Let's go back to San Diego, and to the review that hated me, which went on to say that a song of mine called "You Think You Know Somebody" was phony, and that at the bottom of all of my work you could see a guy wanting to be liked. Almost everybody wants to be liked. But what difference does that make? None. None of the other people wanting to be liked paid a person to go out and find other people so that the other people would judge them (you) in public.

Just you, you're the only one who did that.

So the person judging you thinks you just want to be liked? You asked for their opinion, and you got it. They hate you, and they just told you why.

And you should be grateful. You're on the road singing.

Sounds like you might have a gig going. Singing gigs end, but they don't end because a girl hates you. That doesn't mean her opinion is invalid. But your opinion of her opinion is kind of invalid. And I wish I'd known that a long time ago. 'Cause if I had, maybe I could have gotten some motivational speaking engagements, talking to young people about surfing and dropping out of school and doing drugs.

High five.

CHAPTER 19

EAST NASHVILLE
SKYLINE

I have pain in my back and heart, so something called a "pain-killer" was bound to appeal. For a time, I let those pills become the second most important thing in my life, next to my marriage. When did it happen? Well, I can tell you. After I did an album called *Happy to Be Here*, I got obsessed with soul music that came out on a Memphis label called Stax Records, stuff by Otis Redding and Wilson Pickett and people like that. I also got obsessed with being numbed out on painkillers. Right away, I noticed that these pills aren't named very accurately, because they don't actually kill the pain. They are pain-maskers that also somehow manage to make you, the person taking the pills, become accustomed to the mask to the point where you need it all the time. When the mask starts to wear off, you've got to put it right back on. It's not as dramatic as it sounds. It can go on for years, and often does. Some people live their whole lives on these pills, with those masks.

I was one of them, for a little while. I decided the painkillers were so good that I didn't want to drink or smoke, or do much of anything else. That lasted about six weeks, and during those six weeks I discovered and completely fell in love with songs by Randy Newman. Will Kimbrough gave me a Newman record called *Bad Love*, and to this day it blows my mind. He came to play in Nashville, and I went to the show, and the day after that I went to the record store and bought every Randy Newman album.

So there I was, wearing my mask, discovering great music that changed me for the better. The only trouble with my life of Otis and Randy and pills was that I wasn't writing. One night at the Leaping Frog Inn in Calaveras County, California, I decided to smoke a joint and have a beer. The first night I smoked, I wrote a song. The next day, we played Santa Cruz at the Fat Fry, which is a festival that the best radio station in the world, KPIG, puts on. At that festival, I wrote a song called "Beer Run" during my friend Robert Earl Keen's set. The next day, I wrote another one, called "New Connection." That's when I decided to quit quitting pot and everything else.

"Beer Run" actually started with something a bass player named Keith Christopher said when we were recording. We ran out of beer, and Keith said, "B double E, double r-u-n, beer run!" I said, "Can I have that for a song?" and he said I could. So I did. Watching Robert Earl at the Fat Fry, I saw a couple of kids in the crowd who looked like they'd come from Texas and looked like they were expecting a little different concert than the one they were getting.

Robert Earl's concerts in Texas are full of college kids who sing along. In Santa Cruz, it's older people who smoke pot and listen closely. These kids weren't sure what to make of it. They seemed like they wanted to take their get-drunk-and-sing-along energy and impose it on the crowd, which can be a fun thing to do: I know this from experience. But it didn't work. I watched them kind of give up on that and dial into what was happening in Santa Cruz. In my head, I started making up this idea that somebody had gotten them stoned, and soon I had a song. I played it for Robert Earl, because it talks about him and I wanted to make sure he saw it as the honor I was trying to make it. I sing it as a love song to Santa Cruz and KPIG and Robert, not as a song about beer. And some people assume for some reason that I don't like that song, but I have just as much of an emotional attachment to that as to any of the other songs I have made. The words go like this:

BEER RUN
By Todd Snider

> B double E double R-U-N beer run
> B double E double R-U-N beer run
> All we need is a ten and a five-er
> A car and a key and a sober driver
> B double E double R-U-N beer run
>
> A couple of frat guys from Abilene
> Drove out all night to see Robert Earl Keen
> At the KPIG Swine and Soiree dance

They wore baseball caps and khaki pants
They wanted cigarettes, so to save a little money
They bought one off this hippie that smelled kinda funny
The next thing they knew, they were pretty hungry
And pretty thirsty, too

B double E double R-U-N beer run
B double E double R-U-N beer run
All we need is a ten and a five-er
A car and a key and a sober driver
B double E double R-U-N beer run

They found a store with a sign that said their beer was coldest
So they sent in Brad 'cause he looked the oldest
He got a case of beer and a candy bar
Walked over to where all the registers are
Laid his fake ID on the counter top
The clerk looked and turned to look back up and stopped
He said, "Son, I ain't gonna call the cops
But I'm gonna have to keep this card."
The guys both took it pretty hard

B double E double R-U-N beer run
B double E double R-U-N beer run
Oh how happy we would be
Had we only brought a better fake ID.
B double E double R-U-N beer run

They met another old hippie named Sleepy John
Claimed to be the one from the Robert Earl song
So they gave him all their cash, he bought 'em some brews
Was a beautiful day out in Santa Cruz

They were feelin' so good it should have been a crime
The crowd was cool and the band was prime
They made it back up front to their seats just in time
So they could sing with all their friends
"The road goes on forever and the party never ends."

B double E double R-U-N beer run
B double E double R-U-N beer run
All we need is a ten and a five-er
A car and a key and a sober driver
B double E double R-U-N beer run

Before I recorded "Beer Run," I played it on a syndicated radio show called *Bob & Tom* in Indianapolis. It was the original morning zoo show, funny guys who like to have musicians on. So I played "Beer Run" on their show and, as they say in show business, the phone lines lit up. They kept playing that recording of me playing it on their show, and people started asking me for it, and then I put it on a record called *New Connection*.

Most people go into art because wherever they are and whatever they're doing, they don't feel heard or understood.

From the outside looking in, this job I do looks just like a can't-miss opportunity to be heard and understood. It is my experience that my job can help people be heard, but that what usually happens is the complete opposite of being understood. Then the artists either kill themselves or find out that their art, rather than helping them be understood, actually taught them to accept being misunderstood. The key to my job is understanding that I'm not going to be understood the way I want to, even though I signed up because I wanted to be understood, and learning to accept that disparity. It's not the easiest thing to swallow, that one. It's easier to swallow than a shovel and a ditch, but not as easy as something else I'm great at, like karate. The sad part in "Beer Run" is that I feel an element of Robert Earl's pain, standing up there while these little dramas go on among all the people who are crowded around by the stage, not understanding him. Also, there's something a little sad—to me, though it doesn't have to be to you—about those kids. They went a long, long way out of their way to try to escape their reality. Maybe it's sad to me that people have to find a way to escape their reality, when they could just mask it with little pills.

After that "Beer Run" song came out, for the first time since I started singing there'd be some college kids coming by and mixing in with the liberal, NPR types and the pot-smoking hippies who came to listen and scratch their chins. I didn't mind these alpha male types coming by, and it was easy to predict what they were going to want to talk with me about. It was "Beer Run." Sometimes they'd yell things about it during my show, and I didn't mind that, either. People have been yelling at me during my shows since I was twenty. I'm not wild about people yelling at me when I'm at home, but if you pay that money to come into the show, you can do whatever the fuck you want to do. If the police come up to you, maybe you've gone too far, but only too far for the police, not too far for me.

The only thing that got on my nerves a little bit about "Beer Run" wasn't the fault of the college kid who thought I would really like it if he yelled "Beer Run" the whole time. You know damn well that kid wasn't trying to bum anyone out. He thought everyone was going to like him yelling for that song, or he wouldn't have yelled for it. What bugged me was the other people who would naturally assume those kids were "ruining the shows" for me, and who would roll their eyes in scorn at the kid who was just trying to have fun.

I have yelled at Jerry Jeff Walker. Judge the judgmental, and what am I?

And you can yell at me, that's for motherfucking sure. And you can sure as motherfucking sure yell at me to play songs. When I make up some song and someone asks me to play that song and I know how it goes, there's not going to come a day when I'm not going to play it. I've got more songs than I can play every night, so everybody spends a little time on the bench on our team, but I don't have any songs I don't like to play.

I was watching the Giants play the Dodgers, which is never a nonimportant game. You may occasionally have gotten the idea from these pages that I am a little hard on sports. But baseball's not a sport. It's an art. I will not argue this point. If you try to argue with me, I will reply with a fart.

Another one, even.

While I was watching that game, the phone rang, and it was Al Bunetta. Al is John Prine's manager, and he was running the record label I was on, which was called Oh Boy. He was concerned, because there was a new song, just out, by George Jones and Garth Brooks. It was called "Beer Run." He thought we had a pretty good case to get money or something, because we'd already had a song out called "Beer Run."

I was not concerned. I was financially well-off enough to have the special baseball package that lets you see all the Giants games on TV, and, anyway, Tom T. Hall said if you get your song stolen you should think of it as a compliment: you've just written something worth stealing. Maybe you can do it again.

To be clear, I am not saying anyone stole the song Keith Christopher and I made up. I'm saying that the idea that someone stole that song was presented to me on the telephone while I was watching a baseball game.

I told Al that I didn't care what happened, so long as I didn't have to get dressed up and go to town or have dinner with somebody I didn't know. I'd rather sing for money than dine for money. Also, I was thrilled. You mean something's coming out of the mouth of George Jones, the greatest country singer of all time, that might have something to do with me? Shit. An honor. And Garth Brooks, a nice guy who also happened to have sold more country records than anyone in the history of history, was singing a song with the same title as the one I was singing? Great.

I don't know what all Al did about any of this, but when he came back he told me he'd met with some people, and it had been decided that nobody took anything from anybody. Turns out different songs can have a certain amount of the same notes, and you can't copyright a title. That was great with me, the guy who completely took the melody from Arlo Guthrie's "Alice's Restaurant" because I had a story to tell that reminded me of "Alice's Restaurant." Arlo Guthrie hasn't hassled me, even a little bit. I wish he would. I'd love to meet him.

A few years and one Giants World Series title later, I was with my friend Peter Cooper at an event in Nashville. We have events most every week in Nashville, where we honor ourselves. And then we have award trophy shows every couple of months, too, so you can watch us honor ourselves from the comfort of your own living room.

You're welcome.

I was grateful to be invited to be a part of a show honoring Tom T. Hall. Peter and I were in the green room, which is the little room I might have mentioned a while ago when I told you the Bill Elliott story. But at this show, because Tom T. was being honored, the green room was even splashier. The carrots were cut real funky cool, the towels weren't the same ones they use in the kitchen, and the ranch dip was fancier.

Also, they had whiskey, which Peter and I noticed right away. We were drinking the whiskey when Peter looked across the room and said, "Hey, I think that's the guy that wrote the other 'Beer Run' for George Jones and Garth Brooks."

I said, "Let's go hassle him."

I think Peter said that might not be a great idea, but it was hard to tell what he was saying 'cause of all the funky-cool carrots and gourmet ranch dip in his mouth.

I walked up to the guy and said, "I'm Todd Snider," and after I said my name, he said, "You wrote 'Beer Run' too."

In my mind, I thought, "Yeah, and you took it from me." So with my mouth, I said, "Yeah, you took it from me."

Actually, that's not what I said, though I've told people at my shows that's what I said.

What really happened is I kicked him in the balls and un-loaded my free whiskey in his face and had to be dragged out of there by my collar, as I screamed, "You rat prick, you owe me money and you will pay it to me someday!" He looked embarrassed, probably for himself.

Really, though, I just asked him about his other songs. I made him list a few of them off, and he had a shitload. He'd written a ton of great stuff, and one of his songs was a beau-tiful ballad that Garth Brooks had a big hit with, a song called "If Tomorrow Never Comes."

As Peter and I went off to get our drinks refreshed, I came up with an idea for a song of my very own. It's called "If Tomorrow Never Comes."

IF TOMORROW NEVER COMES
By Todd Snider

If tomorrow never comes
I won't give a damn
If tomorrow never comes
I will not be afraid to meet my maker
Just the way that I am
You can't prove anything
But one thing is true
If you can steal from me
I can steal from you

Any kind of heaven everybody doesn't get in
Won't seem like a heaven to me
They tell you that the Garden of Eden was perfect
But you couldn't even eat off the apple tree
And for heaven's sake look out for that snake
Lying to your woman constantly
Adam must have scratched his head
Looked up and said
Lord this just isn't doing it for me

If tomorrow never comes
I won't give a damn
If tomorrow never comes
I don't want to be afraid
To come and meet you just the way that I am
I can't do anything I'm dying too
If tomorrow never comes
Tonight will have to do

I say I don't ever claim to know what's going on around here
I don't even know where I'm from
I know where I'm going when I get to where I'm going
What I'm doing when I get done
You tell me I'm forgiven if I need to be
I say permission ought to come that easily
I'm piling cores up underneath this apple tree
Singing oh Lord have mercy on me

If tomorrow never comes
And tonight is all I got
If tomorrow never comes
I don't want to be afraid
To come and meet you just the way that I'm not
Can't do anything
And then you die
Judge the judgmental and what am I?

Either way I'm every guy I ever tried not to be
I want everything as good as it gets
I've learned nothing but that there is another sunrise coming
All but one of the times it sets

And if tomorrow never comes
Tomorrow never comes
If tomorrow never comes
Tomorrow never comes
If we were all good people
We could work in perfect rhythm
If worms had daggers
Birds wouldn't fuck with them

Okay, back to the painkillers.

I was traveling around and playing shows, and a producer named R. S. Field was helping me make a record called *New Connection*. We made that record, and I thought it was pretty good, because I was finally using some things John Prine had showed me about poetry and vulnerability. I wrote more love songs than I usually do, because I think a song from one person to another person about love or unrequited love is the height of depth. The politics stuff is shallower than that, even though some people see it the opposite way.

I didn't have a lot of input into that record, other than the songs and placing my trust in R. S. Field. That's the only time I said to the producer, "Do whatever you want, and call me when it's time to sing." I loved what he did, and he helped me find some musicians I'll stay with for the rest of my life. I was pretty out of it the whole time that record was being made. They said it took a long time to get the pot smell out of the basement where we recorded. Then when the record was done, I went on a tour and kept on with the painkillers and the pot. That two-year period, 2003 and 2004, those are the years that got me a reputation I'll carry with me right up until the day this book tops the best-seller list. After that, I'll be considered an erudite raconteur whose stories illuminate the hidden corners of the human experience. But until then, I'll be the loose cannon guy that Tommy Womack (my friend and great songwriter) tells people he saw gut a pigeon, smoke it, and then do a dance for Satan. Not true: I made Skip Litz gut the pigeon.

My tour manager at the time used to call me "Freak Show," because every time he'd come to my room there'd be weirder and weirder people there. With hard drugs, the places you have to go to get them makes your life a constant adventure traveling through what is inevitably going to be a disaffected, disenfranchised, dysfunctional social group. You are stepping into a world that's not technically allowed to exist. It's a little like the art world, because to get into this world you have to be broken. This was something I did for awhile. I'd wind up in some basement, with some guy with a nickname who was showing me his knife collection or his snake or something.

One night, we were in Florida, and I had been having stomach trouble. I played at a festival, and I went up and did my best, but when I got done they were booing. I couldn't believe it. I was sitting on the floor in the dressing room, stunned that this was happening. I told my tour manager, "Get me out of here, immediately." We jumped in the car and headed back to the hotel. The next day, I got the paper on the way to the airport, and they had a review of my show that said I had rudely blown off my encore to a roaring crowd. The next day, I went to a doctor, and then I went to sleep, and when I woke up I was in rehab again.

That time, rehab lasted about two weeks. After it, I had a couple of other relapses. They'd give me different drugs to come down off the drugs I was on, and I wasn't very good about not taking the ones I wasn't supposed to take anymore. I kept nodding out during the recording of my next record, *East Nashville Skyline*, but I was there and awake a lot more than on the one R. S. Field helped me with. I was present this time, and I led. When we finished the album, I was supposed to go on a West Coast tour, one with well more than a dozen shows. I'd canceled a bunch of earlier shows because of the stomach thing, and this was supposed to be the triumphant return to sobriety and noncancellation. Getting ready for that, I was at home and mixed up the wrong drugs and some wine. I took the drugs I was supposed to take, then got a little drunk and took the drugs I wasn't supposed to take. And things swirled out of control from there.

I woke up in an ambulance. They were pounding on me. My wife was there, and she was crying because she thought I might die. That was the first time it really occurred to me in a deep way that this was affecting someone else. Ever since then, I have tried and so far not failed, to at least not get so reckless that I would die.

I went to sleep in the ambulance and woke up again in the hospital, with cops around me. They said I'd tried to kill myself, which is illegal. So I was in a lot of trouble. Also, the drugs I had were illegal.

But I had to do those shows. They were my triumphant return to sobriety. The morning after this happened, I went in front of a board of six doctors, and I explained to them what it would mean to me to miss those shows. They actually prescribed more drugs, enough to get me through that tour, because they knew I couldn't kick drugs out there. I had to promise to kick when I got home and to prove it with six months of piss tests.

The fear I'd seen from my wife was motivation for me.

I always thought that it was going to end soon. I was on a self-destructive thing that hadn't been very well thought out. I was doing what a lot of people do, and it was starting to get old, and I was starting to get old. I'd never counted on that.

When that record, *East Nashville Skyline*, came out, some people seemed to really like it. And there was a realization that I was on my sixth or seventh time around the country, and that more people were coming out than had come out before. It was starting to feel like this was going to be what I was going to do. Prine had told me that five albums make you a lifer. I'd done that, and it was starting to look like in spite of my best efforts that I hadn't derailed this thing. I'd finally made a record I didn't hear any crap about. I had no idea how I'd done it, and I knew I had to do it again.

Let me clarify. I'm not saying that I was a success, or that I am one now, or that there's any such thing. But some people think when you have some "success," that the success brings relief. It's usually almost the opposite. The night of the Super Bowl, the winning coach looks pretty happy. The next morning, he realizes that the best he can do is what he just did. Time to climb that mountain again, and what does that look like? Looks like a pain in the ass.

East Nashville Skyline was the first time I did exactly what I meant to on a record. It was the first time I found my own little thing. And so maybe I will admit that doing what you mean to do is some sort of success. But, again, success doesn't bring relief.

Drugs bring relief.

Tommy Womack did a record a few years back called *There, I Said It!*, and all his friends and people he'd never met told him it was the best thing he'd ever done. He got on the cover of the *Nashville Scene* newspaper.

Success, sure. Relief, surely not: He followed that one up with an album called *Now What?*

My next act involved red wine and reefer, and a fairly extended period of drama-free good times. No ambulance rides, for sure. I made up the next record, *The Devil You Know*, with a bunch of friends, most of whom lived in the neighborhood. And when we weren't making the record up, we were laughing a lot.

It took a while, but we made an album we all really liked. When it came out, other people said nice things about it, and reviews started appearing in some of the magazines I subscribe to. That's when I found out they still make you pay for the subscription, even when they're writing about you. End of the innocence.

We got asked to go on Jay Leno's *Tonight Show*, which was a ton of fun. We went out to Los Angeles, rehearsed for a day, met celebrities, and partied balls. Then we went to the studio, and Leno showed us his motorcycle. If this motorcycle had been a suit, it would have been one of those rhinestone jobs that the country stars used to wear. "That's a killer motorcycle," I told Leno.

"It's ridiculous. Absolutely ridiculous," Leno said, with a little shame in his voice.

When we got booked on Leno's show, I was very nervous. I grew up watching *The Tonight Show*, and sometimes I get a little (by "a little," I mean "overwhelmingly") starstruck. When we did the sound check, I never felt like I got fully acquainted with what was happening. During the show itself, I thought we played good. When they first announced my name, though, the screen went to a close-up of my face where I looked kind of Manson-y. And not Marilyn Manson, either. Charles. But that's what I look like. I have to walk around with that face all the time, but now it was being delivered to the nation via hi-def close-up.

You actually play the Leno show in the early afternoon. It happens very quickly in real time. Right before I went on, the guy who opened the curtain said, "If this goes well, maybe you can get some shoes." And then I was on—we were all on—and three minutes later, we were done.

After the show, we went up to the roof of the hotel where we were staying in Hollywood, and we played JJ Cale on a boom box and boogied down for hours, waiting for the show to come on the air at 11:30 p.m. LA time. We paid the security people some money to let us stay on the roof, but they still kicked us off after awhile. I went back to my room with a bunch of friends, and we danced a little bit and then passed out before the show and didn't see it. When we got home late the next day, though, everybody was looking at me weird and telling me I'd bugged my eyes out. But one of my heroes, Bobby Bare, also called and said he loved it. I'd never met him before.

If someone says to me, "You bugged your eyes out on Leno," I say, "Well, you didn't." That works great, but only for some of my friends.

The same day I got home and heard the complaints, someone else called and said David Letterman wanted me to be on his show. So I went on his show, and I thought that went well, too. But when I got home from that, everyone in the neighborhood said, "You spit on the stage. That's the Ed Sullivan Theater stage, where The Beatles played."

I didn't really spit, though. I wouldn't do that. I love the Beatles. And I love David Letterman, and the Top Ten List, and Biff Henderson and Mujibur and Sirajul. I wouldn't spit on that stage. Well, I wouldn't *spit* spit. I did have to spit my guitar pick out of my mouth, so I could play my harmonica. I put my pick in my mouth so I could reach down and get my harmonica, and then once I had my harmonica, I needed my mouth for that. So I spit my pick out. Come to think of it, I guess I could have just dropped my pick out of my hand.

So, to people who say, "You spit on the Letterman show," I say, "You didn't." That works both for people who have never been on Letterman and for people who were smart enough to drop their pick before playing their harmonica.

CHAPTER 20

HILARIOUS

It seems like a long time ago that I told you about Bob Mercer, who ran Jimmy Buffett's record company.

Bob Mercer was good to me. He never sold me a bill of goods. He sold me to other people as a bill of goods. Over the years, he lost a lot of other people's money on me. Which was fun, for me.

Bob's most-repeated word was "hilarious." He said it long and slow and British. When I'd have a tantrum and walk off-stage and try to quit the tour, he thought that was hilarious. When I'd make a record he liked, that was hilarious. When I'd show up late or without shoes, that was hilarious. When he'd convince a record company that I was worth signing and paying, that was hilarious.

After I did an album called *East Nashville Skyline*, he took me out to dinner with people I didn't know, from Universal Records, and he sold them on a bullshit deal that hinged on the idea that *East Nashville Skyline* had been reviewed well. Not that it had sold well, mind you. Just that it had been reviewed well. Look up the best-selling albums of all time, and you'll find stuff by Meat Loaf, Shania Twain, Celine Dion, and Britney Spears, and none of these was reviewed well. Look up the best-reviewed albums of all time, and you'll find a bunch of stuff you won't find in your best-selling albums search. The two categories don't overlap significantly. Getting a record contract based on "reviewed well" is like getting a wife based on "no significant criminal history." But that was the magic of Bob.

Bob was the guy I would call and talk to, even when other people were working in the "people I call and talk to" position. He managed me, even when I had other managers. When Bob wasn't officially managing, I'd talk to another manager, tell Bob what the other guy said, and Bob would tell me what to say back. He never left my life, though I worried that he would. When I left Margaritaville records and Jimmy Buffett, I came back to Bob and told him, "I think I may have made a mistake." Right away, he said, "No, this is good, and we're still family, and I'll still help you." Well, almost right away. The first thing he said was, "Hilarious."

At the dinner, Bob explained to the Universal Records people about how great the last record was, and how he couldn't even imagine what the new record was going to be about. Then he turned to me and said, "So, what's it about?"

I said I hadn't even started it yet.

He said, "Hilarious." But then, when some of the other guys were looking the other way, he leaned in and whispered into my ear, "Don't you dare dry up on me now, you little fucker."

I was in fact drying up on him, but then I undried. I wrote some new songs. I played them for my friend Peter Cooper, who said he liked them, and then I went into a studio and recorded some demos to send to Bob. The demos sort of evolved into a record. One of the songs was called "All That Matters," and we cut it first as a demo. Then we cut another version that somebody in the studio said might be better for radio, and Bob said to go with the demo version. He knew getting on the radio was not going to happen. If that had been a possibility, we might have gone with the radio version, got to the other end of that rainbow, and blown what money we made, gleefully. Hilariously, even.

One song, "Happy New Year," we tried to cut like a rocker. Bob said, "No, make it an acoustic thing. What difference does it make what you say if no one can hear you?"

The record we made was called *The Devil You Know*. From what people yell at me to play during concerts, *The Devil You Know* might be the album of mine that people liked the best. I don't argue with that or about anything people think about what I do or who I am. That part isn't up to me. I agree with everybody when they tell me what's good, or what I'm like, or how I sound. It would do me no good not to agree.

With *The Devil You Know*, I was excited that when it came out, my wife's painting got to be the album cover. Record companies usually want a close-up picture of your face on the cover, and I thought for sure that changing this and going with my wife's painting instead would be a sticking point. As it turned out, they were very quick to agree that maybe the cover shouldn't show my face, which was strange, because twelve years earlier, when my first album came out, they were all about my face. It couldn't have been the decade-plus years of touring. I know that for certain. I look like a goddamn angel.

It didn't make sense at all. Still, I was happy for Melita. Times change, I guess.

Making *The Devil You Know* was a good time. We got to be on TV. We made a movie. We drank a fuckload of wine. We had fireworks shows every Fourth of July, and we even made it snow one night in East Nashville. It was 52 degrees out, but we called the local TV station and told them there was a blizzard outside the Three Crow Bar. We weren't sure if they believed us until we saw that they were reporting it as fact, on the local news. There is a record of it snowing in East Nashville, on a night that it was impossible for it to have snowed. Whenever anyone says to me, "So I guess you're proud of yourself," this is the reason I can say, unreservedly, "Yes."

That said, I had a hard time making another record right after *The Devil You Know*. I was panicking sometimes and needed to get to the source of what it was that was making my life more difficult when it shouldn't have been. There was something eating at me, and part of it was that I was fighting overconfidence. Another part of it was that I was fighting underconfidence. I was writing down everything I saw, thinking that I could turn it into a song. And because *The Devil You Know* had done well, I was motivated to do well again. I felt like I had to beat myself, which hurts.

And so I made a record that never came out, called *Crank It, We're Doomed*. Bob Mercer said that might've been the best work I'd done, but nobody else in my camp liked it, at all. I include myself in that group. I was working on a bunch of songs, some about politics, some that were about stories, and some that were ridiculous rock music. I felt unmoored and uncertain, and there were changes all around me

So I turned to my manager, Burt Stein.

Bob had told me to go meet a guy who he then informed me would be my new manager. "He's named Burt Stein," Bob said. "Report to him on Monday."

I did. And that was years ago. Burt is a great guy, and he was the last real gift that Bob made me. He didn't send me to Burt with a casual sense of recommendation. It was more that he had picked Burt and that he was right to do so. And he was.

By this time I had a pile of more than twenty songs, but I was confused about what to do with them. "These are too political," I told Burt.

"Well, the political ones might be a lump, man," Burt said.

I said, "What if I put them in one album, and call it *Peace Queer?*"

He said, "Damn, now you have to do it."

So then we had the idea for a trilogy: first, the *Peace Queer* album with political songs, then the one full of stories, then the one full of ridiculous rock music. I told Bob about the trilogy idea, and he said, "Hilarious." I went over to Doug Lancio's studio and finished up *Peace Queer*, shot a cover photo showing Eric McConnell holding a gun to my head, and wrote a bio with a friend of mine who pretended to be network television reporter Cokie Roberts. Actually, he or she didn't pretend. And you can't copyright a name. Here is the bio that Cokie wrote:

PEACE QUEER, THE BIO
By Cokie Roberts

I was told to meet Todd Snider at the 3 Crow Bar at 1 o'clock in the afternoon. This was impossible, as Todd Snider was not at the 3 Crow Bar at 1 o'clock in the afternoon. But he showed up at 1:45, sweating and claiming to be followed. As Todd is not normally a paranoid person (ed. note: this is not true, he is quite paranoid), I wondered aloud whether his pursuers were angry that he is releasing *Peace Queer*, an album filled with politically charged, potentially divisive material.

He said, "No, that's not it at all. Actually, I was a little too close to that Tonya Harding and Nancy Kerrigan thing. For some of us, that'll never be over. Never."

None of which brings us to the matter at hand. I'm hired to do a job here. Swear to God, he's calling this thing *Peace Queer*. So I ask, why *Peace Queer*?

"What, too commercial?" he said. "I don't care. My intention is to outsell *Thriller*. And not just the Michael Jackson one. Ultimately, I believe this record will sell 6.8 billion copies. That's not one in every home. That's one in every hand. Well, roughly every other hand, 'cause most people have two hands. And on the day that happens, I guarantee America and parts of Canada world peace."

A pipe dream? Hardly, for fans of rock 'n' roll, folk, country and Americana music have long been held in Snider's sway. His last album, 2006's *The Devil You Know*, landed him on *The Tonight Show with Jay Leno* and *Late Night with David Letterman*, and it appeared on numerous year-end Top 10 lists. Sitting across from him at the 3 Crow, his personal charisma is in evidence.

And how.

The humble, youthful man from Beaverton, Oregon, is a real swashbuckler. And *Peace Queer* is just the beginning of his typically unique vision. It is the first in a trilogy. Even as we celebrate the release of *Peace Queer*, Snider is already working on the follow-up, with Rolling Stones producer Don Was. After that, there will be a rock album called *Shit Sandwich*.

"I'm gonna make it in real time," he said, his piercing blue-grey (sometimes they seem green, too) eyes shining towards a success-filled musical future.

For now, though, we're here to discuss *Peace Queer*. And *Peace Queer* is, assuredly, the bomb. The album's cover, which depicts Snider being held at gunpoint by a shirtless hippie, nods to the violence that is at the heart of all peaceful endeavors.

"Clearly, anyone who looks at the photograph can tell that I had been abducted by an international league of peace queers and forced to write protest music. You know, for their cause," he said. "But, write this down 'cause it's true and it's important: I grew sympathetic to their cause. In fact, the more often we paused for the cause the more sympathetic I grew. Maybe I was Patty Hearst shifted, but I don't care. I'm in. I believe in our mottos and can't wait to hear our slogan."

Indeed, the mottos are telling.

"Our first motto is 'Thou Shalt Not Kill,'" Snider explained. "Our second motto was, 'Thou Shalt Not Steal,' but then we realized we'd kind of lifted the first motto. So we dropped the second motto and just went with the one."

Peace Queer starts with revelry, and the album includes a Civil War sea shanty, a plaintive cover of 1960's classic "Fortunate Son," a spoken-word number, a rocket-fueled meditation on contemporary culture ("Stuck on the Corner"), and a Fred Sanford-ish funeral dirge. The emotional centerpiece of the album is the wistful "Ponce of the Flaming Peace Queer."

"We're very proud of that one," Snider said. "It ties up the story."

Story?

Yes, story.

"It begins like the Iraq War began: by declaring victory and then plowing forward into the long night," Snider said. "We started our drive with an end-zone dance. *Peace Queer* is a six-song cycle, starting with a song called 'Mission Accomplished.' In six sentences, the record goes like this: Here's the kid being told everything's going to be great. Here's the reality of that. Here's that kid when he comes home a sad and banged-up and angry 'winner.' Here's the breakdown of why

I think that's happening. Here's the guy in our culture that I think is causing that to happen, and it's not a president. And then here's what I think is going to happen to that guy. And then we roll credits."

Upon *Peace Queer*'s release, listeners will hear Snider assisted by Patty Griffin, Kevn Kinney, Don Heron, Doug Lancio, Will Kimbrough and other luminaries. It's a record of brevity, humor and hope.

"Things happen in this album besides you being told that war is wrong, with a beat," Snider said. "I don't know that war is wrong. I just know that I'm a peace queer, and I'm totally into it when people aren't fighting, in my home, at the bar where I hang out or in a field a million miles away. It's a drag to hear that people are punching each other or hurting each other.

"As an International Peace Queer, I believe that world peace is the responsibility of the individual," he continued. "I'm not saying I'm necessarily a role model. But I will say that everybody has to do their part. And you can look at me for an example, if you must. I haven't killed anybody in 12 years."

On the heels of the bio, we made up a movie where my friends tried to debunk my fake story about how the album got made. In my mind, putting razzmatazz around it was making it more palatable. As my wife says, "You've got to put the aspirin in the ice cream and not be a thunderhead about your ideas." I was concerned about the lyrics being too political, but I felt like giving it the *Peace Queer* title and a funny cover and a funny movie and a bullshit bio sort of pillowed the antiwar message, which I worried had been done to death already.

Then I set out to make a story record, one that would make Kent Finlay glow. Kent didn't like bullshit rock songs. He liked Shel Silverstein story songs, like "Boy Named Sue." I thought, "I'm going to do a record with no theme, just songs that Kent will like. And I'm going to do it with the best producer there is." I told Burt Stein that I thought I needed a producer, and he said, "What about Don Was?" Right, Don Was. The guy who produced The Rolling Stones. Maybe we should call Phil Spector instead. And while we're at it, let's get Bob Dylan to come write a bunch of songs. Burt said, "Don called here yesterday. He's a fan of yours, and he remembers you from the time when you were in the studio with Garth Brooks."

At the time, Don was on tour. He said I could come on the bus, hang out, and do some shows. I got out there, and we started talking about why anyone would make an album. We agreed there was no good reason at all to make albums, and we agreed that if there was no good reason to do it, that it could be a tremendous amount of fun.

Don and I went to a Milwaukee Brewers baseball game, and two different people yelled at me, screaming that I was a faggot. Don said, "That's a weird part of your energy: angering jocky people."

It was, and it is.

Don asked me if I wanted to be on the radio, and I said, "No, I just want to be like Tom Waits or something."

After the game, we went back to the hotel and recorded about twenty songs into one microphone. The next day, we thought about putting that out. But I kept telling him how I wanted there to be this full-band sound, and he started saying we could get a great band together, with Jim Keltner playing drums. Keltner had played with Bob Dylan, most of the Stones, most of The Beatles, James Taylor, Carly Simon, and a zillion others. I loved his drumming. I was over the moon about recording with Jim Keltner. So we went out to Hollywood, and Bob Mercer and Pamela Des Barres came out, as did Randy Jackson and Tracy Chapman and others. They were there to say hi to Don. Keltner played drums, and he'd memorize the lyrics to a song in one pass, and reference his questions about the drumming to the lyrics. I'd never seen that before.

We made the album, and Mercer really liked it. He liked most of my records. There was one called *New Connection* where he called me and went, "Pretty good record, although I think we all get that you're in love, and 'Beer Run' maybe didn't need the full cast of background shouters." That's the first album he came close to dismissing, which set me out working on the *East Nashville Skyline* record. I dedicated that next one to him, and I made it just so he could sit next to his pool and giggle.

But at this point, Bob was not well, health-wise, and he was not going to challenge me anymore. He was just going to love me, which was fair enough. He didn't have the energy to do both. I'm glad he chose love.

We put that album out. It was called *The Excitement Plan*, and it did good too, for a guy like me. But at the same time there was another current running, one that was happening in my own family. My sister was going through a divorce, and as everyone came to her support, it started to feel to me like somehow I was getting boxed out of my family. Then there was an article in the *New York Times* that embarrassed my mother.

And so my problems with my mom extended to problems with my sister and brother, and to the worst heartache I'd ever had. I wound up going through three divorces at one remove— my brother, my sister, and my mom—and then in the middle of all that, Bob Mercer died.

I went to the funeral, where we were all instructed to wear bright colors. It was at Capitol Records, a famous round building in Hollywood where Frank Sinatra recorded his hits.

Every heavyweight you could imagine in music was there to talk about Bob. They said that he was at EMI in London when nobody at EMI could get The Beatles to talk to them. So the head guy said, "Who's the youngest guy here?" Well, that'd be Bob, in accounting, who had gotten his job as a bean counter after working at a potato-chip company. They sent him down to try to get The Beatles to say what it was that they wanted. A job that is now called "A&R" was born, and the "recording budget" and "promotion budget" all came from that.

Then, partly because of Bob, everything changed. People at the record companies had all worn suits to work, and to record. Bob told them that The Beatles and other people didn't want that to happen anymore. Try to find a suit at a recording session today, and you will fail.

Bob took on higher and higher jobs at the record company, until he was Paul McCartney's manager. One day, Paul said, "I need you to come out to the house." Bob took the three-hour trip out to Paul's house and knocked on the door. Paul opened the door and said, "You're fired." Then he shut the door, and Bob drove three hours back home.

Bob got given the reins to the record company, and his theory was to trust young people. "It's not about what I think," is what he thought. "Hire young people who are mad for the world, and listen to them." One day, young people brought in a band called the Sex Pistols, and Bob couldn't get his head around them. But the kids loved them, so he said, "I'll sign them." Then the bass player spat on him, and he said, "That's a step too far." He fired them, and they hated EMI after that. They spit first, and hated later. Quite a trick.

Bob went on to produce Pink Floyd's concert, "The Wall," after which Jimmy Buffett hired him to run his record company, Margaritaville. The reason Jimmy knew Bob is because Jimmy's first wife, Margie, was Bob Mercer's second wife. They stayed friends through all of that, which tells you something about Bob and Margie and Jimmy.

At some point, I started to realize that Bob and Margie had become my parents, in more than a metaphorical way. Kent Finlay had been the first one to suggest to me that I could be whatever I wanted, in a real way, but he didn't have as easy a time living out those words as Bob Mercer did. Bob lived those words out as if there was no other choice, and for him there probably wasn't. He was an animal, like Hunter S. Thompson said about his lawyer. He was the last of the great water buffalo types who could go through a wall headfirst, come out the other side, and look good doing it. I was told that Bob Mercer had died, but I won't believe that until I have gnawed on his skull with my very own teeth, because it still hasn't gotten too weird for me.

That last thing is what I should have said at his funeral. Instead, I just sang. But I sang Bob's favorite songs, which were Bob Marley's "One Love," Bill Withers's "Lean on Me," and The Beatles' "All You Need Is Love."

After the funeral, I rode around with Bob's son, Jackson. I don't know Jackson as well as I'd like. But he has the guitar that I wrote my first album with, and he feels like a brother to me.

Bob always encouraged me and told me that being myself was smarter than being smart. That was a relief, and I don't think I'd still be working without that advice. Every time I ever stepped in a pile of dog shit, Bob Mercer was there to say, "Hilarious," as opposed to "Oops." It was always, "We should get a great whiff of this." Not, "We should clean this off your shoe."

This advice guided me, because it was the light I needed to look at so that I didn't start thinking I should look at other lights. If you're going to be in commerce, why would you even come near art? There are eight billion more certain ways to make money than with art. But if you're going to be in art and you want it to stay fun, you have to take Bob's approach. I don't want to over-pat myself on the back, but if I'm going to ever give myself credit for anything, it's that I understood that being foolish and unprofessional and gleeful and irrational and overdramatic and unfounded and illogical was what I was supposed to do as an artist. Bob ratified that, a million times.

Some people think that attitude is ungrateful, but it's actually the opposite. And working harder at the songs isn't the way to be grateful, even though I do work hard at the songs. Living the songs and being the songs is the best way for me to show gratitude. Getting up at nine in the morning and working on verses in a structural way is part of it, and I do that, but going out after the show to find some story that ought to get told is still the best way to honor what's been given to me. I feel sad for the ones who have died doing this, but I don't feel anything for the ones who don't risk total catastrophe, and I think both of those things come from Bob and Margie Mercer.

Since Bob's death, Margie has served as my advisor, and she is exactly like him. She meditated and he medicated, and they came to the exact same conclusions. When something good happens to me, I tell Margie Mercer, and she doesn't make me feel like I'm bragging. I usually tell her things, like, "I'm going to be in a movie, playing myself, being on drugs the whole time." Or, "I'm going to write a book about Jimmy Buffett throwing fruit at me and all the other shit I fuck up."

And Margie says, "Hilarious."

This is not a success story. It's just a story.

If there's something to win, I'm pretty sure I've got it around here somewhere. I've got a lot of trophies. They're from a phase I went through, where I stole a lot of trophies.

After *Peace Queer* and *The Excitement Plan*, I worked for a week-end on lyrics to an album called *Shit Sandwich*, for a band called Elmo Buzz & The Eastside Bulldogs. I came up with eight songs about chicks and cars and partying hard, and we went into a studio where part of our deal was that we were sup-posed to show some people who'd paid to be there what the recording process was like. We were supposed to show them how to correctly track a song. Instead, we showed them how to put back thirteen bottles of wine and fifteen joints and poorly record eight songs over the course of three hours. That was the end of what I called the "Crank It, We're Doomed" trilogy.

After that, I told myself I wasn't going to write songs any-more. I didn't feel like writing songs was good for me. In fact, I thought it was hurting. I started to feel like it was something I'd better let go of. "Just stop," I thought. "Stop trying to be understood, and stop giving all day, everyday, to poems."

When you peel away all the bullshit reasons you would do a song and only use the right reasons, and only try to say what you mean and not say cool stuff that makes you look good, it's not the funnest fucking thing in the world. It often requires an assessment of things you'd rather not assess. But I didn't stop. Because I like the things that come from not stopping more. Because I am greedy and results oriented.

To do this thing, even at the smallest folk music house in Phoenix, you have to talk about the girl who broke your heart, and you have to not give her a cool name or add cigarettes into your story about her. If I didn't have to really put my heart into this, I wouldn't. But if you don't, you lose the gig. Simple as that.

And I love the gig. I love the travel. I love the attention. I love the free buffet tray. I love the clapping and the posters and the bus. I love trying to think of what to wear. I love making a set list, and I love doing the liner notes. I love being in the paper. I love all of it. There's not a part of it that I don't love and won't miss when it's gone. In a sense, then, I've come to do exactly what I didn't want to, which is to do it for the rewards. I didn't know the rewards would be so cool, or that the process would be so hard.

John Prine says it starts off like tying your shoe, and that it ends up being like brain surgery. From the outside, it looks like tying your shoe, even when it's brain surgery. Bob and Margie Mercer knew it was brain surgery and told me it was like tying your shoe. And tying your shoe, they said, was hilarious.

CHAPTER 21

TOO SOON TO TELL

If you ever find yourself in some old Texas town
Look for my old buddy Jack out driving around
He's in a beat-up Ford, he's got a band in the back
Every time he pulls over another place gets packed
People going crazy, people going wild
There's just something about country music Texas style

—From "Nashville," by Todd Snider

Used to be that Jack Ingram and I couldn't get arrested. I mean, we tried and everything. True story.

It was 1996. I was on my second album tour. Someone told me about a young guy from Texas who liked me and wanted to open. We gave him fifteen shows, and he was excited to be opening for us and couldn't believe that we had a bus.

Then the first show came, and there were about twenty people there, which I don't think he expected. Sometimes it's twenty people and sometimes it's eight hundred. Fun either way.

About a week or two into the tour, Jack and I knew we were going to be really good friends. The friendships between musicians happen quickly, and in a different way than most people's friendships. When you're in music, you might see your closest friends in the world six times a year. They are intense relationships, both brief and enduring. My friend and neighbor Kieran Kane, I see him more out of town than in town. He lives four doors down.

One night, Jack and I found ourselves in Phoenix, Arizona. I don't remember the name of the club, but it had saddles or buckles in the title. It was a country bar. This posed a problem, in a sense, as both Jack and I wanted to be too country for rock and too rock for country. Every year, a dozen new kids decide they're going to make that thing work. That year, we were two of them. By Celine Dion standards, it has never, ever worked.

So we were both concerned about the belt buckles, the hats, and the nonironic western shirts we saw in front of us that night. Jack and his band went out there before I did. We got nervous and were passing a bottle of Jack Daniel's back and forth before the show. He was the opener, which meant that I had about forty-five more minutes of drinking time.

It also meant that I observed certain problems cropping up. One of them, which I noticed right after Jack and his band started, was that the thing where the buckle people tried to line dance to his songs was not working. The buckles started getting frustrated, and then they started heckling him. I knew our band was even less country than his band, so I figured they were going to murder me. I was pretty drunk by the time I went on, and I just went right at them. I did the "Play a Song and a Half and Tell Everyone to Go Fuck Themselves" show, thinking at least I'd be mildly memorable.

I told those people I felt like I was at Applebee's, which was supposed to be some not-very-good joke, and then I walked out the back door into the night, in frustration, like a turd. Jack followed after that, with the bottle. We were both down.

One of us said, "We can't even get arrested in this town," which is an old showbiz expression meaning, "I am not popular here."

Then we decided we'd try to get arrested.

We saw the police station, and it had a little man-made pond in front of it. So we jumped in the pond, in all our clothes. While we splashed around in there, the cops were coming and going in their cars. We were clearly trespassing, and clearly in their pond, and they didn't care. They acted like they couldn't see us. It was just like the gig.

So then we went back to the hotel and dove into the pool there. Then we decided we were going to wake up somebody at the hotel, and we started climbing up the side of the building, via the balconies. We got up about four floors, and then people started coming out of the hotel and it became kind of a thing.

We couldn't get arrested in Phoenix. But we could, for sure, get kicked out of a hotel there.

That night cemented our relationship in a big way. After that, we talked all the time, and wrote lots of songs together, and were just good friends. Then Jack started getting hits as a country singer, on the radio, which made me both proud and jealous. Jack got a little backlash over his hits. People in Jack's native Texas, in my opinion, seem to want their heroes to keep a hand tied behind their back all the time. I guess that's a rodeo thing, but I think it's fucking ridiculous. They actually hold it against their favorite singers when they get discovered by other people and start making some real money. They call it "selling out," which is what I try to do every night of my life. If you're from Texas and you start doing well, some of the people who supported you on the way up will suddenly start questioning your motives. I don't understand this at all. We don't know what's in a person's heart, or what that person considers art. If we don't like what they're doing, we can leave them alone and go listen to what we do like.

Country music these days is really done by teamwork, and some people don't like that, and I understand why. But the idea that anyone who's doing well in country music is being told by a record label who to be and what to sing, well, that just ain't happening. I have people who I ask whether I should wear this shirt or that shirt, and that's not that big a deal. But the work is too hard to do it if you're acting phony. If you don't like something you hear on the radio, don't tell yourself that it's the record label singing to you now. Some of those Texans who were onboard with Jack at the beginning thought that when he was having hits later on it was because he was singing something he was told to sing. That doesn't happen. You wouldn't believe the songs Jack turned down. There were probably a hundred where the label said, "This will be a hit" and Jack said, "Nah, not for me."

I can defend Jack all day long, but the truest thing I can say is that if I'd been in his shoes, I'd have walked the same mile, and anyone who told me they didn't like it could bark my hole and use my dick for a walking pole. Jerry Lee Lewis said that. But enough about Jerry Lee.

My friend Jack, the guy who opened for me, became a star. When I was on the road and met people who wanted to talk about Jack, it would often be like they wanted me to attack him and wanted there to be a rivalry. And if it wasn't that, it would be people who squinted thoughtfully and asked, "When are you going to do that?" Like I could make a phone call and suddenly be on the radio or collecting awards. I can only imagine what the center of the Jack Ingram storm must have been like. I wasn't anywhere near the middle, and it was in my life, all the time.

There is jealousy. I have it with all my friends, and I just go ahead and tell them. That's the only real cure, and there's nothing wrong with it when you tell them. It's a compliment. It doesn't get received as competitive. When I was younger, I was in awe of songs I heard from people I'd never met. Now I know the people doing the songs I'm in awe of. That makes me happy, but it's not always the best feeling in the pit of your stomach when you like one of your friend's songs better than your own. I've had that feeling with Jack, but not only Jack, not by a long stretch. I've had it with Will Kimbrough and Tommy Womack and Tim Carroll and Peter Cooper and Kevin Gordon and Dan Baird and a lot of others. They make me so proud it hurts.

A magazine asked me to write something about Jack. I wrote that not long ago, in Texas, there was a young singer-songwriter who wanted to be a star but kept getting told he was going to be more of a cult guy who might get his songs sung by some of the bigger stars. I wrote that most people, myself included, hear something like that and say, "Thank-you." But this guy heard that and said, "No, I don't care if you think I'm Guy Clark. I'm George Jones, and I'm not giving up just 'cause you're telling me to." That person went back to Texas with the information he'd gotten about what people thought he could do, and he changed the way he looked and changed the way he sounded. His old fans were uncertain about the new sound.

But his new fans . . . well, there were so many more of them. Eventually, the smarter people realized that the second version of this guy was probably the truer version. And from then he went on to have a number one country hit.

That man's name: Willie Nelson. See how I did that?

Jack ended up going on national television at the awards trophy show, singing a song he and I made up. I got to feel like I was part of country music history, and Jack cemented himself as a country music celebrity.

A celebrity. Who opened for me. I taught him everything he knows, and some stuff he already knew. A celebrity. And celebrities have celebrity golf tournaments. Which is why I've told you all this: because I wanted to set up the part of this story where I absolutely and completely dominated Jack Ingram's celebrity golf tournament, leaving Matthew McConaughey, Roger Clemens, Lance Armstrong, and a bunch of other suckers in the dust.

Look it up. Or read on.

—

So Jack told me he had a celebrity golf tournament, and I said, "How come I'm not in it?" He said, "Because it's a celebrity golf tournament."

I started humming "Beer Run," which did nothing for him.

I told him I was a celebrity, because they run small print in the newspaper that says it's my birthday when it's my birthday.

He looked in the paper and said, "Today is Lauren Tewes's birthday."

I said, "Who's that?"

He said, "Exactly."

By the way, I found out later that Lauren Tewes played cruise director Julie McCoy on the TV series *The Love Boat.* So, technically, she's a thousand times more of a celebrity than I am. But enough about Lauren Tewes.

A couple of weeks later, Jack called and said that Steve Fromholz had dropped out. Jack wanted to know whether I'd do his celebrity golf tournament.

I said, "Sure."

Actually, it was more of a fallen-celebrity golf tournament, featuring Roger Clemens, Ricky Williams, Lance Armstrong, and Vince Young. They satisfied the tournament's quota of fucked-up jocks. Then it was me and Bob Schneider and Hayes Carll and Jack and Matthew McConaughey. And then rich people who wanted to play with those people.

The weekend kicked off with a celebrity concert that Friday night featuring John Mellencamp. At the concert, they auctioned off a bunch of shit. They even auctioned off a night with Jack for a fuckload of money. I could tell that whole thing made him uncomfortable, but they generated $800,000 for a kids' charity all in one night.

Mellencamp played what I thought was a great set, and the appreciation of his performance grew the further back you got in the arena. The front row was rich people sitting on their hands. The back row was regular people, standing and clapping and singing, in full awareness of the fact that Mellencamp was playing classic after classic. It was, "Remember this? I wrote it. Here's another I wrote. Wrote this. Wrote this, too."

It was jaw-dropping, and without an encore.

After the Mellencamp show, Jack said we could meet the 'Coug. I wanted to ask him about something he'd said on *The Colbert Report* on Comedy Central. On Colbert, he walked out and said, "This is the old Babyface Nelson place, right?" and I knew that was from the movie about Hunter S. Thompson, *Where the Buffalo Roam*. I told my wife that someday I was going to meet Mellencamp and ask him about *Where the Buffalo Roam* and that we were going to get along great.

We got backstage, and Mellencamp was off in a private room. The band was out by the deli tray, where they always are, doing shots. The bandleader, Mike Wanchic, saw me and told me that John listens to my albums and that he might want to say hello. Of course, I was already going to get to say hello, because I was with Jack and had taught Jack everything he knows. Also, because Steve Fromholz dropped out of the celebrity golf tournament.

So we went back and saw John Mellencamp. He's a cool, tough, Woody Guthrie type, and he was smoking a cigarette. He said, "Man, you've got some good songs." I was already starstruck, and now I was elated to the point of nervousness. Then he turned to his right and said, "You've got to meet this guy, Todd Snider. He writes good songs." The guy to his right was Matthew McConaughey, a famous actor whose movies I always loved and whom I would come to consider my friend the very next day. Now, though, I was double starstruck.

I said to John, "When you were on Colbert, was that *Where the Buffalo Roam*?"

He said, "How'd you remember that?"

I started to tell him the whole story about seeing the movie and meeting Hunter and Hunter physically attacking me, but instead I just said, "I'm a big fan."

I was double starstruck, and then triple starstruck when I noticed Vince Young was in the room.

It was cool to get to ask Mellencamp stuff. He said he thought Elvis Costello was his generation's best songwriter, and he asked me a bunch of questions about myself.

I asked him when he wrote songs, and he said these days it's probably just if there's a ton of money involved. He's more into his painting and into performing than writing now. After that talk, I went and told my wife that I just got to talk to those guys for forty minutes, and I was so charged up from John Mellencamp knowing who I was that I didn't sleep at all. I watched TV the whole night, replaying my conversation with Mellencamp.

A few minutes after I finally fell asleep, it was time to get up and go be in that celebrity golf tournament.

I had it set up so I would have pot and percodan when I got to town. Pants on the ground. So, in the hot sun, because of my backaches, I took a pretty strong painkiller, or so, and proceeded to fucking dominate.

Unlike a lot of other times, when I think one thing is happening in my head but another thing is happening in real life, here I actually, in reality, fucking dominated. I was on a team of five guys, and I was supposed to be their celebrity. Upon hearing that, they audibly expressed their disappointment. Perhaps they were expecting Steve Fromholz. One guy even used the word "screwed." But they were really funny, and pretty good at golf. I don't really know how to play golf, I just play. I learned it the same way I learned guitar. The guys on my team said my swing was all jacked up, but the balls kept hitting fairways. They acted like that was some kind of big deal, but I think sports are easy. How hard is it to take a stick and whack it against a ball? It's not. How hard is it to take a stick and make a ball roll over to that hole? Easy as fuck, brother. I've played Carbondale.

So, with my leadership and watchful eye over my young teammates, we shot eighteen under par and won the whole fucking tournament.

After we were done, I walked into the pro shop to take a leak the way the pros do, and McConaughey saw me and yelled, "How'd it go out there, Todd?" I went into my Fred Sanford dance and said, "I don't know if you've glanced up at the leaderboard." Then he started doing that same dance and he went, "What's it say?" I said, "Team Todd Snider my honky!"

We had to wait for Hayes Carll and Roger Clemens to finish. When they came in, they were not up to snuff. The trophy went to Team Todd Snider. McConaughey had to give me the trophy, and they asked me to make a speech.

I held the trophy up and said, "All of you doubted me. Every last motherfucking one of you."

That wasn't true, though. Coach Mack Brown of the University of Texas Longhorns did believe in me, the whole time. It was his pep talks and my skill and leadership that took Team Todd Snider to the top.

From there, we all went back to the hotel, because that night we were going to play a show. I'd been in the sun all day long, on this pain medication, and was smoking pot during the tournament, too. Lance Armstrong had shown me a way to do it so that I wouldn't get caught for at least a couple of years.

I told Lance that I don't see why jocks are so weird about drugs. If steroids took five seconds off the songwriting process, I would have been so balloon-headed that there wouldn't be a nonconvertible car that would work for me. Managers would expect every songwriter to take them, and they would drop us if we stopped taking.

I don't get jocks. It's easy, and they're pussies about drugs. Ride a bicycle? Please. I did that when I was eight.

So by this time in the afternoon, I was a champ, and I was supposed to be taking a nap before my show. But I'd just won a golf tournament, I'd taken some pills, I felt like my victory speech was good, I'd just met all these famous athletes, and I was overwhelmed with it all. I was not going to catch any sleep.

We got to the concert that night, and I took another pain pill. I took it, sincerely, for my back, but also to wake up. Pot and pills either knock you out or pick you up. If they pick you up, you're a constant contestant for trouble.

I went down to the gig, and there were a few dressing rooms. One of them was a big room where most of the people were. But I went back to a smaller room where Guy Clark was. Guy is a legendary songwriter, so beloved down in Texas that they still say that he's their state's greatest songwriter, even though he moved to Nashville in 1971. Guy Clark is great and old and crotchety. I went to his house one time, played him a song, and he looked me in the eye and said, "I don't get it." Guy has never damned anyone with faint praise. But "I don't get it" is better than the worst thing Guy can say about your song, which is "cute." "I don't get it" means Guy doesn't get it. "Cute" means "Fuck you, you no-talent, chicken shit dumb ass."

I had a hat on that had flowers on it. My friend Amanda Shires had sewn the flowers on. Guy looked at me and said, "Are those flowers in your hat?" In fact, I affirmed, they were. He said, "Why?" and I didn't answer. But he was sweet to me and let me sit there and hang out with him. Then Radney Foster came in, and we were all taking turns playing this new guitar Guy had built. The guitar sounded great, and we were all catching up, away from the big room with all the celery sticks.

Then in came Kris Kristofferson. He walked into the room, then kind of jogged up and hugged me and said, "I love you, boy." Radney had Guy's guitar, and he played a song called "The Man You Want," and then he handed it to me. I said, "Kris, what key is 'Stairway to the Bottom' in?" That's a Kris song I love, but then again I love all of them. I was going to play his song for him there in that room. But Kris said, "No, sing me whatever your new song is." I played one called "Too Soon to Tell," with my heart pounding out of my chest.

TOO SOON TO TELL
By Todd Snider

> Low, grey clouds rollin' over my head
> I'm walkin' up a hill to get my fortune read
> I can still take rejection but it does get harder to do
> I wish I could show you how you've hurt me
> In a way that wouldn't hurt you too
>
> Tennis shoes hangin' from a telephone wire
> I've got a little money; I could get a little higher
> I was alright awhile, but you know how it goes
> Everything in moderation, including moderation I suppose
> I never did like the people where I was employed
> They was always out to get me 'cause I'm paranoid
> Now I'm workin' for myself
> And that don't pay a lousy dime
> If what we're here to do is learn to forget
> I'm gonna need more time
>
> It's too soon to tell, too soon to tell
> It's too soon to tell, too soon to tell

It's too soon to tell, too soon to tell
By and by

It's too soon to tell what's gonna happen to you when you die
It's too soon to tell what we'll ever avenge
They say that living well is the best revenge
I say bullshit, the best revenge is to win
This isn't over, we're going to meet again

And good Lord if you're up there, you sure got some nerve
Seems like even the wicked get worse than they deserve
We're afraid to die every goddamn one of us
I swear to God it's like you're makin' fun of us
Not worth keepin, or too good to keep
You got a better kinda secret, better wait 'til I'm asleep
And if you're so God almighty then what's with all this
  mystery?
Yes I wanna trust ya buddy, but you're clearly keeping secrets
  from me

It's too soon to tell, too soon to tell
It's too soon to tell, too soon to tell
It's too soon to tell, too soon to tell
By and by
It's too soon to tell what's gonna happen to us when we die

At the fortune teller's on the second floor
In bright red letters hangin' off of the door
It said "closed," I think it might've been some kinda sign
Don't give up on me baby; I think I could be losin' my mind
I've just met too many people that I love too much

They're scattered all over; I could never stay in touch
With travelin', almost forever it seems
You too will wake up one morning with a lot more memories
    than dreams

Low, grey clouds rollin' over my head
I'm walkin' down the hill without my fortune read
I can still take rejection but it does get harder to do
I wish I could show you how you'd hurt me
In a way that wouldn't hurt you too

In the middle of my singing that song, Kris laughed and said, "God is happy." I felt like I held my own in that moment, with three guys I'd looked up to for a long time. Guy didn't give me a "cute," or even an "I don't get it." Seemed like he got it.

Kris played first when the real show started. He silenced three thousand people and brought tears to the eyes of at least a thousand. Ingram had built the bill backward: legends first, me and Hayes Carll and Bruce Robison at the end. Guy came up right after Kris, and he killed. It's one thing to watch a rock band knock people on their ass, but another thing to watch a poet do it. Kent Finlay and I watched this together, and Kent was crying his eyes out.

When Kris and Guy got done, I went back to that little room and sat with Guy while the rest of the show went on. Kris stayed on the side of the stage the whole time, taking it all in. They piped in the music, so Guy and I could hear everybody. At one point, somebody played a song that was a litany of cuss words. It was more a comedy bit than it was a song. I could feel Guy wrenching up, and I said, "Man, our generation doesn't really try as hard as yours. Sorry." And he cracked up at that.

When it was my turn to go on, Guy said, "Go break a heart." I was looking down on cloud nine, from two days of constant stimulation, and the set I did with Hayes and Bruce felt good. People seemed to receive it well, and Kris was watching the whole thing and smiling. At the end, when we were all back onstage together and people were clapping, Kris told me it was one of his favorite nights of music in his life. A lot of really good songs got played that night, by a whole lot of people.

So when it was over, I was roaring. As I walked off the stage, I shook hands with the people who were reaching out. I get handed joints a lot, by the way. You might be surprised to shake someone's hand and find that there's now a joint in your hand. Not me, brother. Happens all the time. "That's why your life stinks, but my life is just like a dream," goes one of my favorite David Olney songs.

Walking off, a guy handed me what I thought was a joint, but that upon further inspection turned out to be cocaine.

It was 12:30 in the morning. I needed to go to sleep so I could get up at 5 a.m. for my flight.

But I had a different plan.

Safety third.

I went back to my room, and Melita was drinking some wine. I did about four lines of cocaine, took a shower, and threw up. Then we went to the airport and flew home. I slept about three hours when we got back to the house, but I couldn't sleep any longer. I took another pain pill and went down to this little area in East Nashville where all the stores are, and me and my friend Sergio Webb played guitar all afternoon, just for people walking by.

I went to bed around 9 p.m., got up the next morning, and felt great. Then we got up to go the airport again, this time to go to Canada. As we rode to the airport, I didn't have sunglasses on and I felt like the sun was really zapping me. As soon as we were going through the line where you get your ticket and drop off your baggage, I said "I have to sit down." So I sat, and the security guys asked if I needed help. I told the guy I was traveling with to call Melita to come get me. I sat about ten minutes in the security area. They wanted to get me an ambulance, but I said I didn't want to do that.

Melita picked me up and insisted that we get to the hospital. We got there, and my heart rate was insane. The doctors really freaked out. They were worried, and they said I was walking wrong, and there was a moment of fear that it could be bone cancer or lung cancer, which runs in my family.

At the hospital, I stayed five hours to get my heart right and get hydrated. They finally sent me home and told me I had to go see my doctor the next day. When I did that, he made me do a CT scan. I was told I had to wait until 5 p.m. the next day to find out if it was bone cancer.

He didn't call until 6.

I've been going to this doctor for years, and one time I asked him what it was like to tell someone something serious. He said, "I just do it at the end of the day, so I can go and have a drink right after."

When I met with my doctor, he asked me to tell him what all happened before I collapsed at the airport. I told him the story, all of it: Jack, Mellencamp, Kristofferson, McConaughey, and the Fred Sanford dance. All the stuff I just told you. And he said he had to leave the room and go look at some more charts.

He came back with a sad look on his face. "I think it's serious this time," he said.

"What do you mean?" I said.

He paused. My heart skipped. "I'm afraid," he said, "that you're stupid, and I don't think there's anything we can do about it." He said that thing I first thought was a joint and then thought was cocaine was in fact cocaine and a bunch of something else. "You're stupid," he repeated. "People who do cocaine are stupid. People who do cocaine that is handed to them for free by someone they don't know and won't ever see again, that's a new kind of stupid. There isn't really a cure for that. You are stupid. Don't take cocaine from strangers any more, and we won't be having any more of these episodes."

"Cool," I said. "High five."

He left me hanging.

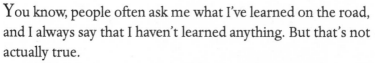

You know, people often ask me what I've learned on the road, and I always say that I haven't learned anything. But that's not actually true.

Build a man a fire, and he'll be warm for the night. Set a man on fire, he'll be warm the rest of his life.